GLOBAL AIDS CRISIS

A Reference Handbook

Other Titles in ABC-CLIO's
CONTEMPORARY
WORLD ISSUES
Series

Books in the Contemporary World Issues series address vital issues in today's society such as genetic engineering, pollution, and biodiversity. Written by professional writers, scholars, and nonacademic experts, these books are authoritative, clearly written, up-to-date, and objective. They provide a good starting point for research by high school and college students, scholars, and general readers as well as by legislators, businesspeople, activists, and others.

Each book, carefully organized and easy to use, contains an overview of the subject, a detailed chronology, biographical sketches, facts and data and/or documents and other primary-source material, a directory of organizations and agencies, annotated lists of print and nonprint resources, and an index.

Readers of books in the Contemporary World Issues series will find the information they need in order to have a better understanding of the social, political, environmental, and economic issues facing the world today.

GLOBAL AIDS CRISIS

A Reference Handbook

Richard G. Marlink
and Alison G. Kotin

CONTEMPORARY
WORLD ISSUES

A B C CLIO

Santa Barbara, California
Denver, Colorado
Oxford, England

Library of Congress Cataloging-in-Publication Data
Marlink, Richard G.
    Global AIDS crisis : a reference handbook / Richard G. Marlink and
Alison G. Kotin.
        p.   cm. — (Contemporary world issues)
    Includes bibliographical references and index.
    ISBN 1-85109-655-8 (hardback : alk. paper) — ISBN 1-85109-660-4
(e-book)   1. AIDS (Disease)—Handbooks, manuals, etc.   2. AIDS
(Disease)—Epidemiology—Handbooks, manuals, etc.   3. World
health—Handbooks, manuals, etc.   I. Kotin, Alison G. II. Title.   III.
Series.

    RA643.8.M36 2004
    614.5′99392—dc22

                                                            2004021402

08 07 06 05 04   10 9 8 7 6 5 4 3 2 1

This book is also available on the World Wide Web as an eBook. Visit
abc-clio.com for details.

ABC-CLIO, Inc.
130 Cremona Drive, P.O. Box 1911
Santa Barbara, California 93116-1911

This book is printed on acid-free paper ∞.
Manufactured in the United States of America

Contents

Preface

A t the end of 2003, 40 million people worldwide were living with HIV and AIDS. Eight million were infected with HIV during 2003 alone, and 3 million people died of AIDS-related causes. Of these 40 million, nearly 70 percent are living in sub-Saharan Africa.

HIV has not spared any country, but instead has heightened our awareness of the connections between individuals, nations, regions, and continents. As the HIV epidemic evolves, policy makers, health care workers, community leaders, and others must recognize that the virus will never be contained among "risk groups" such as intravenous drug users or sex workers, but instead must be frankly addressed in all sectors of society. Responses to HIV have the potential to exacerbate or to reduce societies' negative assumptions about race, class, sexual orientation, and gender roles. Our response to the worldwide epidemic will be successful only if it is crafted in a spirit of collaboration, innovation, acceptance, and respect.

Global AIDS Crisis presents an overview of the worldwide HIV epidemic, comparing experiences of and responses to HIV and AIDS across nations. We focus on drawing parallels between challenges experienced in different regions along with ground-breaking solutions for preventing new infections and caring for those living with HIV. It would be impossible to address HIV and AIDS equally in every country; therefore this book seeks to highlight and examine themes that unite diverse regional experiences with the epidemic virus such as access to care and treatment, vaccine design and scientific discovery, and health and human rights. Parallels between national challenges and responses help to show the epidemic from a truly global perspective, and to illustrate how international partnerships provide hope in the difficult battle against AIDS.

Chapter 1 presents a history of the HIV epidemic, from the first cases of AIDS recorded in African countries to present-day scientific, political, and educational responses around the world. The chapter also includes an overview of the human immunodeficiency virus itself, including discussion of origins and ancestors of the virus, modes of transmission, prevention techniques, and advances in treatment. Chapter 2 addresses specific challenges in the fight against AIDS from social, scientific, and political perspectives, examining regional case studies to illustrate global trends. Issues covered in Chapter 2 include stigma and discrimination, access to care and treatment, government responses to the epidemic, and HIV vaccine design.

Chapter 3 is a chronology of events related to HIV and AIDS in the world from 1959 to late 2003. The timeline includes items from scientific and news sources, presenting both a social history of the virus and a chronology of scientific and medical discoveries. Selected events and trends draw parallels between different regions' experiences with HIV and AIDS, as well as illustrate instances of international collaboration. Chapter 4 is made up of short biographical sketches of individuals who through activism, political involvement, scientific research, and other means have raised awareness about HIV and promoted successful responses to the epidemic both locally and worldwide. Chapter 5 is made up of tables, figures, and statistics that illustrate the epidemic trends discussed in Chapters 1 and 2, and provides an overview of the history, present, and future of HIV and AIDS from a global perspective.

Chapters 6 and 7 provide lists of print and electronic resources for further scholarship on issues related to HIV and AIDS, as well as lists of support and education resources for people living with HIV and AIDS, people affected by the virus, activists, and policy makers. These organizations, publications, and primary sources allow interested readers to explore the history and impact of the epidemic in greater depth, and, if they wish, to become involved in the fight against HIV and AIDS.

We hope that Global AIDS Crisis will inspire readers to question their assumptions about HIV and AIDS, to feel confident discussing the virus and its worldwide impact, and to continue to learn about HIV as the world's epidemic evolves in the future. We would like to thank the staff and partners of the Harvard

AIDS Institute for their support, assistance, and expertise during the process of writing this book. The Harvard AIDS Institute is dedicated to promoting research, education, and leadership to end the AIDS epidemic, with research and education partnerships in Botswana, Brazil, China, Puerto Rico, Senegal, South Africa, Tanzania, Thailand, and other regions worldwide.

Richard G. Marlink and Alison G. Kotin

Notes

UNAIDS. AIDS Epidemic Update, December 2003. Geneva, UNAIDS.

1

Introduction

Human immunodeficiency virus (HIV), the retrovirus that causes acquired immunodeficiency syndrome (AIDS), has proved that there is nowhere in the world from which we are remote and no community from which we are disconnected. By 2003 HIV was present in every country on the globe. Claiming more lives than the black plague, World War I, and World War II, HIV has spread quickly along international transportation routes, through large towns and rural villages, between sexual partners, and among family members.

Although the HIV epidemic has shown that no part of the world can be considered "isolated" from the international community, it has also become clear since the virus was identified in 1983 that the epidemic is influenced by the specific social, economic, and political realities of the communities affected. These different conditions have taught activists, epidemiologists, health care workers, and others to see the AIDS pandemic not as a uniform event, but as a dynamic "mosaic" of epidemics. The responses from government, community members, health care infrastructure, and the international community to each of these microepidemics provide lessons about how seemingly disparate parts of the world can experience a similar epidemic pattern and how these lessons in turn can build worldwide partnerships. Over the long term, HIV and AIDS cannot be fought successfully if the virus and its effects are not addressed from a global perspective, with an understanding of the connections among every community and country affected.

The Genetics and Virology of HIV

HIV is a retrovirus, part of the "Retroviridae" family of viruses distinguished by their ability to replicate by converting viral RNA (the virus' genetic template) to DNA (the host organism's genetic information), using host cells' energy and chemical resources. All Retroviridae acquire and alter host DNA, mutating rapidly once infection has occurred. Unlike HIV, not every member of the Retroviridae clan triggers illness in those it infects. Some retroviruses have been present in their chosen host species for millennia, evolving over time until their genetic information has become part of their host's DNA makeup (Gifford and Tristem, 2003; Coffin, 1991). Other retroviruses that have originated more recently can cause a wide range of symptoms, including extreme weight loss (wasting), neurological disorders, cancer, and immunodeficiency as in the case of HIV (Coffin, 1991).

HIV exhibits more genetic diversity than almost any other retrovirus. After HIV enters a host's body, viral particles (virions), consisting of two strands of RNA in a protein "envelope," bind to the outer surface of the host immune cells (such as T-lymphocytes) that usually work to identify and neutralize antigens in the body. Once an HIV virion infects a host cell, the viral RNA is converted into DNA through the process of "reverse transcription," which is controlled by the viral enzyme reverse transcriptase. Within the cell, viral DNA becomes integrated with the DNA of its host, rendering the infected cell invisible to the immune system. Once HIV's DNA has been replicated, new copies of the virus "bud" out of the original cell. Although it requires many steps, this process takes place quickly—in an untreated patient with HIV, more than a billion new virions can be produced in a day (Kalichman, 1998; Simon and Ho, 2003).

HIV's extraordinary genetic diversity can be attributed in large part to the inaccuracy of the reverse transcription process. Unlike the more complex process of cellular DNA transcription that takes place within the human body, viral RNA transcription to DNA cannot "proofread" as new DNA is created, and consequently a number of genetic deletions, insertions, repetitions, and splicings are likely to take place during the viral replication process. Not every mutant variety of HIV produced this way will be viable or transmissible, but the likelihood that numerous variants of the viral strain responsible for the initial infection will develop *in vivo* (within a living host) is high.

Currently eleven subtypes of HIV-1 ("Group M" labeled A through J, and the genetically outlying "Group O") and six subtypes of HIV-2, the second AIDS virus, have been characterized (Expert Group, 1997). Worldwide, subtypes A, B, C, D, and the recombinant A/E account for 95 percent of new HIV-1 infections, with more than 85 percent of HIV-1 infections in 2001 from subtypes A, B, and C (Osmanov et al., 2000). In 2000, subtype A was most prevalent in Central and Northern African countries, with the highest rates of infection in Western countries, such as Nigeria, Côte d'Ivoire, and Cameroon, where subtype A accounts for approximately 80 percent of total HIV infections. Subtype B remains predominant in developed regions such as Europe, the United States, and Australia, although other subtypes are also prevalent in all these regions. Subtype C is now responsible for more than 50 percent of worldwide HIV infections, including about 3.2 million new HIV infections in sub-Saharan Africa, and 770,000 in southern Asia per year (UNAIDS [HIV epidemic update], 2001). In areas of the world where the AIDS epidemic is newly established and spreading quickly, such as Eastern Europe and the Middle East, several subtypes dominate, suggesting that originally disparate strains of HIV do not remain isolated over time.

Some viruses have the ability to "seal" a cell they have infected, preventing other viral particles from entering, or coinfecting, that cell. HIV lacks this ability, not only allowing hosts to become infected with multiple other viruses, but also opening the way for an individual to become simultaneously infected with more than one HIV subtype. When this HIV coinfection takes place, the mutations that occur during reverse transcription can allow two strains of HIV to "recombine" within a single host cell. When viral transcription is complete, a hybrid strain emerges from the infected host cell, containing genetic characteristics from both original subtypes. These recombinants are not always viable or able to infect new hosts or cells, but many have proven to be not only virulent, but easily transmissible (Coffin, 1991). By 2000, approximately forty recombinant strains of HIV had been identified, a quarter of which have caused serious epidemics in Africa, Asia, and Eastern Europe (McCutchan, 2000).

Studying recombinant strains of HIV is an important way to understand how the virus moves from one continent, country, or province to another, and also how the virus is transmitted among different population groups. For example, two different recombinants of subtypes B and C were reported in 2000 among intravenous drug users (IDUs) in China, suggesting that HIV might have entered the country via drug trafficking routes from India and Thailand, areas where the same B and C subtypes are common. Nearly identical A/E recombinants have been found in both North Vietnam and southern China. This recombinant strain has been transmitted through the population so rapidly (probably also along heroin trafficking routes) that there has been little time for further mutations to occur (McCutchan, 2000).

In Africa, high HIV transmission rates have led to the synthesis of numerous recombinant HIV strains. HIV on the African continent exhibits more genetic diversity than anywhere else in the world; all known subtypes of HIV-1 and HIV-2 are present in Africa. Because so many subtypes of the virus are present in close proximity, coinfection with multiple strains is common (Expert Group, 1997). By 2000, twenty circulating recombinants of subtypes A, C, and D had been identified in Africa, along with A/G strains, and the A/E recombinant that has created a major epidemic in Thailand. The African A/G recombinant, characterized in 1998, has caused a serious epidemic in western countries such as Senegal, Nigeria, Cameroon, and Gabon, and is responsible for more than 50 percent of all new HIV infections in the region (McCutchan, 2000).

Current HIV subtype research has begun to examine and attempt to quantify the impact of viral subtype on HIV transmission, disease progression, development of AIDS, and survival time. Suspected differences between subtypes are often subtle, which means that it can be difficult to ensure that study findings are attributable to HIV subtype differences alone, without confounding factors, such as human or host genetics, drug use, nutrition, and access to medical care. Disease progression among drug users, sex workers, and heterosexual partners of people living with HIV or AIDS may differ for a variety of reasons aside from viral subtype. In addition, equal prevalence of multiple HIV subtypes within the same subset of a population is rare, because HIV subtypes tend to segregate initially by different groups of risk behaviors. For example, in Thailand the initial epidemic in Bangkok among IDUs was associated with subtype B, whereas the northern Thai epidemic associated with heterosexual transmission was primarily A/E infections (Hu et al., 1999).

HIV spreads regardless of national boundaries and available health care, therefore lessons learned about the effects of a specific subtype or recombinant from a single region can be relevant in an international context. The fact that an HIV A/E recombinant spread more efficiently among Thai commercial sex workers than subtype B did among either sex workers or intravenous drug users in the same country suggests that some HIV subtypes might infect more successfully than others (Essex et al., 1997; Hu et al., 1999). A 1996 study investigated HIV's entry into "Langerhans' cells," which are responsible for alerting the body to the presence of infectious agents in the cervix and vagina, or on the penis. Langerhans' cells are a part of the human immune system, which HIV attacks readily, and in the laboratory the study group found that the Thai A/E recombinant not only infected Langerhans' cells more quickly and easily than subtype B, but also continued to replicate in infected cells longer (Soto-Ramirez et al., 1996). From this evidence, the study group hypothesized that the Thai A/E recombinant may have the potential to be transmitted more quickly and effectively than subtype B through heterosexual intercourse (which brings Langerhans' cells into contact with infectious bodily fluids). HIV surveillance data also lend credence to the overall hypothesis that subtype B is less likely to be transmitted heterosexually, because 90 percent of all heterosexual HIV transmissions take place in areas where non-B subtypes are common—sub-Saharan Africa, India, and Thailand (Weniger et al., 1994; Piot and Laga, 1994; UNAIDS, 2001). If this theory is correct, it is possible that the introduction of a non-B subtype of HIV into an area without a heterosexual epidemic as serious as that in Southeast Asia and southern Africa could lead to a dramatic increase in HIV infections.

Modes of HIV Transmission

HIV cannot be transmitted via casual contact, such as a shared drinking glass or a handshake. Instead transmission is linked to more intimate contacts involving shared bodily fluids during birth, breast-feeding, sexual intercourse, drug injection with previously used equipment, or contaminated blood transfusions. Along with biological factors related to a host and the virus itself, transmission can be influenced by sociocultural factors, so that the risk of infection varies widely among individuals and communities (Royce et al., 1997). Because many factors and behaviors can influence the likelihood of HIV transmission, prevention measures must be carefully tailored to the targeted population. In addition, because HIV transmission often occurs through interpersonal connections, situations that disrupt social mores and relationships have the potential to greatly influence how and where the virus will spread.

Four routes of HIV transmission account for nearly all infections worldwide: sexual intercourse between HIV-infected and -uninfected individuals, mother-to-child transmission during pregnancy or labor and via breast milk, transfusions with HIV-infected blood, and injection with contaminated equipment (Kalichman, 1998). Rather than causing infections among isolated risk groups, these modes of transmission show the links among all groups and sectors of society. For example, in Eastern Europe and Southeast Asia, the first recorded cases of HIV were among IDUs and commercial sex workers. Subsequent waves of the epidemic have led to infections in the spouses and partners of IDUs, the clients of infected sex workers, and subsequently their spouses and partners. Once the AIDS epidemic involves the general population via sexual transmission, the likelihood of mother-to-child transmission of the virus increases, leading to a new cycle of infection among infants and young children (UNAIDS, 2003).

Sexual Transmission

Although early cases of AIDS were diagnosed in gay men in the United States, heterosexual transmission of the virus now accounts for the majority of new HIV infections worldwide. Sexual transmission is most efficient via anal sex and from male-to-female during vaginal intercourse. Although oral sex is far less risky for HIV transmission than vaginal or anal penetration, HIV can still be present in the saliva of infected individuals, raising the risk of transmission via oral sex above zero (Edwards and Carne, 1998). Condoms and other latex barriers have been shown to be effective in preventing the transmission of HIV virions during sex, presenting one simple, and highly effective, prevention option (Kalichman, 1998). Because women, particularly sex workers, are often unable to insist that their partners use condoms during sex, prevention science has begun to focus on the development of vaginal microbicides that would prevent the transmission of HIV even without the use of a condom (Potts, 2000).

The odds of acquiring HIV via sexual transmission increase considerably when either sexual partner is infected with another sexually transmitted disease (STD) (such as genital herpes, gonorrhea, or chlamydia) (Plummer et al., 1991; Quinn et al., 1986). Sores caused by STDs, even if they are not visible to the naked eye, provide entry points for the virus into an uninfected host and increase the likelihood that blood will be transferred from one partner to another during sex. STDs like chlamydia that do not create sores or abrasions still facilitate HIV transmission by causing tissue in the genital tract to become inflamed or thinned (Cameron et al., 1989; Plummer et al., 1991).

In 1994, a group of British and Tanzanian researchers conducted a study in the rural Mwanza region of Tanzania to determine the effects of STD treatment on HIV incidence. Recognizing that local medical infrastructure did not allow for complex laboratory or diagnostic procedures, the study group trained local health care workers in simple "syndromic" techniques, in which they matched the clinical symptoms patients displayed to the most likely STD diagnosis and treatment. When the study began in 1991, average HIV prevalence in the region was 3.8 percent, and syphilis prevalence was 8.7 percent (Grosskurth et al., 1995). When data from the Mwanza study was analyzed, the group found that in communities that received the STD treatment intervention, new HIV infections had declined by 42 percent over two years. This reduction was consistent for both men and women who had received STD diagnosis and treatment, but among the control communities, where no special STD services were offered, annual HIV incidence remained constant. This study was the first controlled clinical trial to evaluate a community-based HIV prevention measure, and has shown that reductions in STD infections and access to condoms can result in dramatic decreases in new HIV infections. Instead of attempting only to change the sexual practices of study participants, the study group emphasized syndromic STD treatment, health education, and access to appropriate medical care. The design of this study is significant for resource-scarce countries in sub-Saharan Africa and elsewhere, because it models an effective and comparatively low-cost health intervention that does not require extensive health care infrastructure before implementation (Grosskurth et al., 1995).

Mother-to-Child Transmission

Mother-to-child transmission of HIV has contributed significantly to the epidemic's increase worldwide, particularly in developing countries. Without medical intervention, between 15 and 40 percent of all infants born to HIV-infected mothers will be HIV-positive at birth, which translates to between 300,000 and 400,000 babies born with HIV every year around the world (Altman, 1998; Connor et al., 1994). As early as 1985, scientists noted that mothers could infect babies with HIV during pregnancy, labor, delivery, and via breast milk (Altman, 1998; Ziegler et al., 1985). Until 1998 scientists studying HIV-infected pregnant women were unsure of when between conception and delivery the virus was most likely to be transmitted from mother to infant. This uncertainty did not prevent a group of virologists from discovering and testing the first successful antiretroviral therapy to prevent mother-to-child transmission in the early 1990s (Connor et al., 1994).

In 1991 and 1992, scientists studying HIV models in mice and monkeys noted that zidovudine (also known as AZT, the first antiretroviral drug developed) could block viral transmission from mother to infant during pregnancy, labor, and delivery. The next year, a group of French and U.S. scientists began the first clinical trial to determine whether zidovudine could prevent mother-to-child transmission of HIV among humans. The AIDS Clinical Trials Group 076 (ACTG 076) study group enrolled healthy, HIV-infected, pregnant women, giving half the group a regimen of zidovudine and half a placebo (Connor et al., 1994).

In the ACTG 076 zidovudine group, women took the drug twice a day for approximately eleven weeks prior to labor, and during labor they received zidovudine intravenously. Babies born to the mothers in this group were given zidovudine as well, four times per day for six weeks after delivery (Connor et al., 1994). Mothers enrolled in the study did not breast-feed their babies in order to avoid another avenue for HIV transmission (Connor et al., 1994). At the end of the study thirteen babies in the zidovudine arm of the study were infected with HIV, compared with forty in the placebo arm. This significant reduction in mother-to-child transmission of the virus signaled a dramatic advance in HIV prevention strategies.

The findings from the ACTG 076 study brought hope to many HIV-infected pregnant women and couples hoping to have children despite one partner's infection, but the cost of and infrastructure needed for zidovudine therapy in 1994 was prohibitively high for implementation in most developing countries. Concerned that poor women might never gain access to this potentially life-saving advance, a group of Thai and U.S. scientists began a new study in Bangkok in 1996. Using ACTG 076 as a model, the Bangkok study team modified zidovudine regimes to be shorter, to involve fewer doses per day, and to require no injections. This short-course model tested in women from Bangkok lowered rates of mother-to-child transmission by about 50 percent to a less than 10 percent overall transmission rate. The study group noted that most instances of mother-to-child HIV transmission take place just before delivery, targeting zidovudine therapy to a narrower window of time. In addition, analysis of study findings showed that mothers with high viral loads were more likely to transmit the virus to their babies, demonstrating that zidovudine's preventative effectiveness might lie in the drug's short-term ability to significantly reduce the number of HIV virions in an HIV-infected person's blood (Shaffer et al., 1999).

HIV transmission was reduced by approximately 66 percent in the ACTG 076 study, showing that short-course zidovudine therapy is slightly less effective in preventing infections in infants during pregnancy, labor, and birth. Balanced with this comparison, however, is the importance of the availability of a safe, successful, and affordable HIV prevention intervention for pregnant women in developing countries. Compared with the ACTG 076 regimen, the short-course regimen modeled in Bangkok is three to sixteen times less expensive, and because it does not require intravenous delivery of drugs, it can be implemented widely, even in regions lacking extensive medical infrastructure. UNAIDS announced the results of the Bangkok trial in 1998 and within weeks had begun to host international meetings of donors and policymakers to plan how this prevention intervention could be implemented in the developing world (Shaffer et al., 1999).

Although the Bangkok study offered a comparatively inexpensive and greatly simplified prevention option, studies have continued to further refine the "short course" strategy in cost, simplicity, and efficacy. In the summer of 1999, a group of Ugandan and U.S. scientists announced the results of a trial using nevirapine instead of zidovudine to prevent mother-to-child HIV transmission. In the Uganda trial, mothers were given just one dose of nevirapine during labor, and the drug was given once to babies after delivery. Not only is this two-dose strategy almost 70 percent less expensive than the short-course zidovudine regimen, it is as effective, reducing mother-to-child transmission to rates as low as 13 percent overall (Guay et al., 1999). Current research studies examine the success of dual- and triple-drug combination therapies for mothers with HIV and their infants, with the aim of reducing mother-to-child transmission rates toward zero while providing solutions that are affordable and feasible in resource-scarce settings. A 2004 study conducted among pregnant women in Thailand has shown that a two-dose, dual-drug regimen containing nevirapine and zidovudine can reduce mother-to-child transmission by a further 80 percent to about 1 percent overall (Lallemant et al., 2004).

Since the completion of the Ugandan trial and other similar studies, nevirapine has become widely acceptable as a simple, low-cost mother-to-child HIV prevention option. Studies conducted in 2004 suggest that this new use for nevirapine might have serious consequences for maternal health over the long run. In a South African study of 623 mothers living with HIV who all received a nevirapine regimen to prevent HIV transmission to their infants, 39 percent of the mothers had developed viral resistance to nevirapine. Among some women these mutations faded over time, but for others resistant viral strains blocked the efficacy of nevirapine in triple-drug antiretroviral regimens. Resistance to nevirapine might also confer resistance to the entire class of nonnucleoside reverse transcriptase inhibitors, thus significantly limiting treatment options for many women. Researchers recommend further exploration of dual- and triple-combination antiretroviral regimens such as the nevirapine and zidovudine combination tested in Thailand to prevent viral mutations (Martinson et al., 2004). The World Health Organization (WHO) and other HIV and health organizations will continue to review these findings in order to update international guidelines on mother-to-child HIV prevention and treatment strategies.

As interventions to prevent mother-to-child HIV transmission during pregnancy and birth become more widely available, the risk of HIV transmission after birth via breast milk requires greater attention. Among women living with HIV who breast-feed, an average of 16 percent transmit the virus to their babies after birth (John-Stewart et al., 2004). In regions where nevirapine or zidovudine regimens have been instituted to prevent mother-to-child transmission, HIV infections from breast-feeding threaten to mitigate any gains in preventing new HIV infections during pregnancy and birth (John, Richardson, and Nduati, 2001). At the same time, breast milk provides important protection for infants from malnutrition, diarrhea, pneumonia, and other childhood diseases. In regions where famine and infectious diseases already contribute significantly to infant and child mortality, protection derived from breast milk is vital to babies' survival. Even in regions where formula feeding is affordable and safe, babies who breast-feed have a lower incidence of illness and death (World Health Organization, 2000). Any public health intervention aimed at preventing mother-to-child HIV transmission after birth therefore should take local traditions, resources, and health priorities into account (Shapiro et al., 2003).

In the United States, the earliest cases of AIDS in infants were reported in 1982 (Anonymous, 1982). Even before the human immunodeficiency virus was characterized, researchers theorized that mothers were transmitting "an as yet unidentified infectious agent" to their babies during pregnancy, birth, or after birth (Scott et al., 1984, 76). In 1985 the first case of HIV transmission via breast milk was documented in the United States when a mother was infected with HIV via a blood transfusion after a cesarean section and subsequently transmitted the virus to her baby several weeks after the birth (Ziegler et al., 1985). In the same year, HIV virions were isolated from breast milk for the first time, confirming breast-feeding as a potential route of HIV transmission even when mothers living with HIV have not progressed to clinical AIDS (Thiry et al., 1985).

The United States Centers for Disease Control (CDC) responded quickly to findings that breast milk could transmit HIV to infants, issuing guidelines in 1985 recommending that pregnant women living with HIV avoid breast-feeding their babies. In addition, the CDC guidelines recommended that women living with HIV attempt to delay becoming pregnant until more information on mother-to-child transmission became available. HIV counseling and testing were recommended for women who were considered to be "at risk" for infection. This group included intravenous drug users, sex workers, hemophiliacs, individuals from countries where heterosexual transmission of HIV was common, and the partners of individuals in these categories. Women who were not part of these groups should not be routinely tested for HIV according to the 1985 guidelines, but could receive counseling and testing if they requested it (Centers for Disease Control, 1985).

The United Nations' Global Programme on AIDS, later renamed UNAIDS, issued its first consensus statement on HIV and breast-feeding in 1992 in collaboration with UNICEF and the

World Health Organization. This document, intended for policy-makers and health care providers, states that breast-feeding should be generally encouraged and supported worldwide (Global Programme on AIDS, 1992). Citing concern over mothers' access to clean water and sterile equipment to safely prepare baby formula in regions at risk for illness or malnutrition, the statement recommended that all women in such settings breast-feed their babies regardless of HIV status. Only women in those areas who had the resources to purchase and properly prepare formula were offered HIV testing and counseling on alternate feeding practices (Global Programme on AIDS, 1992). In regions of the world where famine and infectious diseases did not contribute significantly to infant or maternal mortality, the Global Programme statement recommended that mothers living with HIV be counseled to avoid breast-feeding their babies. In addition, the statement suggests that all pregnant women in these settings be offered HIV counseling and testing before their babies are born (Global Programme on AIDS, 1992).

UNAIDS (formerly the Global Program on AIDS) issued a new set of guidelines on HIV and breast-feeding in 1996. This document begins by stating that control over reproduction and access to current health information should be considered a basic human right for both men and women. Although continuing to recommend that breast-feeding be generally promoted world-wide, the 1996 guidelines state that all men and women should have access to HIV counseling and testing. Pregnant women who test positive for HIV should be counseled on both the benefits and the risks of breast-feeding their babies. In situations where nutritionally adequate alternatives to breast milk are unafford-able or cannot be prepared safely, women should be counseled to breast-feed their infants, because formula feeding will significantly increase the likelihood of infant mortality (UNAIDS, 1996). In addition to addressing HIV transmission via breast milk, the 1996 guidelines note that the surest way to prevent mother-to-child HIV transmission is to lower the incidence of new HIV infections among women. UNAIDS advises that this challenge be addressed through both long- and short-term strategies such as social and financial empowerment, access to safer-sex counseling and techniques including condoms, and treatment for sexually transmitted diseases (UNAIDS, 1996).

In October 2000, the WHO, UNAIDS, UNICEF, and UNFPA issued "New Data on the Prevention of Mother-to-Child Transmission of HIV and their Policy Implications." These recommendations present a more specific strategy for policymakers and health care workers considering the risks of mother-to-child HIV transmission and the benefits of breast-feeding. The WHO states that mothers living with HIV should avoid breast-feeding only in regions where replacement feeding will be "acceptable, feasible, affordable, sustainable, and safe." In all other regions of the world, mothers with HIV should be counseled to exclusively breast-feed their infants (World Health Organization, 2000, 1). In addition to providing general guidelines, the WHO document suggests that formula feeding will be safer if mothers receive counseling and support regularly for two years after their babies are born. All mothers should be given information on correct feeding strategies whether they choose to breast-feed or formula feed (World Health Organization, 2000). Drawing on research conducted among new mothers in developing and developed regions, the WHO recommends that individual countries and provinces conduct evaluations to determine which infant feeding strategies will be most feasible, taking into account available resources, traditional practices, and any stigma associated with HIV infection. This kind of assessment along with public information campaigns will help pregnant women with HIV to determine which feeding method is safest and most desirable for their individual life circumstances (World Health Organization, 2000).

The evolution of international guidelines on breast-feeding for HIV-infected mothers continues to be informed not only by considerations of human rights and access to care, but also by the results of research on HIV, breast-feeding, and infant health conducted in developing and developed regions. A study completed in 2001 in Durban, South Africa, monitored 551 mothers living with HIV and found that the risk of mother-to-child HIV transmission was greatest among women who chose "mixed" feeding methods, supplementing breast milk with formula, water, and other liquids and solid foods. Women who chose to exclusively formula or breast-feed their infants for the first six months after birth (without introducing any other foods or alternating breast milk with formula) had an almost equal risk of HIV transmission. Among mixed feeders, HIV transmission rates were almost twice as high as those recorded among exclusive formula feeders and exclusive breast-feeders (Coutsoudis et al., 2001). This study's findings are significant, because they suggest that in regions where replacement feeding for infants is not feasible, exclusive breast-feeding can provide an equal level of protection against HIV transmission (Coutsoudis et al., 2001). This consideration adds even greater weight to the previously reported benefits of breast-feeding, including reduced infant illness and mortality, wider spacing between pregnancies, and psychological benefit to mothers and children (Global Programme on AIDS, 1992). Counselor training materials and international guidelines now stress the importance of encouraging mothers with HIV who plan to breast-feed not to give their babies any other liquids or solid food until they are six months old (World Health Organization, 2000). In the future, more clinical trials will be necessary to further delineate these findings (Shapiro et al., 2003).

Studies and clinical trails have begun to examine the feasibility of various infant-feeding alternatives in both developed and resource-scarce settings. Researchers and policymakers must now consider which infant-feeding strategies will be safest and most acceptable in specific regions, a determination that is highly dependant on local traditions, resources, and attitudes. A 2003 survey of new mothers living with HIV in Khayelitsha, near Cape Town, South Africa, showed that a majority of these women initially chose to formula feed their babies (Hilderbrand, Goemaere, and Coetzee, 2003). Khayelitsha health facilities offer free infant formula to mothers with HIV, and nearly three quarters of women interviewed had access to electricity and running water, making formula feeding both safe and affordable. Nearly half of all women interviewed had not disclosed their HIV status to any family members, however, making exclusive formula feeding difficult, because this practice is associated with HIV infection among the general population. Women who were not comfortable disclosing their HIV status reported explaining their choice to formula feed their babies by telling family and community members that they had "bad milk," were infected with tuberculosis, had high blood pressure, or were unable to breast-feed owing to career demands (Hilderbrand, Goemaere, and Coetzee, 2003). In Khayelitsha, mixed feeding, consisting of solid foods or other liquids in addition to formula or breast milk, is considered normal, leading some women living with HIV to adopt mixed feeding to avoid speculation about their HIV status. Since mixed feeding might carry a higher probability of HIV transmission and infant mortality than either exclusive formula or breast-feeding, education and efforts to combat stigma will be crucial in regions where health facilities offer free infant formula and encourage HIV-infected mothers not to breast-feed (Hilderbrand, Goemaere, and Coetzee, 2003).

In Botswana, a 2003 study similar to the Khayelitsha survey followed seventy-five pregnant women with HIV to determine their likelihood of either exclusively breast-feeding or exclusively formula feeding their babies. The government of Botswana also supplies free infant formula to mothers living with HIV, although, as in Khayelitsha, the traditional method of feeding in the region is breast-feeding combined with the early introduction of other liquids and solid foods (Shapiro et al., 2003). Among mothers from Molepolole, Botswana, who were assigned to exclusively formula feed their infants, as many as 22 percent either breast-fed at some point or fed their babies solid foods and other liquids. Among mothers assigned to breast-feed, none breast-fed exclusively for nine months, and only 10 percent breast-fed without the introduction of other foods and liquids for the first three months after birth (Shapiro et al., 2003). These findings suggest that government-sponsored replacement feeding programs for babies born to mothers living with HIV are not necessarily effective in preventing mixed feeding either among breast-feeding or formula feeding mothers. In regions where mixed feeding is the norm culturally and formula feeding is rare, mothers with HIV might modify their feeding strategies to avoid disclosing their HIV status, or to follow traditional practices (Shapiro et al., 2003).

In a local context where mixed breast-feeding is considered normal, babies born to mothers living with HIV might be healthier and better protected from infection by exclusive breast-feeding than by a formula-feeding regimen that is difficult to follow consistently (Coutsoudis et al., 2002). In addition, government formula programs can have the unintended consequence of encouraging mothers who are not living with HIV to formula feed their infants. This spillover effect can potentially lead to increased infant mortality in regions where famine or infectious diseases make formula feeding risky, because breast-feeding remains the most beneficial strategy of infant nutrition over all (Coutsoudis et al., 2002; World Health Organization, 2000). Future programs to prevent postnatal HIV transmission from mother to child must consider both the benefits and the risks of replacement feeding to infants whose mothers are living with HIV and to all babies born in the region.

HIV Transmission via Exposure to Contaminated Blood

HIV transmission through contaminated blood transfusions and suboptimal medical practices remains a key area of focus for prevention efforts, particularly in resource-scarce or war-torn regions in Africa, Asia, and Eastern Europe, where medical infrastructure is weakened or nonexistent. Prevention interventions that focus on these modes of transmission include "universal precautions" training for hospital and health care workers, including information on equipment sterilization and reuse and safe handling of blood and tissue products. These precautions are particularly important in settings where war, natural disasters, poverty, and other factors limit the capability of health care facilities.

In China's Henan Province, a rural region located in the central eastern part of the country, commercial blood collection practices have contributed to a fast-moving and serious HIV epidemic. Many people in China consider blood donation to be unhealthy from both a spiritual and a physiological point of view. To make up for this shortage of volunteer donations, Chinese blood banks have been supplied since the early 1980s by rural farmers who are paid to donate their blood (Pomfret, 2001). Paid blood donation often comes with a risk of corruption or exploitation, particularly in areas where money from blood donations makes up a significant part of local workers' yearly income. In Henan Province, blood donors in the 1980s earned an average of US$250 per year from their donations, a sum equal to the average yearly profit of a small farm (Pomfret, 2001).

In 1993, China's health minister, Dr. Chen Mingzhan, announced his support for a plan to export donated Chinese blood and blood products internationally. When blood donation became not only a local medical priority, but also a national industry, demand for blood began to sharply outstrip supply. In order to provide enough blood to meet the growing demand, middlemen, known as "blood heads," began working to bring donated blood from rural farming communities in Henan Province to hospitals and pharmaceutical companies. During the 1990s, blood heads routinely drew blood from multiple donors without sterilizing needles and equipment, a proven avenue of HIV transmission among injection drug users in China and other regions. In addition, blood heads often increased donations by pooling blood from many donors of the same blood type, using a centrifuge to extract plasma, which is used to make gamma globulin and clotting agents. The remaining pooled red blood cells would then be reinjected into the original group of donors, allowing them to give blood again sooner without suffering from anemia or other side effects. In this way, blood from one HIV-infected individual could potentially infect ten to twenty other donors, each of who might donate blood 200 times in his or her lifetime (Rosenthal, 2001).

HIV was first detected in a supply of commercially donated blood in China in 1994, but laws prohibiting the sale of blood and blood products were not put into effect by the Chinese government until 1998. Even in the late 1990s, laws against commercial blood donation were not strongly enforced, as 40–90 percent of regional blood supplies were made up of "bought blood," and voluntary, uncompensated donation remained infrequent (Rosenthal, 2001). By the time HIV was first noted in rural Henan Province, the local epidemic had already reached disturbing proportions. For many years the Chinese government refused to acknowledge the role that commercial blood donation has played in the country's HIV epidemic, and accurate surveillance data for the region is still scant. Studies conducted unofficially by local doctors, often in direct opposition to national and local government, estimate that HIV prevalence in selected villages could range from 20 percent to as high as 80 percent—the highest local prevalence recorded anywhere in the world (Rosenthal, 2000; Rosenthal, 2001).

China's experience with blood collection highlights the importance of ensuring that medical care and procedures are adequately supervised and that a desire for profit or increased medical capability does not overshadow individual well-being. The isolation of Henan Province's farming communities did not prevent HIV from spreading rapidly in the region, but it did hide the epidemic from the public eye for several years. In this instance, risky and possibly unethical medical practices combined with a lack of public awareness about HIV to spread the virus with artificial speed in an otherwise unaffected area.

In clinical settings, the delivery of medical care to ill patients can potentially expose many vulnerable individuals to HIV infection when sterilization and equipment disposal precautions are not closely followed. During the final years of Romania's Communist regime, which ended in 1989, thousands of orphaned or abandoned infants and young children were taken into the care of large state-run orphanages and hospitals. In the late 1980s, a group of Romanian doctors began a clandestine survey of HIV prevalence among hospitalized children and children living in orphanages. Although the Romanian Ministry of Health demanded that no such survey be conducted and that all findings be destroyed, the study continued on a small scale until national HIV surveillance officially began in 1990 (Patrascu and Dumitrescu, 1993).

The first survey of HIV prevalence, conducted by Drs. Patrascu and Dumitrescu, took place in a Romanian hospital where thirty ill children between the ages of four months and twelve years were tested for HIV antibodies. Of this first group of thirty, twelve children tested positive for HIV. Subsequent tests of a larger group of 15,783 children from institutions surrounding Bucharest showed that overall HIV prevalence was 6.8 percent. Within the group, prevalence rates ranged from 0 percent among children between fourteen and seventeen years old to 13.84 percent among children and infants less than three years old. The two doctors learned that among this youngest group of children, most of who were orphaned or abandoned around 1989, malnourishment, anemia, and infections were frequent occurrences. Operating with limited knowledge and medical capacity, doctors and nurses often treated these young patients with injections of medication and, to treat the frequent cases of anemia, many small blood transfusions. National HIV surveillance did not begin in Romania until 1990, so it is very likely that children who received these transfusions were given blood from HIV-infected donors. Injection needles were frequently reused without proper sterilization in these overburdened hospital facilities, allowing transmission of HIV among many children to take place (Patrascu and Dumitrescu, 1993).

In developed countries such as the United States, and in nations such as Thailand and Brazil whose governments have made HIV surveillance a public health priority, blood banks thoroughly screen donated blood and blood products for the presence of HIV. In settings where HIV testing equipment is unavailable or too costly, blood transfusions and medical injections can pose a serious risk of infection. Both health care workers and members of the general public require education on appropriate precautions for donating and collecting blood to ensure that medical care is safe, necessary, and nonexploitative.

HIV Transmission via Injection Drug Use

Injection drug users (IDUs) are often the first community to feel the effects of a country's emerging AIDS epidemic, because HIV infection can be transmitted efficiently to large numbers of people via unsterilized syringes and injection equipment. In addition, because drug use is often more common in areas experiencing social and economic upheaval, increased injection drug use may coincide with breakdowns in health care delivery, human rights abuses, and poverty (Hamers and Downs, 2003). The use, transport, or sale of heroin, cocaine, and other narcotics is illegal almost everywhere in the world, making it difficult to track HIV infections among drug users, even in regions where medical surveillance is possible. In addition, drug users may be unwilling to seek HIV testing, counseling, or medical care owing to social stigma and fear of prosecution.

In India and Thailand, the first wave of the HIV epidemic appeared among injection drug users. In Thailand, the first HIV infections in the country were diagnosed in 1984 and 1985 and were apparently acquired sexually. In 1988, HIV was present at a very low prevalence among Thailand's general population, but tests conducted in 1989 showed that HIV prevalence had jumped to 43 percent among injection drug users over a period of roughly twelve months (Phanuphak et al., 1985; Weniger et al., 1991). Three years later in 1991, India's average national HIV infection level was comparatively low, but HIV prevalence among drug users in selected provinces was as high as 50 percent (Naik et al., 1991). In Manipur Province, which borders Southeast Asia's "golden triangle" of heroin production and transport, the number of HIV infections reported among drug users increased to 2,167 by the end of 1990 (Naik et al., 1991).

Surveillance in Thailand and in the United States has shown that HIV infections initially found only among IDUs do not remain contained within a single community. Infants, spouses, and sexual partners of IDUs are all at risk for infection, and these transmissions help the HIV epidemic move into the general population (Lucas, Chaisson, and Moore, 1999; Weniger et al., 1991). This model cannot reliably predict how HIV will enter a new country, however, because an epidemic among IDUs does not necessarily translate into an epidemic among the general population. In Thailand, the strain of HIV subtype B first characterized among IDUs living with HIV in the late 1980s was not the virus that later caused a heterosexual epidemic among sex workers and their clients. Instead a newly introduced A/E recombinant strain accounts for more than three-quarters of all heterosexual transmission in the country (Ou et al., 1993).

HIV prevention interventions and medical care delivery programs among IDUs are challenging to implement, given that outreach, counseling, and harm-reduction strategies center around behaviors that are usually illegal. In addition, studies in the United States have shown that drug use can adversely affect the success of antiretroviral regimens, resulting in decreased viral suppression, depressed immune function, and faster progression to AIDS (Lucas, Chaisson, and Moore, 1999). Although the direct effects of heroin and other injected drugs on the chemical action of antiretroviral drugs have not been quantified, studies conducted in U.S. cities show that missed clinic appointments and skipped doses of antiretroviral medications contribute significantly to treatment failure among IDUs (Lucas, Chaisson, and Moore, 1999).

In the United States, rates of drug use are high among poor or homeless men and women and sex workers, many of who are members of ethnic minorities. Behavioral studies and outreach programs in these populations show that stress, trauma, and depression in these communities might not only lead to increased levels of IDUs, but might also lead to increased sexual risk taking, even after AIDS education outreach (Nyamathi, Bennett, and Leake, 1995). In the future it will be important to design prevention and outreach programs tailored to the specific needs and social realities of these communities to break down the barriers of stigma and fear of prosecution, which impede access to HIV/AIDS counseling, testing, and care.

The Origins and Ancestors of HIV

HIV belongs to a class of retroviruses remarkable for remaining dormant within their infected host's system for an unusually long period, sometimes more than ten years. These lentiviruses (from Latin *lenti* meaning slow) infect a variety of mammals, including mice, horses, and monkeys (Campbell and Robinson, 1998). Two French veterinarians diagnosed the first lentivirus in a horse in 1904, but it was not until the 1970s that the technology of molecular biology was sufficiently advanced to study lentiviruses' genetic makeup (Campbell and Robinson, 1998). Once these studies began, researchers quickly began to note significant genetic similarities among lentiviruses, as well as similarities in how they affect the health of their hosts.

AIDS was first noted by U.S. clinicians in 1981, and the virus that causes the syndrome was classified two years later as "HTLV-III" (Gallo et al., 1984). At the time, the virus was considered to be similar to the human T cell lymphotropic virus (HTLV) group, retroviruses that attack the body's immune system through T helper cells. Ancestors of the HTLV-I and HTLV-II viruses were previously identified in both humans and monkeys, causing leukemia and neurological disease (Miyoshi et al., 1982; Kalichman, 1998). In 1986, HTLV-III was reclassified as human immunodeficiency virus, or HIV (Kalichman, 1998). This name change acknowledged the difference between HTLV-I and -II and HIV. Unlike the other HTLVs, by 1989 HIV and AIDS had spread to every continent and had proved to be easily transmissible, incurable, and fatal to everyone who became infected.

Some scientists estimate that HIV first infected humans between 1915 and the early 1930s (Korber et al., 2000; Hillis, 2000), a generation before the virus was identified by researchers in the United States. Given the fact that HIV spreads so quickly, even in areas where transportation is limited, other investigators believe that HIV is more likely to have evolved in animal hosts then entered human populations nearer to the time when it was first detected in the early 1980s (Essex, 1997). Currently more than 40 million people worldwide are living with HIV, 70 percent of who live in sub-Saharan Africa (an area that includes Botswana, South Africa, Lesotho, Namibia, and other countries) (UNAIDS, 2002d) not far from where the disease is thought to have originated.

SIV

During the early years of HIV in the United States, scientists at a U.S. primate research center noted that captive Japanese monkeys were becoming ill with the same opportunistic infections and depressed immune system typical of AIDS patients. The subsequnt search for a simian immunodeficiency virus in the wild first focused on Japan as the possible site for the suspected ancestor of HIV, but no similar virus was found in wild Japanese monkeys. Investigators then began to suspect that the Japanese monkeys at the primate center could have been infected by the apparently healthy African monkeys housed in the same facility. Tests of African monkeys living exclusively in the wild showed that many were infected with a simian retrovirus similar to HIV. These findings for the first time strongly suggested that the HTLV-III virus (later dubbed HIV) probably first infected humans through contact with monkeys (Miyoshi et al., 1982; Essex, 1988). This kind of transmission has significant historical precedent, as a variety of viruses, including herpes and influenza, first infected humans through contact with animals (Allan et al., 1992). In addition, both HTLV-I and HTLV-II are present in monkeys—HTLV-I is believed to have originated in Africa, whereas HTLV-II has its ancestors in South America (Essex, 1997).

The HTLV-III virus identified in monkeys, later named SIV for simian immunodeficiency virus, is a lentivirus that shares 40–50 percent of its genetic makeup with HIV (Marcon et al., 1991). Interestingly, although as many as 50 percent of the wild monkeys tested in Africa in the 1980s were found to be infected with SIV, the disease apparently did not cause illness or decrease their population (Kanki, Alroy, and Essex, 1985). At the same time, Asian monkeys infected with this strain of SIV in captivity quickly developed AIDS-like symptoms and opportunistic infections and died (Essex, 1988; Campbell and Robinson, 1998).

Why did SIV-infected African monkeys remain healthy, while monkeys from Asia were so severely affected? Studies of evolutionary theory suggest that strains of SIV have been present among African monkeys for thousands, maybe millions, of years, allowing both the monkeys and the virus itself to adapt until monkeys could be infected with SIV over long periods (possibly even for life) without becoming ill. Evidence for this type of coevolution of a retrovirus and its host has been documented in other species, including rabbits and chickens. Among Asian monkeys, SIV was lethal because it was introduced into the population recently, not allowing time for the host and virus to coevolve (Essex, 1988). Out of the seven most common strains of SIV, five usually affect their native monkey hosts with mild symptoms or none at all, but cause disease and death in monkeys from other regions (Campbell and Robinson, 1998).

HIV could be so fatal to humans because we have not had time to adapt to the virus, which has in turn not yet fully adapted to its new human hosts. The overall goals of a viral organism are both to replicate and to exist over the long term within a host.

HIV is still a relatively inefficient organism in these evolutionary terms, killing those who are infected and therefore shortening its own life span (Allan et al., 1992). *Pan troglodytes,* chimpanzees, commonly infected with the strain of SIV most closely related to modern-day HIV, are members of a genus that is 50,000 years old, raising the possibility that some strains of SIV may have evolved with their hosts over the same timeframe (Allan et al., 1992).

HIV-2

The discovery of HIV-2, the "second" AIDS virus, in Senegal in 1985 provided researchers with further clues about how HIV has evolved from SIV (Barin et al., 1985). Although HIV-1 and HIV-2 are both descended from strains of SIV, genetic analysis shows that one is not descended directly from the other (Korber et al., 1995; Marlink, 1996). Five major simian immunodeficiency viruses have been identified in African chimpanzees, sooty mangabeys, Sykes's monkeys, green monkeys, and mandrills, segregated by species. HIV-1 is a descendant of the chimpanzee virus, whereas HIV-2 is most closely related to the SIV found among monkeys such as sooty mangabeys rather than the great apes (Gao et al., 1994). Genetically, HIV-1 and HIV-2 are about 40 percent similar to each other, whereas HIV-2 is more than 75 percent similar to the SIV endemic among sooty mangabeys. Originally found only in West African countries such as Senegal, Guniea-Bissau, Côte D'Ivoire, and Nigeria, HIV-2 is now present at low levels in the United States, South America, Europe, and Asia (Bock and Markovitz, 2001).

Six subtypes of HIV-2 (designated A through F) have been characterized, along with several recombinant strains (Sarr et al., 2000). HIV-2 subtype A represents the majority of infections worldwide, along with HIV-2 B, which is present less frequently. Unlike HIV-1, non-A subtypes of HIV-2 are difficult to grow *in vitro* (outside a host's body), which prevented the investigation of new HIV-2 subtypes and recombinants until the early 1990s. A 1994 study of HIV-2 subtypes in West Africa suggests that HIV-2 A's ability to grow in laboratory cultures might stem from the fact that subtype A replicates more quickly than the other subtypes of HIV-2. Subtype A is the only type of HIV-2 to cause a serious epidemic and to spread beyond West Africa, where the virus was originally detected. If subtype A does in fact replicate more quickly than other HIV-2 subtypes, it might also prove to be transmitted more easily and to progress more quickly to clinical AIDS than other HIV-2 subtypes (Gao et al., 1994).

Differences between HIV-1 and HIV-2 have become clear as researchers study the two strains of the virus over the long term. HIV-1 and HIV-2 appear to be different in how they are structured, how they affect those who are infected with them, and how easily they can be transmitted. In The Gambia, a study conducted among a group of commercial sex workers in 1991 showed that although HIV-2 did eventually damage a host's immune system, the progression to serious immunodeficiency was significantly slower in those infected with HIV-2 versus HIV-1 (Pepin et al., 1991). HIV-2 is not less pathogenic than HIV-1, instead HIV-2 replicates more slowly, which means that infected individuals are likely to live longer with fewer copies of the virus in their bodies than those infected with HIV-1 (Gottlieb et al., 2002).

HIV-2 is more than 20 percent less likely than HIV-1 to be transmitted from mother to child, and three times less likely to be transmitted through sexual contact (Marlink, 1996). These lower transmission rates might explain why HIV-2 has remained within a relatively compact geographical region and why HIV-2 is spreading more slowly than the HIV-1 epidemic overall. HIV-2 in West Africa might have been present long before it was first identified, remaining undetected as HIV-1 prevalence levels and concurrent opportunistic illness and death increased elsewhere (Marlink, 1996). Nearly twenty years after the virus was identified, cases of HIV-2 remain rare beyond West Africa and can generally be traced back to that region (Bock and Markovitz, 2001).

The Early Years of HIV in Africa

The first reports of people from Africa becoming ill from a disease similar to AIDS began to appear in medical literature about two years after the initial American cases of AIDS were recorded in 1981. Most of these cases were in individuals native to central African countries who lived in or traveled to Europe and were treated in hospitals there. By 1983, the signs and symptoms of AIDS were well known to doctors in Europe and the United States, where the virus was becoming more and more common. Doctors from Sweden, Belgium, and France began to match their past clinical findings from African patients with the newly developed definition of AIDS, suggesting that HIV was likely present in Africa well before it was identified in developed regions.

In 1982, a boy from Zaire died in a Swedish hospital after having been sick with infections typical of AIDS since he was five months old (Nemeth et al., 1986). When his blood was tested, he was found to have been infected with HIV, probably since he was born in 1974, although there is no information to show that his mother was also HIV positive (Nemeth et al., 1986). In 1977, a mother from Zaire brought her son to a Belgian hospital to be treated for the illnesses that often accompany an immune system that had been depressed by HIV. Although her son recovered, the mother soon fell ill with similar symptoms and died in 1978 within six months of coming to the hospital (Vandepitte, Verwilghen, and Zachee, 1983). In 1985, doctors from Belgium and Rwanda examined three Rwandan brothers and their parents, all of who were in different stages of illness, and found that all were infected with HIV (Jonckheer et al., 1985). The family's oldest son was born in 1977, and was probably infected with HIV at birth. His twenty-nine-year-old mother could potentially have become infected with HIV nearly two decades before the virus was characterized (Jonckheer et al., 1985).

Looking back, a group of Belgian researchers noticed that the incidence of cryptococcosis (a fungal infection that is a common opportunistic infection associated with AIDS in Africa) in Zaire had begun to increase dramatically after 1980 (Vandepitte, Verwilghen, and Zachee, 1983). Two years later, another group of researchers working in Zambia and Uganda noted that a new and far more aggressive type of Kaposi's sarcoma (a form of cancer that is a common opportunistic infection in AIDS patients in the United States) had become prevalent around 1983 (Bayley et al., 1985). Unlike in the United States, Kaposi's sarcoma in Africa is a relatively common cancer among those who are not infected with HIV, progressing slowly and generally remaining nonlethal. By contrast, the new form of Kaposi's sarcoma identified in Uganda and Zambia spread quickly within the body and proved fatal. When the patients with this new form of Kaposi's sarcoma were tested for HIV, almost 90 percent were found to be infected with the virus (Bayley et al., 1985).

By 1986, increased availability of accurate HIV tests revealed that HIV was spreading quickly in the United States, infections had been identified in seventy-four African countries, and the virus had been detected in intravenous drug users in Thailand

(Quinn et al., 1986; Essex, 1997). By the end of the decade, HIV was present on every continent and probably in nearly every country in the world. Ten years after the virus was first identified, HIV and AIDS were a worldwide reality.

HIV Becomes a Global Epidemic

HIV is sometimes considered a "foreigner's disease," originating elsewhere and imported into previously isolated communities by travelers, refugees, and expatriates. Although this supposition in many ways suggests a desire to pin blame for the spread of the disease on outsiders, studies conducted on every continent show that those who travel frequently are at an increased risk for infection with HIV (Hawkes and Hart, 1993). In regions where the epidemic is comparatively new, such as Eastern Europe and Southeast Asia, the spread of HIV through the general population has been observed to be linked to patterns of seasonal migration, international shipping, sexual networking, and urban growth. In African countries where HIV surveillance did not commence until some years after the epidemic was well established, clear trends can still be seen in the routes of virus transmission from country to country, from town to town, and from cities to small villages and farming communities.

The advent of the HIV epidemic has prompted many countries, including the United States, to limit the entry of immigrants or visitors living with HIV or AIDS. The global prevalence of the virus, along with a lack of evidence that other sexually transmitted diseases can be prevented in this way, suggests that this policy is not based in meaningful or effective public health strategies. International travel has increased exponentially since improved flight technology expanded commercial airline service in the 1940s and 1950s. In addition, long-distance, work-related migration has become common in many parts of the world. In this context of increased global mobility, the key to international HIV prevention might lie in a knowledge of how the virus is transmitted in specific regions, rather than limiting movement across national borders. In 1949, the World Health Assembly issued a statement regarding infectious disease, encouraging countries to focus their efforts on improving medical care and infrastructure, rather than regulating entry of individuals at their borders (World Health Assembly, 1949).

African Trade Routes and Migrant Workers

Migration from rural communities to large cities and towns in Africa increased dramatically during the years leading up to and following World War II. Between 1940 and 1961 the population of Kinshasa (capital of the Democratic Republic of the Congo) increased nearly ten-fold from 49,000 people to 420,000 as forced resettlement, the need for work, and the turmoil of war compelled thousands to migrate (Chitnis, Rawls, and Moore, 2000). This rural-to-urban migration pattern continues in the present, as laborers travel from small communities to highways, cities, mines, and large farms in search of seasonal work. Many of these migrant laborers, truckers, and miners return home for a period every year before travelling to a distant work site.

As HIV and AIDS began to spread rapidly across southern Africa during the 1980s and 1990s, surveys showed that the highest concentrations of infection were consistently found in cities and along major trading routes. In Uganda, where HIV was first identified in 1982, a study conducted ten years later found that HIV prevalence along main roads and in major trading centers was three to five times higher than in rural villages (Serwadda et al., 1992). A similar study conducted in Tanzania showed that even in a country with lower average HIV infection rates, HIV prevalence in urban areas was higher: 11.8 percent compared with only 2.5 percent in rural settings (Barongo et al., 1992). Both studies also indicate that people at the highest risk for HIV infection are those who travel frequently, earn a higher income, are more educated, and have more sexual partners than their peers (Serwadda et al., 1992; Barongo et al., 1992). Tracking the spread of the epidemic, researchers turned their attention to workers within Africa who pass through major cities and move along trading routes from shipping ports such as Mombasa, Kenya, to more rural, inland areas.

Long-distance truck drivers and their assistants represent one of the most mobile groups of male workers in Africa. Frequently away from home for extended periods, drivers provide an important source of revenue to roadside businesses such as bars and hotels, making highways and truck stops centers of both commerce and social activity. Employees in these roadside establishments are likely to be members of the surrounding community, and women who work as "bar girls" or in hotels often supplement their income through commercial sex work, which can be a more lucrative option than manual labor (Haygood, 1999). HIV prevalence is often extremely high among these women, with documented rates of up to 76 percent prevalence in Uganda (Carswell, Lloyd, and Howells, 1989).

A study conducted in Lyantonde Province, Uganda, in 1989 surveyed HIV prevalence among truck drivers and their assistants who transport goods from port cities to inland regions. Overall HIV prevalence was found to be 35.2 percent in this group, compared with 9.2 percent in a control group of local residents (Carswell, Lloyd, and Howells, 1989). In Kenya, a study conducted among truck drivers and their assistants between 1991 and 1992 found that an average of 26 percent were HIV positive, although among drivers from central African countries where the HIV epidemic has been present the longest, the HIV infection rate was as high as 42 percent (Mbugua et al., 1995). Older men earning higher salaries were also more likely to be infected than their assistants, implying that this group had more access to bars, hotels, and sex workers near truck stops on major roads.

Truck drivers and roadside workers are not an isolated group, but instead the first link in a chain of travel and communication connecting major shipping ports and cities with rural villages and farms. Many drivers and migrant workers are married but can only visit their families infrequently, between work seasons or during short vacations. In a 1985 study conducted in Rwanda, 36 percent of commercial sex workers' clients were married soldiers or truck drivers who were frequently away from their homes and families for extended periods. Additionally, customers of the sex workers in this cohort reported an average of thirty-one sexual partners per year, compared with a control group of nonmigrating men from the surrounding community who reported an average of three partners (Van de Perre et al., 1985). This pattern of increased sexual activity among individuals who travel long distances for work increases the likelihood that wives and other partners who remain at home will be exposed to HIV. This risk in turn can lead to an increase in mother-to-child transmission of HIV, effectively introducing the virus into all sectors of the population.

HIV prevalence near African highways and in cities is generally far higher than in more isolated settings, owing to increased contact with travelers from other countries or regions (Wawer et al., 1991; Serwadda et al., 1992). The same principle holds true on a more localized level as individuals move away from their home villages to work or study in cities and later return, speeding the spread of HIV away from main roads and into rural communities. In Kenya, although HIV prevalence in rural areas remains lower than in cities or trading posts, rates of HIV there have increased from 0.17 percent in 1987 to 13 percent in 1997. This rate of infection is only slightly lower than the prevalence of 14 percent recorded in Mombasa, Kenya's major shipping port (Mbugua et al., 1995; UNAIDS, 2002c).

Drug Trafficking in Southeast Asia

Genetic characterization of HIV subtypes can yield important information about where the virus is spreading and the routes along which it travels. A good example of this comes from the borders of Myanmar (formerly Burma), Vietnam, Laos, Thailand, and China—the so-called golden triangle of East Asian narcotics trafficking. Along with Afghanistan, this region has been an epicenter of opium poppy and heroin production since the nineteenth century. Currently, Myanmar, Laos, and Afghanistan are the three largest opium producers in the world. Myanmar produces almost 90 percent of all opium poppies processed and exported in the region, and international export of heroin constitutes a significant proportion of the country's gross national product (GNP), although opium poppy production is illegal across Southeast Asia (Beyrer et al., 2000).

Heroin is transported via clandestine shipping routes from Myanmar into cities in China's southwestern Yunnan and Xinjiang Provinces, then on into India and Vietnam, three countries where HIV epidemics began to flourish among communities of injection drug users in the early 1990s. In 1994, 90 percent of all China's reported HIV and AIDS cases were in Yunnan Province, which is home to only 5 percent of China's population. These early cases in Yunnan were HIV-1 subtype B infections almost exclusively, from a strain closely related to the B subtype prevalent in Myanmar (Yu et al., 1999). In 1995, a shift occurred in Yunnan when a strain of subtype C and a new B/C recombinant began to predominate among IDUs. Two years later, the same HIV-1 B and B/C epidemics among IDUs were noted in Xinjiang Province. The subtype C in Yunnan and Xinjiang is genetically most closely related to a strain found in northern India, which is another heroin production region (Yu et al., 1999). Surveillance therefore suggests that between 1995 and 1997 drug traffic entering China transmitted new HIV subtypes from India as well as Myanmar to the local population. The new subtypes and recombinants were then transmitted from one province to another. In this way, without knowing exactly where a regional epidemic began, surveillance can trace a viral strain's movement, origins, and approximate age.

International Tourism

Tourism accounts for a significant proportion of international travel and for decades has been one of the world's major sources of revenue. The World Tourism Association documented approximately 100 million people traveling legally across national borders in 1985, 457.3 million by 1990, and 696.7 million in 2000. In 2000, these nearly 700 million travelers spent approximately 475 billion U.S. dollars abroad, primarily in Europe, Eastern Asia and the Pacific, and the Americas (World Tourism Organization, 2003).

Demographic studies have not yet fully quantified the effects of international tourism on the global movement of the HIV epidemic, but the size and economic power of the tourist industry make this an important area for further study. In keeping with its 1949 statement, in 1987 the World Health Organization recommended against universal mandatory HIV testing for all international travelers. Aside from the numerous legal and ethical concerns such a strategy would raise, the financial and human resources that would be necessary to screen all travelers entering a country would be prohibitive, particularly in less-developed regions of the world. Although several countries, including China, India, the United Kingdom, and West Germany, did seek to limit or prevent the entry of HIV-infected visitors during the late 1980s, most nations have focused energy on educational activities and safer-sex promotions among tourists and visitors (Lange and Dax, 1987). Despite public health testimony against such a law, the United States continues to prevent people living with HIV and AIDS from immigrating into the country.

Many tourists meet new sexual partners while traveling, forming relationships both with fellow tourists and with members of local communities. Tourists are an important source of revenue for hotels and entertainers, and also for male and female sex workers. A study conducted in the Dominican Republic suggests that tourists visiting from outside the country are often considered to be wealthier than local customers, and are therefore sought after as clients both by commercial sex workers and by entertainers (Forsythe, Hasbún, and De Lister, 1998). A similar study conducted among the Pacific Island states shows that sex workers seek out tourists as potentially lucrative clients, and visitors to the islands might come specifically to engage in commercial sex (Lewis and Bailey, 1992/1993).

"Sex tourism," when travelers visit a region or country specifically to take advantage of the local sex industry, has been documented worldwide: in South and Central America, Southeast Asia, the Pacific Islands, and elsewhere. Regardless of the legality of prostitution in these regions, the tradition of tourists seeking out both male and female sex workers among local populations demonstrates the importance of adequate educational and prevention measures among both commercial sex workers and travelers. In the Dominican Republic study, tourists were surveyed to determine their perceptions of HIV prevalence in the community and their own risk for infection. In addition, tourists were asked to state their opinion on a potential educational campaign on safer sex practices aimed at travelers entering the country. The study found that a majority of tourists were aware of their risk of exposure to HIV infection and would be comfortable receiving educational materials on HIV and other STDs from travel agencies, hotels, and elsewhere (Forsythe, Hasbún, and De Lister, 1998). In Jamaica and among the Pacific Island states emphasis is also placed on seeking alternative forms of employment for sex workers, many of who are migrants from rural areas seeking employment (Figueroa et al., 1995; Lewis and Bailey, 1992/1993).

Studies conducted in the late 1990s have shown that tourists are unlikely to consider local HIV prevalence when choosing a destination to visit. This signals a shift in perception over the last two decades of HIV's presence in the world—between 1981 and 1983, tourism in Haiti dropped more than 85 percent owing to publicity about the island's HIV epidemic (Lewis and Bailey, 1992/1993). As global awareness of how HIV can and cannot be transmitted increased over subsequent decades, the fears that prevented tourists from visiting Haiti and other high-prevalence regions in the early 1980s have diminished. Although research is currently scanty, worldwide the HIV epidemic does not seem to have deterred tourists from embarking on international travel, or from visiting any specific regions (Forsythe, Hasbún, and De Lister, 1998).

Continued scholarship regarding modes and trends in HIV transmission has contributed to a shift in conceptualization of HIV risk in the global community. Rather than identifying risk groups or high-risk regions to be avoided, health care workers, travelers, and governments are beginning to target risky behaviors. This perspective helps to decrease the stigma surrounding sectors of society and regions of the world where HIV prevalence is high, and simultaneously strengthens prevention efforts among all subgroups of the population. As modes of transmission change worldwide, this approach will prevent avoidance of HIV-affected communities and complaisance among traditionally low-prevalence groups and nations (Lange and Dax, 1987; Lee, Bell, and Hinojosa, 2002).

Civil War and International Conflict

The risk of HIV transmission within a community increases when infrastructure, social organization, and access to basic survival necessities are interrupted or destroyed. In armed conflict situations, civilians are often unable to access food, clean water, and shelter, and medical care and health facilities are often unavailable. In situations where a war has forced people either to become refugees crossing national borders in search of asylum, or displaced persons within the borders of their own country, sexual abuse, prostitution, unsafe medical practices, and increased drug abuse all facilitate the rapid spread of HIV. Women and girls are particularly vulnerable to sexual abuse and HIV infection in these conflict settings, as systematic rape becomes a weapon of war and sex an item to barter for food, transportation, or protection (Mworozi, 1993).

In central and southern Africa, where HIV prevalence remains the highest in the world, civil wars in Angola, Uganda, Mozambique, Sudan, Sierra Leone, and Somalia have led to refugee migrations and large-scale human rights abuses. In Rwanda, the 1994 genocide of the Tutsi people carried out by the Hutu resulted in 800,000 deaths over four months. In addition to mass murder, Hutu soldiers systematically raped thousands of Tutsi women and girls, intentionally spreading HIV to the uninfected (Donovan, 2002). HIV prevalence has risen to more than 11 percent in Rwanda, with reported cases of AIDS more than tripling between 1993 and 1996 (UNAIDS, 2000b).

In Angola, surveys of military personnel conducted in the late 1980s showed that HIV and STD prevalence in the military was significantly higher than in the general population. During the years of Angola's civil war, HIV prevalence was highest in the northern part of the country, but after the war, prevalence began to rise in southern Angola, first as refugees fled fighting in the north and later as soldiers returned home (Santos-Ferreira et al., 1990). This "bipolar" transfer of increased HIV prevalence from one part of a country to another has been observed in Uganda and Mozambique as well as in Angola and could easily take place in other regions outside of Africa where civil unrest is accompanied by large-scale forced migration and troop movements.

In Uganda, HIV prevalence is highest in the southern provinces of Rakai, Masaka, and Kampala, and in the northern province of Gulu. The movement of HIV from north to south within Uganda's borders has been attributed to international trucking, as well as to the movements of migrant workers. Neither trucking nor labor migration, however, can fully explain the timing and direction of Uganda's early AIDS epidemic (the first reported cases of AIDS in Uganda were in 1983). For six years after the Ugandan dictator Idi Amin was deposed in 1979, the ruling Ugandan National Liberation Front (UNLF) continued to recruit and conscript soldiers, focusing primarily on tribes living in the high-HIV-prevalence northern provinces. These new recruits were deployed near Uganda's southern border, probably contributing significantly to the increase in HIV infections in that area in the 1980s (Smallman-Raynor and Cliff, 1991). Uganda provides a good example of how internal displacement during a war can quickly spread HIV across a country by speeding up the pace of migrations that might have taken place more slowly via commercial routes. Internal migration cannot be prevented during war or in peacetime, but the dislocation and societal disruptions of armed conflict add additional elements of HIV transmission risk and dramatically increase the number of vulnerable travelers.

Long-term civil wars in Asia have led not only to population displacement, but also to international trafficking of human beings and increases in drug exports and the commercial sex trade. Myanmar remains one of the leading producers of opium and cocaine in the world, with the bulk of opium crops grown in the eastern Shan states, near the borders of Thailand and China.

Although technically illegal, heroin production, shipping, and sales account for a significant portion of Myanmar's GNP and supply a livelihood for a majority of northeastern peasant farmers. Never fully politically integrated with the rest of the country during the colonial era or in the present day, the eastern Shan states of Myanmar have been engaged in a conflict against the country's central government since the end of British rule in 1948. The government of Myanmar has responded to insurgencies and the formation of rebel military groups by destroying crops in Shan state, mandating forced migration and isolation of communities, and practicing intimidation tactics, including systematic sexual abuse of women and girls, executions, and torture (Beyrer, 2001).

As ethnic Shans continue to seek ways to flee the region, women and adolescent girls are often lured into sex work with promises of factory, domestic, and restaurant jobs in Thailand across Myanmar's eastern border. As illegal aliens in Thailand, Shan sex workers have little or no autonomy and are often subject to coercion and harassment from Thai authorities, customers, and brothel owners. HIV infection ranges from 50- to 70-percent prevalence among Shan women, who make up the majority of workers in Thailand's "lower-class" sex establishments. These refugee women are often in debt to their employers and are therefore unable to negotiate safer sex practices, such as condom use, or to refuse clients. In addition, Shan women are not able to take advantage of Thailand's rigorous HIV prevention interventions among sex workers owing to language barriers, lack of personal autonomy, and high rates of illiteracy. Physicians and human rights workers in Myanmar have observed that trafficking and exploitation of Shan women and girls will probably continue as long as political instability in Myanmar prevents refugees from finding stable housing and employment (Beyrer, 2001).

A long-term civil war can result in a nation's isolation from neighboring regions and the international community. During a conflict, communication becomes more difficult and foreign workers and visitors might avoid the region. In Nicaragua, a political coup in 1979 followed by years of social unrest and economic sanctions imposed by the United States left the country cut off from its South and Central American neighbors, with little international support for social and medical infrastructure. The civil war in Nicaragua, initiated by the Frente Sandanista de Liberación Nacional's overthrow of the current military regime, left 300,000 displaced persons in the country between 1980 and 1987. Rates of sexually transmitted infections among refugees were estimated to be high at the time, and sexual abuse of displaced women and girls was common, although medical surveillance data collected after the coup is far from complete. Sanctions imposed by the United States contributed to a 40-percent decrease in funding and support for health care infrastructure between 1987 and 1993 (Low et al., 1993).

As in eastern Africa and Southeast Asia, the conditions prevalent in Nicaragua after the war could have contributed to a significant and quickly spreading AIDS epidemic. The first case of AIDS diagnosed in Nicaragua, however, was not reported until 1987, nearly six years after initial cases were reported in neighboring countries (Low et al., 1993). Subsequently, rates of HIV have risen in the general population, but as of 2000, median HIV prevalence in Nicaragua was only 0.2 percent. Compared with nearby countries such as Honduras, Panama, and Guatemala (where national HIV prevalence in 2000 was 1.6 percent, 1.5 percent, and 1.0 percent, respectively), Nicaraguan HIV prevalence is surprisingly low. Female sex workers have been hardest hit by AIDS in Nicaragua, but even in this group where rates of other sexually transmitted diseases are high and risky sexual practices are common, HIV prevalence was only 1.6 percent in 1990, the last year that the community was surveyed (UNAIDS, 2000a).

Did a civil war and several years of economic sanctions temporarily protect Nicaragua from a large-scale AIDS epidemic? A 1993 study conducted in Nicaragua, Guatemala, El Salvador, Costa Rica, and Honduras noted that the countries with high levels of international tourism had correspondingly higher median HIV prevalence countrywide than their more isolated neighbors. In addition, countries receiving the most bilateral aid from the United States between 1981 and 1989 (El Salvador, Costa Rica, and Honduras) recorded the highest HIV-prevalence levels in the region in 1990. The temporary effect of Nicaragua's civil war and subsequent severing of diplomatic relations with the United States was that the country was shielded from imported HIV infections from North America, where HIV prevalence remains higher than in any Central American country (Low et al., 1993). Currently the virus is spreading quickly in Nicaragua, and although absolute numbers of new HIV infections are still low, prevalence is rising steadily, with few indications that adequate prevention and care services are available (UNAIDS, 2000a).

In the United States and other developed countries, warfare can potentially import new HIV strains and subtypes both from neighboring countries and from other continents. This possibility raises serious concerns in regions where the HIV epidemic has been slowed (in Europe and North America, for example) that the introduction of new HIV subtypes and recombinants into the general population could lead to a large-scale epidemic outbreak. Studies of the comparative virulence and infectivity of different HIV-1 subtypes support this speculation, suggesting that with the introduction of subtypes such as HIV-1 C and HIV-1 A/E, a new heterosexual epidemic could begin in developed countries (Lasky et al., 1997).

A study conducted among French service personnel deployed to foreign posts between 1987 and 1995 found that of sixty-one HIV-infected individuals, more than 60 percent were infected with non-B strains of HIV. The remaining infections, although HIV-1 subtype B, were of a strain genetically distant from the B subtype common in France and the rest of Europe. The majority of all HIV infections occurred in Djibouti, a small East African country that hosts several European military bases and is home to both North American and European expatriates and military personnel. Among HIV-infected members of this group, the non-European strain of HIV-1 subtype B predominates, suggesting that expatriates and others in the community were infected with a B subtype native to eastern Africa. These infections likely occurred through sexual contact with local sex workers and other members of the surrounding community (Lasky et al., 1997). Even in peacetime, armed forces stationed on foreign soil do not remain isolated from local communities. HIV prevention messages and interventions are urgently needed to ensure that military travel overseas does not contribute to a new HIV epidemic, either at home or abroad.

Over the long term, conflict situations are likely to result in a loss of medical surveillance data for the region in question, making an assessment of health care needs, HIV prevalence, and disease spread difficult. Available statistics on AIDS prevalence and incidence in war-torn African, Asian, and South American countries are at best out of date and at worst provide no real picture of the situation countrywide. For this reason, it is important to remain aware that predictions of disease trends and sources might not tell the whole story.

Wars increase HIV risk for all parties involved, from civilians to military service personnel. Along with an increase in the risky sexual behaviors and sexual abuse of women and girls associated with military occupation, armed conflict can have a detrimental effect on local health infrastructure, leaving thousands of people without access to adequate medical care. This scenario is particularly serious in the context of the HIV epidemic, because breakdowns in health care delivery prevent implementation of even the simplest prevention measures, such as education, voluntary counseling and testing, and condom distribution.

Where Is HIV Now?

Worldwide, 42 million people were infected with HIV and living with AIDS at the end of 2002. The Joint United Nations Program on HIV and AIDS (UNAIDS) estimates that another 45 million people could become infected by 2010 (UNAIDS, 2003). The decades leading up to the discovery of HIV saw changes that have contributed significantly to the pattern of the epidemic's spread, including increasing international travel, improved transportation and shipping routes in developing countries, struggles for national independence, and famine. Currently new epidemics of HIV are beginning in China, India, Russia, Eastern Europe, and elsewhere, but so far this increasing burden of disease in some areas has not led to any leveling off of prevalence or deaths in other settings. Although sub-Saharan Africa no longer represents the area of the epidemic's fastest growth, this region, which is home to only about 10 percent of the world's population, is also home to 70 percent of all people living with HIV and AIDS in the world (UNAIDS, 2003).

In Africa the HIV epidemic is older than elsewhere: Genetic studies have clarified that both HIV-1 and HIV-2 originate from viruses infecting nonhuman primates native to western and central Africa, confirming this as the virus's place of origin (Vidal et al., 2000). Despite the epidemic being so well established in the area, HIV prevalence has continued to rise to more than 30 percent prevalence among sexually active age groups in Botswana, Lesotho, Namibia, Swaziland, and Zimbabwe (UNAIDS, 2003). All epidemics eventually reach a plateau stage where prevalence stops rising, but in areas such as sub-Saharan Africa the epidemic is so severe the plateau prevalence could be higher than infections in one out of every three people.

Although the prevalence of HIV in the population is low compared with the total number of people infected in sub-Saharan Africa, the AIDS epidemic is growing fastest in Eastern Europe and Central Asia. Intravenous drug use is widespread in Russia and the countries on its borders, particularly among young people and prisoners. In Lithuania, Belarus, and the Ukraine, rates of drug use are particularly high, along with rates of HIV, but the epidemic has not remained within this IDU community. Heterosexual intercourse now accounts for a major proportion of total HIV transmission in this region, so that HIV now affects all sectors of society (UNAIDS, 2003).

Could the explosion of HIV and AIDS cases in Eastern Europe be predicted? Thailand's rate of HIV is the highest in the Asian Pacific region, followed closely by Cambodia and Myanmar. Unlike the Russian and Eastern European epidemic, HIV is well established in Thailand, with the first cases diagnosed in 1985, just four years after the first cases of the new "gay cancer" later identified as AIDS were reported by American medical journals (Phanuphak et al., 1985). Thai injection drug users were the first group in the country to become infected with HIV, but within five years the virus was common among the country's large community of commercial sex workers and increasingly prevalent among their clients and clients' wives, girlfriends, and families. In countries such as Indonesia and Cambodia, where drug use in the general population has soared in the wake of social and political turmoil, similar cycles of infection have moved through the population (UNAIDS, 2003). It might be that Eastern European nations can learn from the Thai epidemic, targeting prevention measures to populations who will soon be particularly vulnerable to infection and planning how to care for those who are already infected.

Looking at an overview of worldwide HIV prevalence in 2003, the areas of highest HIV prevalence (sub-Saharan Africa, Central America, the Caribbean, western Asia) stand out strongly, but another story is unfolding in regions where prevalence still appears to be low. In India and China, average national HIV prevalence is still below 1 percent, but a closer view reveals significant differences among regions and clear warnings of risk (UNAIDS, 2003). In India, average national HIV prevalence is about 0.8 percent, a figure that is deceptively low, as India's population is one of the largest in the world. The 0.8 percent HIV prevalence in India means that approximately 3.97 million people are living with HIV or AIDS in the country, accounting for more than 9 percent of all people living with HIV and AIDS in the world (UNAIDS, 2002b).

As in India, China's HIV epidemic has followed a different course in almost every region of the country, with the highest prevalence in the country's southern states. Although overall HIV prevalence in the country is 0.1 percent, prevalence among communities of injection drug users ranges from 44 to 85 percent in the provinces of Yunan and Xinjiang (UNAIDS, 2002a). Among rural farmers who participated in commercial blood selling during the 1980s and 1990s, unofficial surveillance estimates that HIV prevalence could be as high as 80 percent in some communities. A significant percentage of China's population consists of people who travel long distances to work, thus raising the risk of HIV spreading into the rest of the country (UNAIDS, 2003). Additionally, as the movement of the Thai epidemic shows, explosive increases in HIV prevalence among drug users can lead to a similar increase in prevalence among the general population.

In South America, where the AIDS epidemic has been present since the 1980s, the national response has been significant in many countries. Government-subsidized antiretroviral medications are provided in five South and Central American countries (first in Brazil, and more recently in Argentina, Costa Rica, Cuba, and Uruguay), and this region continues to set worldwide precedents for access to AIDS care and treatment (UNAIDS, 2003). Initially, the South and Central American HIV epidemic mirrored that of the United States and Europe, with the highest HIV prevalence among men who have sex with men. Although this group is still disproportionately affected, surveillance published in 2003 shows that since the epidemic's beginning in the region, the ratio of men to women infected with HIV has changed from 3 to 1 to 2 to 1. This shift indicates that although rates of HIV infection among men have not changed, more women are becoming infected (UNAIDS, 2003). In countries like Brazil, Honduras, Uruguay, and Argentina, drug use has also increased, particularly among prison inmates and in areas of social and political turmoil. The dynamics of the HIV epidemic in South America are changing, but effective surveillance and strong government involvement can help a public health response to move as quickly as the virus.

The HIV epidemic has changed in high-income countries over the two decades since the virus was first identified in the United States. Deaths from AIDS in wealthy North American and European countries have decreased since highly active antiretroviral therapy regimens became available to the general population in the late 1990s, and quality of life among people infected with HIV has improved. At the same time, as the epidemic continues in these regions over the long term, new communities and sectors of the population are being affected. Once found primarily among gay and bisexual men, intravenous drug users, hemophiliacs, and partners of those who were infected, HIV is now common in all sectors of the population, with prevalence rates rising fastest among young women and ethnic minorities. Among adolescents who become infected with HIV in the United States, more than half are girls, and AIDS is now the leading cause of death among African American men between the ages of twenty-five and forty-four (UNAIDS, 2003). In Europe, surveillance shows that between 1997 and 2000, heterosexual transmission of HIV increased by 59 percent (UNAIDS, 2003). As the face of the epidemic changes, prevention, care, and treatment tactics must change as well. Perhaps lessons learned from the heterosexual HIV epidemics in Asia and Africa can help high-income regions develop new prevention strategies.

In the United States, new kinds of long-term prevention interventions will now have to be crafted to reach the communities initially most affected by HIV and AIDS in the 1980s. Although HIV transmission among gay men has decreased thanks to information campaigns, counseling, grassroots activism and support, and other prevention strategies, this community has consistently been disproportionately affected by the virus. Unprotected sex between men remains a major risk factor for infection in countries such as the United States, Canada, and Australia. It has been suggested that the wide availability of antiretroviral medications in these developed nations has led to feelings of complacency among young people who did not come of age during HIV's early decades (Stall et al., 2000). Prevention messages developed during the 1980s might not only fail to reach young, sexually active people today, but might no longer seem relevant to older men who have lived for twenty years with the knowledge of HIV's presence among neighbors, friends, and loved ones. Increases in the incidence of sexually transmitted diseases such as gonorrhea and syphilis among gay men in many U.S. cities suggest that current safer-sex and prevention messages are no longer effective. As anti-retroviral therapy slowly becomes more available to populations worldwide, the importance of battling complacency about the virus among all communities and age groups will increase as well (UNAIDS, 2003).

The global HIV epidemic has never been static or pre-dictable. Since the earliest cases of immune deficiency and HIV were diagnosed in Europe and the United States, the virus has spread quickly and has continually confounded expectations about which individuals are most at risk for infection and how different sectors of society are related. HIV was first assumed confined to gay and bisexual men and hemophiliacs when it was characterized in the early 1980s. HIV affected African families and travelers even before the virus was identified, however, with AIDS-like symptoms detected in children, parents, and individuals as early as the late 1970s. Worldwide, young, heterosexual women and members of ethnic minorities are currently at dis-proportionate risk for HIV infection as compared with the general population. As members of the World Health Organization and UNAIDS observed in new guidelines to prevent mother-to-child HIV transmission, women and children will continue to be at heightened risk for HIV infection until social and economic inequalities between genders can be addressed and mitigated. Overall, new HIV epidemics flourish in regions where political, economic, and social influence is disrupted or shared unequally among different sectors of society. A global perspective is neces-sary to understand the movements of HIV and AIDS in the pre-sent, and an appreciation of the effects of international relations, war, poverty, migration, and access to medical care and educa-tion on transmission is necessary to combat the virus.

References

Allan J. S., E. M. Whitehead, K. Strout, et al. Strong association of simian immunodeficiency virus (SIVagm) envelope glycoprotein heterodimers: possible role in receptor-mediated activation. *AIDS Research and Human Retroviruses,* 1992; 8(12): 2011–2020.

Altman, L. K. AIDS brings shift in UN message on breast-feeding. *New York Times,* 26 July 1998.

Anonymous. 1982. Unexplained immunodeficiency and opportunistic infections in infants—New York, New Jersey, California. *Morbidity and Mortality Weekly Report* 31(49): 665–667.

Barin, F., F. Denis, J. S. Allan, et al. 1985. Serological evidence for virus related to simian T-lymphotropic retrovirus III in residents of west Africa. *Lancet* 2(8469): 1387–1389.

Barongo, L. R., M. W. Borgdorff, F. F. Mosha, et al. 1992. The epidemiology of HIV-1 infection in urban areas, roadside settlements, and rural villages in Mwanza Region, Tanzania. *AIDS* 6: 1521–1528.

Bayley, A.C., R. Chiangsong-Popov, A. G. Dalgleish, et al. 1985. HTLV-III serology distinguishes atypical and endemic Kaposi's sarcoma in Africa. *Lancet* 1 (8425): 359–361.

Beyrer, C. 2001. Shan women and girls in the sex industry in Southeast Asia; political causes and human rights implications. *Social Science and Medicine* 53: 543–550.

Beyrer, C., M. H. Razak, K. Lisam, et al. 2000. Overland heroin trafficking routes and HIV-1 spread in south and South-East Asia. *AIDS* 14: 75–83.

Bock, P. J. , and D. M. Markovitz. 2001. Infection with HIV-2. *AIDS* 15 (suppl. 5): S35–S45.

Cameron, D. W., J. N. Simonsen, L. J. D'Costa, et al. 1989. Female to male transmission of human immunodeficiency virus type 1: Risk factors for seroconversion in men. *Lancet* 2 (8660): 403–407.

Campbell, R. S. F., and W. F. Robinson. 1998. The comparative pathology of lentiviruses. *Journal of Comparative Pathology* 119: 333–395.

Carswell, J. W., G. Lloyd, and J. Howells. 1989. Prevalence of HIV-1 in east African lorry drivers. *AIDS* 3: 759–761.

Centers for Disease Control. 1985. Recommendations for assisting in the prevention of perinatal transmission of human T-lymphotropic virus type III/Lymphadenopathy-associated virus and acquired immunodeficiency syndrome. *Morbidity and Mortality Weekly Report* 34(48): 721–733.

Chitnis, A., D. Rawls, and J. Moore. 2000. Origin of HIV type 1 in French Equatorial Africa? *AIDS Research and Human Retroviruses* 16(1): 5–8.

Coffin, J. M. 1991. "Retroviridae and their replication." In *Fundamental Virology*, edited by B. N. Fields, D. M. Knipe, et al. New York: Raven Press, pp. 1437–1500.

Connor, E. M., R. S. Sperling, R. Gelber, et al. 1994. Reduction of maternal-infant transmission of human immunodeficiency virus type 1 with Zidovudine treatment. *New England Journal of Medicine* 331(18): 1173–1180.

Coutsoudis, A., K. Pillay, L. Kuhn, et al. 2001. Method of feeding and transmission of HIV-1 from mothers to children by 15 months of age: Prospective cohort study from Durban, South Africa. *AIDS* 15(3): 379–387.

Coutsoudis, A., A. E. Goga, N. Rollins, et al. 2002. Free formula milk for infants of HIV-infected women: Blessing or curse? *Health Policy and Planning* 17(2): 154–160.

Donovan, P. 2002. Rape and HIV/AIDS in Rwanda. *Lancet* 360(suppl. 1): S17–S18.

Edwards, S., and C. Carne. 1998. Oral sex and the transmission of viral STIs. *Sexually Transmitted Infections* 74(1): 6–10.

Essex, M., and P. J. Kanki. 1988. The origins of the AIDS virus. *Scientific American* 259(4): 64–71.

Essex, M. 1998. State of the HIV pandemic. *Journal of Human Virology* 1: 427–429.

Essex, M. E. 1997. "Origin of acquired immunodeficiency syndrome." In *AIDS: Biology, Diagnosis, Treatment, and Prevention,* fourth edition, edited by V. T. DeVita, S. Hellman, and S. A. Rosenberg. New York: Lippincott-Raven, pp. 3–14.

Essex, M. E., L. Soto-Ramirez, E. Renjifo, W. K. Wang, T. H. Lee. 1997. Genetic variation within human immunodeficiency viruses generates rapid changes in tropism, virulence, and transmission. *Leukemia* 11(suppl 3): 93–94.

Expert Group of the Joint United Nations Programme on HIV/AIDS. 1997. Implications of HIV variability for transmission: Scientific and policy issues. *AIDS* 11: 1–15.

Figueroa, J. P., A. Braithwaite, E. Ward, et al. 1995. The HIV/AIDS epidemic in Jamaica. *AIDS* 9: 761–768.

Forsythe, S., J. Hasbún, and M. B. De Lister. 1998. Protecting paradise: Tourism and AIDS in the Dominican Republic. *Health Policy and Planning* 13(3): 277–286.

Gallo, R. C., S. Z. Salahuddin, M. Popovic, et al. 1984. Frequent detection and isolation of cytopathic retroviruses (HTLV-III) from patients with AIDS and at risk for AIDS. *Science* 224(4648): 500–503.

Gao, F., L. Yue, D. L. Robertson, et al. 1994. Genetic diversity of human immunodeficiency virus type 2: Evidence for distinct sequence subtypes with differences in virus biology. *Journal of Virology* 68(11): 7433–7447.

Gifford, R., and M. Tristem. 2003. The evolution, distribution and diversity of endogenous retroviruses. *Virus Genes* 26(3): 291–315.

Global Programme on AIDS. 1992. Consensus statement from the WHO/UNICEF consultation on HIV transmission and breast-feeding. *Weekly Epidemiological Record* 67(24): 177–184.

Gottlieb, G. S., P. S. Sow, S. E. Hawes, et al. 2002. Equal plasma viral loads predict a similar rate of CD4 T cell decline in HIV Type 1- and Type 2-infected individuals from Senegal, West Africa. *Journal of Infectious Diseases* 185: 905–914.

Grosskurth, H., F. Mosha, J. Todd, et al. 1995. Impact of improved treatment of sexually transmitted diseases on HIV infection in rural Tanzania: Randomized controlled trial. *Lancet* 346: 530–536.

Guay, L. A., P. Musoke, T. Fleming, et al. 1999. Intrapartum and neonatal single-dose nevirapine compared with zidovudine for prevention of mother-to-child transmission of HIV-1 in Kampala, Uganda: HIVNET 012 randomized trial. *Lancet* 354(9181): 795–802.

Hamers, F. F., and A. M. Downs. 2003. HIV in central and eastern Europe. *Lancet* 361:1035–1044.

Hawkes, S. J., and G. J. Hart. 1993. Travel, migration, and HIV. *AIDS Care* 5(2): 207–214.

Haygood, W. Prostitution plays key role in fueling Africa's AIDS crisis. *Boston Globe* 11 October 1999.

Hilderbrand, K., E. Goemaere, and D. Coetzee. 2003. The prevention of mother-to-child HIV transmission programme and infant feeding practices. *Southern African Medical Journal* 93(10): 779–781.

Hillis, D. M. 2000. How to resolve the debate on the origin of AIDS. *Science* 289(5486): 1877–1878.

Hu, D. J., A. Buvé, J. Baggs, G. Van der Groen, and T. J. Dondero. 1999. What role does HIV-1 subtype play in transmission and pathogenesis? An epidemiological perspective. *AIDS* 13: 873–881.

John, C. G., B. A. Richardson, and R. W. Nduati. 2001. Timing of breast milk HIV-1 transmission: A meta-analysis. *East African Medical Journal* 78(2): 75–79.

John-Stewart, G., D. Mbori-Ngacha, R. Ekpini, et al. 2004. Breast-feeding and transmission of HIV-1. *Journal of Acquired Immune Deficiency Syndromes* 35(2): 196–202.

Jonckheer, T., I. Dab, P. Van de Perre, et al. 1985. Cluster of HTLV-III/LAV infection in an African family. *Lancet* 1(8425): 400–401.

Kalichman, S. C. 1998. *Understanding AIDS: Advances in Research and Treatment*. Washington, DC: American Psychological Association.

Kanki, P. J., J. Alroy, and M. Essex. 1985. Isolation of T-lymphotropic retrovirus related to HTLV-III/LAV from wild-caught African green monkeys. *Science* 230(4728): 951–954.

Korber, B., E. E. Allen, A. D. Farmer, and G. L. Myers. 1995. Heterogeneity of HIV-1 and HIV-2. *AIDS* 9(suppl A): S5–S18.

Korber, B., M. Muldoon, J. Theiler, et al. 2000. Timing the ancestor of the HIV-1 pandemic strains. *Science* 288(5472): 1789–1796.

Lallemant, M., G. Jourdain, S. Le Coeur, et al. 2004. A randomised, double-blind trial assessing the efficacy of single-dose perinatal nevirapine added to a standard zidovudine regimen for the prevention of mother-to-child transmission of HIV-1 in Thailand. Presented at: Programme and Abstracts of the 11th Conference on Retroviruses and Opportunistic Infections, 8–11 February, San Francisco. Abstract 40LB.

Lange, W. R., and E. M. Dax. 1987. HIV infection and international travel. *American Family Physician* 36(3): 197–204.

Lasky, M., J. L. Perret, M. Peeters, et al. 1997. Presence of multiple non-B subtypes and divergent subtype B strains of HIV-1 in individuals infected after overseas deployment. *AIDS* 11: 43–51.

Lee, D., D. C. Bell, and M. Hinojosa. 2002. Drug use, travel, and HIV risk. *AIDS Care* 14(4): 443–453.

Lewis, N. D., and J. Bailey. 1992/1993. HIV, international travel, and tourism: Global issues and Pacific perspectives. *Asia Pacific Journal of Public Health* 6(3): 159–167.

Low, N., M. Egger, A. Gorter, et al. 1993. AIDS in Nicaragua: Epidemiological, political, and sociocultural perspectives. *International Journal of Health Services* 23(4): 685–702.

Lucas, G. M., R. E. Chaisson, and R. D. Moore. 1999. Highly active antiretroviral therapy in a large urban clinic: Risk factors for virologic failure and adverse drug reactions. *Journal of the American Medical Association* 131(2): 81–87.

Marcon, L., N. Hattori, R. C. Gallo, and G. Franchini. 1991. A comparison of genetic and biologic features of human and non-human immunodeficiency lentiviruses. *Antibiotics and Chemotherapy* 43: 55–68.

Marlink, R. 1996. Lessons from the second AIDS virus, HIV-2. *AIDS* 10(7): 689–699.

Martinson, N., L. Morris, G. Gray, et al. 2004. HIV resistance and transmission following single-dose nevirapine in a PMTCT cohort. Presented at: Programme and Abstracts of the 11th Conference on Retroviruses and Opportunistic Infections, 8–11 February, San Francisco. Abstract 38.

Mbugua, G. G., L. N. Muthami, C. W. Mutura, et al. 1995. Epidemiology of HIV infection among long-distance truck drivers in Kenya. *East African Medical Journal* 72(8): 515–518.

McCutchan, F. E. 2000. Understanding the genetic diversity of HIV-1. *AIDS* 14(suppl. 3): S31–S44.

Miyoshi, I., S. Yoshimoto, M. Fujishita, et al. 1982. Natural adult T-cell leukemia virus infection in Japanese monkeys. *Lancet* 2(8299): 658.

Mworozi, E. A. 1993. AIDS and civil war: a devil's alliance. Dislocation caused by civil strife in Africa provides fertile ground for the spread of HIV. *AIDS Analysis Africa* 3(6): 8–10.

Naik, T. N., S. Sarkar, H. L. Singh, et al. 1991. Intravenous drug users—a new high-risk group for HIV infection in India. *AIDS* 5(1): 117–118.

Nemeth, A., S. Bygdeman, E. Sandström, et al. 1986. Early case of acquired immunodeficiency syndrome in a child from Zaire. *Sexually Transmitted Diseases* 13(2): 111–113.

Nyamathi, A. M., C. Bennett, and B. Leake. 1995. Predictors of maintained high-risk behaviors among impoverished women. *Public Health Reports* 1995. 110: 600–606.

Osmanov, S., C. Pattou, N. Walker, et al. 2001. Estimated global distribution and regional spread of HIV-1 genetic subtypes in the year 2000. *Journal of Acquired Immune Deficiency Syndromes* 29: 184–190.

Ou, C. Y., Y. Takebe, B. G. Weniger, et al. 1993. Independent introduction of two major HIV-1 genotypes into distinct high-risk populations in Thailand. *Lancet* 341: 1171–1174.

Patrascu, I. V., and O. Dumitrescu. 1993. The epidemic of human immunodeficiency virus infection in Romanian children. *AIDS Research and Human Retroviruses* 9(1): 99–104.

Pepin, J., G. Morgan, D. Dunn, et al. 1991. HIV-2 induced immunosuppression among asymptomatic West African prostitutes: Evidence that HIV-2 is pathogenic, but less so than HIV-1. *AIDS* 5:1165–1172.

Phanuphak, P., C. Locharernkul, W. Panmuong, and H. Wilde. 1985. A report of three cases of AIDS in Thailand. *Asian Pacific Journal of Allergy and Infectious Immunology* 3: 195–199.

Piot, P., and M. Laga. 1994. "Epidemiology of AIDS in the developing world." In *Textbook of AIDS Medicine,* edited by S. Broder, T. C. Merigan, and D. Bolognesi. Baltimore, MD: Williams and Wilkins, pp. 109–132.

Plummer, F. A., J. N. Simonsen, D. W. Cameron, et al. 1991. Cofactors in male-female sexual transmission of human immunodeficiency virus type 1. *Journal of Infectious Diseases* 163(2): 233–239.

Pomfret, J. The high cost of selling blood. *The Washington Post* 11 January 2001.

Potts, M. Thinking about vaginal microbicide testing. 2000. *American Journal of Public Health* 90(2): 188–190.

Quinn, T. C., J. M. Mann, J. W. Curran, and P. Piot. 1986. AIDS in Africa: An epidemiologic paradigm. *Science* 234: 955–963.

Rosenthal, E. In rural China, a steep price of poverty: dying of AIDS. *The New York Times* 28 October 2000.

————. Deadly shadow of AIDS darkens remote Chinese village. *New York Times* 28 May 2001.

Royce, R. A., A. Sena, W. Cates Jr., et al. 1997. Sexual transmission of HIV. *New England Journal of Medicine* 336(15): 1072–1078.

Santos-Ferreira, M. O., T. Cohen, M. H. Lourenço, et al. 1990. A study of seroprevalence of HIV-1 and HIV-2 in six provinces of People's Republic of Angola: Clues to the spread of HIV infection. *Journal of Acquired Immune Deficiency Syndromes* 3: 780–786.

Sarr, A. D., J. L. Sankalé, A. Guèye-Ndiaye, et al. 2000. Genetic analysis of HIV type 2 in monotypic and dual HIV infections. *AIDS Research and Human Retroviruses* 16(3): 293–298.

Scott, G. B., B. E. Buck, J. G. Leterman, et al. 1984. Acquired immunodeficiency syndrome in infants. *New England Journal of Medicine* 310(2): 76–81.

Serwadda, D., M. J. Wawer, S. D. Musgrave, et al. 1992. HIV risk factors in three geographic strata of rural Rakai District, Uganda. *AIDS* 6: 983–989.

Shaffer, N., R. Chuachoowong, P. A. Mock, et al. 1999. Short-course zidovudine for perinatal HIV-1 transmission in Bangkok, Thailand: A randomized controlled trial. *Lancet* 353(9155): 773–780.

Shapiro, R. L., S. Lockman, I. Thior, et al. 2003. Low adherence to recommended infant feeding strategies among HIV-infected women; results from the pilot phase of a randomized trial to prevent mother-to-child transmission in Botswana. *AIDS Education and Prevention* 15(3): 221–230.

Simon, V., and D. D. Ho. 2003. HIV-1 dynamics in vivo: Implications for therapy. *Nat Rev Microbiol* 1(3): 181–190.

Smallman-Raynor, M. R., and A. D. Cliff. 1991. Civil war and the spread of AIDS in central Africa. *Epidemiology and Infection* 170: 69–80.

Soto-Ramirez, L., B. Renjifo, M. F. McLane, et al. 1996. HIV-1 Langerhans' cell tropism associated with heterosexual transmission of HIV. *Science* 271: 1291–1293.

Stall, et al. 2000. The gay 90s: a review of research in the 1990s on sexual behavior and HIV risk among men who have sex with men. *AIDS* 14(suppl 3): S101–S114.

Thiry, L., S. Sprecher-Goldberger, T. Jonckheer, et al. 1985. Isolation of AIDS virus from cell-free breast milk of three healthy virus carriers. *Lancet* 11: 891–892.

UNAIDS. HIV and infant feeding: An interim statement. 1996. *Weekly Epidemiological Record* 71(39): 289–296.

———. 2000a. Epidemiological fact sheets on HIV/AIDS and sexually transmitted diseases 2000 update: Nicaragua. Available at: http://www.who.int/hiv/pub/epidemiology/pubfacts/en/. Accessed March 25, 2004.

———. 2000b. Epidemiological fact sheet on HIV/AIDS and sexually transmitted infections: Rwanda 2000 update. Available at: http://www.who.int/hiv/pub/epidemiology/pubfacts/en/. Accessed March 25, 2004.

———. 2001. AIDS epidemic update, December 2001. Available at: http://www.who.int/hiv/pub/epidemiology/epi2001/en/. Accessed: June 16, 2004.

———. 2002a. Epidemiological fact sheets on HIV/AIDS and sexually transmitted diseases 2002 update: China. Available at: http://www.who.int/hiv/pub/epidemiology/pubfacts/en/. Accessed March 26, 2004.

———. 2002b. Epidemiological fact sheets on HIV/AIDS and sexually transmitted diseases 2002 update: India. Available at: http://www.who.int/hiv/pub/epidemiology/pubfacts/en/. Accessed March 26, 2004.

———2002c. Epidemiological fact sheets on HIV/AIDS and sexually transmitted diseases 2002 update: Kenya. Available at: http://www.who.int/hiv/pub/epidemiology/pubfacts/en/. Accessed March 26, 2004.

———. 2002d. AIDS epidemic update, December 2002. Available at: http://www.who.int/hiv/pub/epidemiology/epi2002/en/. Accessed March 25, 2004.

———. 2002e. Report on the global HIV and AIDS epidemic UNAIDS/ 02.26E. Geneva: UNAIDS July 2002.

———. 2003. AIDS Epidemic Update 2003. Available at: http://www.unaids.org. Accessed June 16, 2004.

Van de Perre, P., M. Carael, M. Robert-Guroff, et al. 1985. Female prostitutes: A risk group for infection with human T-cell lymphotropic virus type III. *Lancet* 2(8454): 524–526.

Vandepitte, J., R. Verwilghen, P. Zachee. 1983. AIDS and cryptococcus (Zaire 1977). *Lancet* 1(8330): 925–926.

Vidal N., M. Peeters, C. Mulanga-Kabeya, et al. 2000. Unprecedented degree of human immunodeficiency virus type 1 (HIV-1) group M genetic diversity in the Democratic Republic of the Congo suggests that the HIV-1 pandemic originated in central Africa. *Journal of Virology* 74(22): 10498–10507.

Wawer, M. J., D. Serwadda, S. D. Musgrave, et al. 1991. Dynamics of spread of HIV-1 infection in a rural district of Uganda. *British Medical Journal* 303: 1303–1306.

Weniger, B. G., K. Limpakarnjanarat, K. Ungchusak, et al. 1991. The epidemiology of HIV infection and AIDS in Thailand. *AIDS* (suppl. 2): S71–S85.

Weniger B. G., Y. Takebe, C. Ou, et al. 1994. The molecular epidemiology of HIV in Asia. *AIDS* 8 (suppl. 2): S13–S28.

World Health Assembly. 1949. Expert committee on international health and quarantine: Report on the first session (principle 2). *Official Records of the World Health Organization* 19: 5–7.

World Health Organization. 2000. New data on the prevention of mother-to-child transmission of HIV and their policy implications—conclusions and recommendations WHO/RHR/01.28. Available at: http://www.who.int/child-adolescent-health/New_Publications/CHILD_HEALTH/MTCT_Consultation.htm. Accessed February 11, 2004.

World Tourism Organization. 2003. International tourist arrivals by (sub)region. Available at: http://www.hotelbenchmark.com/frames.htm?http%3A//www.hotelbenchmark.com/Features/articles/020130WTO.htm. Accessed June 16, 2004.

Yu, X. F., Y. Shao, C. Beyrer, et al. 1999. Emerging HIV infections with distinct subtypes of HIV-1 infection among injecting drug users from geographically separate locations in Guangxi Province, China. *Journal of Acquired Immune Deficiency Syndromes* 22: 180–188.

Ziegler, J. B., D. A. Cooper, R. O. Johnson, J. Gold. 1985. Post-natal transmission of AIDS-associated retrovirus from mother to infant. *Lancet* 1(8434): 896–898.

2

Problems, Controversies, and Solutions

HIV remains one of the most complicated and costly diseases in the world, even after more than twenty years of study and research into the virus and its effects. In confronting AIDS, individuals and communities must also come to terms with their own ideas and traditions regarding family, class, race, and gender roles. As rates of HIV infection grow, particularly in regions such as sub-Saharan Africa, Eastern Europe, and Southeast Asia, the presence of the virus promises to have a profound effect on societies, communities, and individual relationships. Issues such as the stigma associated with HIV infection in many regions clearly show the connections between societal acceptance and individuals' ability to access medical care and other forms of support. Gaps between rich and poor, at both the community and the national level, are exacerbated by growing demands for complex and expensive medical interventions to treat HIV and AIDS. Policymakers are left to make difficult decisions about allocation of funds, often in the face of other serious public health threats, and frequently without sufficient precedent to adequately predict the results of their decisions. At the same time, HIV and AIDS have led to the creation of new international partnerships as pioneers in research, policy, and fund-raising seek to bring the benefit of their experience to severely affected regions. These partnerships, though beneficial, raise ethical and practical questions that, in some cases, are being considered for the first time. HIV and AIDS can debilitate families and individuals, but at the community and national levels the social, financial, and structural effects of the virus might be equally serious.

Stigma and Discrimination

The metaphors used to describe HIV and AIDS reflect feelings of fear, blame, and uncertainty: war, victimization, crime, and punishment (Aggleton and Maluwa, 2000). In an article published in 1990, approximately a decade after AIDS was first identified in the United States, a group of French researchers stated that "AIDS is not the keystone of our society, but it is the metaphor for our contradictions" (Manuel et al., 1990, 23). Government, community, and family responses to HIV and AIDS worldwide have demonstrated these contradictions, reacting to the threat of infectious disease with fear, compassion, and more ambivalent responses. Often it is not HIV itself, but a society's preconceived ideas about who is at risk for infection that influence how individuals and communities respond to people living with HIV and AIDS.

Considering individual and community responses to HIV and AIDS from a psychological perspective shows that many negative reactions to those who are infected stem from the coping mechanisms individuals develop to handle stress. Responses to a perceived threat often include attempts to escape, regulate, or deny a source of fear, or to displace anxiety onto an easily defined object. In the case of HIV, these strategies lead to rejection of infected family members, denial, refusal to tolerate "deviant" behavior or alternative lifestyles, and stigmatization of groups or communities seen to be at fault or at risk for infection (Gilmore and Somerville, 1994). Because HIV is a terminal disease with no known cure, intense fear often surrounds a diagnosis of HIV or AIDS, which in turn can affect how people living with HIV and AIDS are regarded and cared for by others. In the past, other diseases such as the black plague, cholera, polio, syphilis, leprosy, tuberculosis, and hepatitis B have provoked similar responses (Gilmore and Somerville, 1994).

The concept of "stigmatization" was codified in 1963 by the sociologist Erving Goffman, who defined it as a process of discrediting individuals perceived as different based on traits or identity (Aggleton and Maluwa, 2000). In practical terms, discrimination is an expression of stigma, transforming class, gender, ethnicity, sexual orientation, and other characteristics into concrete social inequalities (Parker et al., 2002). For example, because HIV is transmitted primarily through sexual contact, and because the virus was first perceived among groups considered sexually deviant, such as gay men and commercial sex workers, HIV infection remains associated with nonnormative sexual behavior. Once this association has been solidified, denial of medical care to people living with AIDS and infringements on the human rights of people living with HIV can be justified as an appropriate response to deviant or illegal behavior (Parker et al., 2002). Positive responses to people with HIV and AIDS at the national, community, and family level have been documented worldwide. As long as the virus remains associated with stigmatized communities or behaviors, however, responses to those who are infected will be affected by class divisions, gender roles, race, and standards of "appropriate" sexual expression (Warwick et al., 1998).

Reactions to HIV infection and people living with AIDS differ depending on cultural, economic, and geographic context, but several themes in both positive and negative reactions have emerged from international surveys of stigma. A study conducted simultaneously in Thailand, Tanzania, India, and Mexico in the mid-1990s found that although the specifics may differ, perceptions of gender roles, appropriate sexual behavior and orientation, and socioeconomic status all influenced how HIV and AIDS were regarded in community settings. Economic resources were shown to have a direct impact on the quality of care people living with HIV and AIDS will receive. Across all four countries, study respondents felt that private medical care was of higher quality than public services and facilities, but the cost of hospitalization, drugs, and examinations in the private sector was generally more than most low-income families could afford. When families care for relatives with HIV or AIDS at home (a common approach to care in resource-scarce settings), a family's economic situation often dictates the level of care and support they are able to offer (Warwick et al., 1998).

Women and men who took part in this four-country study reported a range of reactions from family members after revealing their seropositive status. In Thailand, Mexico, India, and Tanzania, where HIV is primarily transmitted heterosexually, the virus is considered to be an STD and therefore traditionally associated with extramarital or premarital sex. Women from India reported that they often face intense scrutiny when revealing their HIV status to family members and must prove that they were infected accidentally rather than as a result of marital infidelity. Men in India rarely faced such questioning when their seropositive status was revealed. In Mexico, women reported a similar dynamic, adding that if an HIV-positive woman is suspected of promiscuous behavior or infidelity, family members might refuse to care for her, regardless of the actual circumstances of her infection (Warwick et al., 1998). In situations where women are not confident that they will receive support from family and community members upon disclosing their HIV status, they might be less likely to seek medical care or to use safer sex practices.

Worldwide, modes of HIV transmission affect how communities and families respond to an individual's disclosure of a positive HIV test result. Negative or unsupportive reactions are usually motivated by social stigma surrounding marginalized sexual identities, nonnormative sexual behavior, and drug use. Often HIV infection is so closely associated with a stigmatized group that the risk of infection from members of other sectors of society is ignored. In Thailand, for example, the government-sponsored "100 percent Condom Program" to prevent new HIV infections focuses almost exclusively on protecting sex between female sex workers and their male clients. Although successful in lowering the risk of STD transmission via commercial sex, the program has not encouraged Thai men to practice safer sex with noncommercial partners, such as wives and girlfriends, who continue to be put at risk for infection. In this way, the close association between HIV and prostitution could be hindering prevention of HIV among Thai women who do not engage in commercial sex work (Havanon, Bennett, and Knodel, 1993).

Just as not all members of a stigmatized or minority group are infected with HIV, not all people who are living with HIV and AIDS are members of traditionally recognized risk groups. In regions where HIV infection is associated with a specific or deviant identity, people who become infected with the virus could face a double stigma, both as affected by disease and as a perceived member of a marginalized group. In both North and South America, HIV and AIDS were first diagnosed and characterized primarily among gay men (Castro et al., 1998; Gilmore and Somerville, 1994). Heterosexual sex is now the most common mode of HIV transmission worldwide, but in the United States and in other regions in North and South America, HIV-infected men are often still assumed to be gay. Conversely, the same stigma can lead to the assumption that all gay men must be either HIV-positive or at high risk for infection. This cycle of blame and prejudice can seriously affect the care and support people living with HIV and AIDS can expect from family members and health care services in regions where gay, lesbian, and bisexual identities are stigmatized (Herek and Capitanio, 1993; Gilmore and Somerville, 1994).

In the late 1990s, a study conducted in Ciudad Netzahualcóyotl (Netza) and Mexico City began to define the links between sexual orientation and family responses to HIV infection in Mexico. Netza is an urban community outside of Mexico City, a majority of whose residents are immigrants from other parts of the country seeking employment in the capital. The unemployment rate is about 56 percent in Netza, which means that many families live in a constant state of social and financial "emergency" (Castro et al., 1998). The gay community in Mexico City was also surveyed for the study, because many of these men have moved to the capital from Netza. Researchers found that the families of gay men from Netza generally reacted negatively to a relative "coming out" as homosexual, although a number of families became more accepting over time. In Netza, HIV infection is closely associated with homosexuality, so men who come out as gay are often assumed to be leading an "immoral lifestyle" and to be at high risk for HIV infection. Conversely, men living with HIV or AIDS are often stigmatized because they are assumed to be gay (Castro et al., 1998).

Gay men with HIV in Netza often return home to live with their immediate family after becoming ill, because home-based care accounts for the majority of care available to people with AIDS in the area. Although families are generally willing to care for HIV-infected members, gay men are often allowed to return home only on the condition that their sexuality remains hidden from the community and sometimes with the stipulation that their illness not be attributed to AIDS. This discomfort with discussions of homosexuality and HIV infection stems from families' fears of being stigmatized by the surrounding community, and it can lead to profound social isolation for people living with AIDS and their caretakers. In Netza, families' tenuous economic and social situations can lead members to feel that preservation of accepted gender roles and rules for "appropriate" sexual behavior are necessary to ensure family cohesiveness and safety. In this context, fears and stigma associated with homosexuality and AIDS are nourished by the social and economic realities of the region (Castro et al., 1998).

The first articles devoted to AIDS were published in medical journals in the early 1980s, primarily focused on cases in the United States. Between 1983 and 1988, as the number of articles addressing HIV and AIDS increased and research and policy took on a global perspective, the number of articles related to ethics, human rights, and AIDS doubled every year (Manuel et al., 1990). Many of these articles addressed proposed public health policies, seeking to balance protection of the rights of HIV-positive individuals against the health of society as a whole. Early proposals suggested taking steps, including prosecution of people who spread the HIV virus to their partners; mandatory HIV testing for at-risk groups, such as gay men, sex workers, and drug users; and measures to publicly identify those infected with the virus (Manuel et al., 1990). In the majority of cases, concern for human rights and personal privacy prevented these measures from becoming government policy, but the stigma surrounding HIV and AIDS continues to inform debates on how to prevent the virus from spreading.

The international community first formalized the connections between stigma, discrimination, and the human rights of people living with HIV and AIDS in the London Declaration on AIDS Prevention, ratified in 1988 at the World Summit of Ministers of Health on Programmes for HIV Prevention. This document stated explicitly that discrimination against people with HIV and AIDS and associated stigmatization of groups perceived to be at risk would undermine rather than strengthen public health efforts (World Summit of Ministers of Health on Programmes for HIV Prevention, 1988). Over the next eight years, the World Health Organization (WHO) issued similar statements, and the United Nations convened its first and second "International Consultations on HIV and Human Rights" (Aggleton and Maluwa, 2000). Progress toward ensuring human rights protections for people living with HIV and AIDS remains slow at the national level: In 2001, only 17 percent of the WHO's 191 member states reported specific legislation against HIV- and AIDS-related discrimination (D'Amelio et al., 2001). As antiretroviral therapies become more widely available and international pressure on individual countries to conform to standards of human rights protection continues, it is hoped that institutionalized stigma will decrease. This remains an important area for action, because studies have shown that levels of stigma are lower and people with AIDS are more accepted in countries with explicit HIV and AIDS nondiscrimination policies (Warwick et al., 1998).

Children learn stigmatizing behavior while they are young, repeating beliefs and attitudes modeled by peers, teachers, and parents (Gilmore and Somerville, 1994). The messages conveyed to young people about HIV will in turn affect how they perceive, support, and care for people living with HIV and AIDS in the future. Because the stigma surrounding HIV infection is often closely connected with other types of stigma directed toward ethnic minorities, women, drug users, foreigners, and gay and bisexual men and women, the process of educating children and young adults about AIDS can be controversial.

In July 2002, the Public Broadcasting System (PBS) announced at the XIV International AIDS Conference that the children's television show *Sesame Street* would soon feature an HIV-positive puppet in South Africa. "Kami," who joined the cast of South Africa's *Takalani Sesame* in September 2002, is a five-year-old orphan, infected with HIV in utero. Kami's presence on the show aims to teach young children that they do not need to avoid HIV-infected peers and should offer help and support to friends who are infected with or affected by the virus. Health educators in South Africa hope that the presence of *Takalani Sesame*'s new puppet character will "create a culture of acceptance" among young children in a society that is seen as "very stigmatizing and discriminatory." Approximately 4.7 million people are living with HIV and AIDS in South Africa today (Associated Press, 2002).

Although Kami has been generally accepted in South Africa, U.S. lawmakers and others have objected to her presence on a television program intended for young children. In the weeks after PBS announced Kami's debut, six Republican members of the U.S. House Committee on Energy and Commerce sent an open letter to the company's president stating that an HIV-positive character would be "unwelcome" in the United States. U.S. lawmakers expressed concern that the show was introducing sensitive messages to children at too young an age, explaining that although compassion is a value that should be promoted, HIV and AIDS are not appropriate material for *Sesame Street*'s audience (Tauzin et al., 2002). An editorial published in a Massachusetts newspaper during the same week went further, stating that the introduction of Kami or another character living with HIV into U.S. *Sesame Street* episodes would be "an abomination" and an expression of "political correctness run riot" (Anonymous, 2002b, 1–16). Kami was not infected with HIV through sex or through intravenous drug use, and *Takalani Sesame* does not plan to discuss either mode of transmission on the show. This debate highlights the need for greater clarity in discussions of support for people living with HIV and AIDS to avoid stigmatizing generalizations about "at-risk" groups and common modes of HIV transmission.

In many African settings, early and thorough HIV education is considered to be critical for young people in order to combat the highest HIV prevalences in the world. In Tanzania, where average HIV prevalence is about 8.09 percent in the adult population, infection rates among children and young people are as high as 21 percent in some urban areas. In addition, it is not uncommon for primary school children to become sexually active between fifth and seventh grade, demonstrating the importance of prevention messages aimed at this age group. A 1992 program, implemented in Arusha and Kilimanjaro districts in Tanzania, aimed to provide sixth and seventh graders with information about HIV transmission and prevention, as well as to sensitize primary school children to combat the social stigma that has traditionally surrounded HIV and AIDS in the country. Along with specific information regarding HIV transmission and prevention, students created artwork and performance pieces expressing the importance of tolerance and support for those living with HIV and AIDS and the importance of avoiding risky behaviors. The program also included presentations from local community leaders, religious leaders, and parents to address how to combat HIV in schools and among the general population (Klepp et al., 1997).

At the end of the school year, researchers interviewed 814 of the Arusha and Kilimanjaro students who had received the special HIV education course. Overall, students reported that after the course they discussed HIV and AIDS more frequently and comfortably with their friends and families. Researchers also found that students who had received the course had more accurate knowledge about HIV transmission than those who had not. Boys and girls who had taken the HIV course reported fewer stigmatizing attitudes toward people living with HIV and AIDS than their peers who had not taken the class. Discussion of class material outside of school fostered tolerance and understanding of people living with HIV and AIDS at the community level (Klepp et al., 1997). A key element of future national responses to

HIV and AIDS will be culturally relevant education efforts to break down the fears that often underlie stigma toward people living with HIV and AIDS.

Much of the stigma associated with HIV and AIDS, and the discriminatory actions that stigma can lead to, is based in fear of the unknown and a concern for safety. In diverse contexts research studies and public response show that education can have a quantifiable, positive impact on individual and societal responses to people living with HIV and AIDS and also can significantly increase the effectiveness of prevention messages. When government, provincial, and community-level policies on HIV and AIDS are humane, well-informed, and appropriate to local contexts, people living with HIV and individuals who are uninfected both benefit through better access to health care, prevention, and accurate knowledge about the virus. In most regions of the world, knowledge has proven to be an effective antidote to discrimination against people living with HIV.

AIDS Care, Cost-Effectiveness, and the Economic Impact of HIV

As new resources become available to support efforts to treat and prevent HIV and AIDS in developing countries, policymakers must begin to decide how best to use funds that might still fall short of the support required to fight HIV and AIDS nationwide. Cost-effectiveness analyses have highlighted all aspects of a continuing debate among governments, funders, and nongovernmental organizations (NGOs) over how to stretch insufficient funds for HIV and AIDS care and prevention to benefit the maximum number of people. These studies examine the efficacy of a specific care or prevention strategy (usually qualified in terms of years of life gained through treatment, new HIV infections prevented, or improvements in quality of life) and consider whether this impact justifies the cost of an intervention. Two studies of the cost-effectiveness of funding highly active antiretroviral therapy (HAART) versus funding HIV prevention efforts published in 2002, for example, suggest that in resource-constrained settings prevention should be prioritized over AIDS care and treatment as a more cost-effective strategy (Marseille, Hofmann, and Kahn, 2002; Creese et al., 2002). Replies to these articles and subsequent publications highlight the importance of seeing prevention and care as intrinsically linked and mutually supporting, suggesting that to dichotomize spending decisions based on the assumption that HAART and prevention are mutually exclusive will render both interventions less effective in the long run. Prevention efforts in this context include condom distribution, public education campaigns, STD treatment, ensuring a safe blood supply, and preventing mother-to-child transmission of HIV where possible (Marseille, Hofmann, and Kahn, 2002). HAART therapy consists of a three-drug antiretroviral regimen made up of one protease inhibitor and two reverse transcriptase-inhibiting drugs.

The 2002 articles use literature reviews to compare and evaluate HIV prevention and care programs and to make spending and policy recommendations based on existing data on the cost-effectiveness of a range of HIV and AIDS interventions. The first model compares the costs of HAART treatment for people with HIV and AIDS with the costs of prevention interventions, concluding that prevention might be up to twenty-eight times more cost-effective than HAART. The authors concluded that in the short term, before sufficient funds to fully support both comprehensive treatment and prevention efforts become available, sub-Saharan African countries and other resource-scarce nations should focus support on large-scale prevention initiatives and should seek to confine HAART distribution to smaller pilot studies. The study group argued that more lives would be lost if a "triage" process were not put in place to make sure that funds would be spent to ensure maximum benefit over the long term for minimum expenditure (Marseille, Hofmann, and Kahn, 2002).

The second study concluded from a survey of available cost-effectiveness literature that prevention initiatives provide the greatest impact for the smallest financial investment, making these efforts preferable to more costly HAART regimens. Emphasizing the importance of cost-effectiveness analysis in countries where resources for health care are severely limited, the research group concludes that the most cost-effective kinds of intervention focus on prevention and the least cost-effective include HAART and home-based care programs run by hospital facilities. At the same time, the researchers caution that definitive comparisons of all relevant care and prevention interventions in similar economic settings are still lacking, leaving room for significant variation in costs and cost-effectiveness across different regions of the world (Creese et al., 2002).

These two articles led to a range of responses from policy-makers, researchers, and NGOs, arguing that to advocate funding prevention efforts over HAART for people with HIV and AIDS in Africa is to approach the global fight against the virus with a simplistic strategy. Noting that, in practice, no government has chosen to "strictly enforce tradeoffs" between care and prevention, a group of policymakers from UNAIDS, the World Health Organization, and the World Bank argue that care and prevention interventions are linked within a continuum of health care. The health sector itself has been drastically impacted by high rates of HIV and AIDS among health care workers, and key components of national health infrastructure could collapse if treatment is not available to this population. Additionally, because HIV and AIDS disproportionately affect individuals in their most productive years, without immediate treatment for those already infected, national economic and social development, food production, and security could be seriously compromised (Piot, Zewdie, and Türmen, 2002; Gonsalves, 2002). Members of local and international nongovernmental organizations also wrote to clarify the links between prevention and care interventions, suggesting that each kind of effort not only complements the other, but also strengthens the success of a country's overall plan to fight HIV and AIDS (Goemaere, Ford, and Benatar, 2002; Gonsalves, 2002).

A number of studies presented at conferences on HIV and AIDS in 2002 also suggest that the relationship between prevention and care is complementary, not exclusive. One study examined how four Indian NGOs scaled up delivery of AIDS care and support services, which afforded researchers an opportunity to monitor the effects of HAART availability on the impact of prevention programs. During the two-year study, HIV and AIDS care programs became more numerous and visible in the community and interest in and demand for prevention information increased simultaneously. Noting a number of other positive relationships between an increase in availability of care and prevention, the study's researchers asserted that a "highly beneficial and synergistic relationship" exists between the two activities (Castle et al., 2002). A study released at the Second National Multisectoral AIDS Conference in Tanzania found a similar result. This study's cohort, women receiving drug therapy to prevent mother-to-child transmission, saw access to antiretroviral therapy as a motivator for clinic attendees to be voluntarily tested for HIV and to enter clinical trials (Jacobson, Peter, and Laiser, 2002).

Two other studies presented at the XIV International AIDS Conference in July 2002 call for prevention programs to accompany treatment and care. The first study was conducted in response to an increase in high-risk sexual behavior among individuals undergoing medical treatment for HIV infection, suggesting that antiretroviral therapy must be complemented by educational interventions to prevent HIV infection rates from increasing (Gordon et al., 2002). A second study of eight Zambian businesses planning to provide care for HIV-infected employees suggested that in addition to improving disease management, it would be in the companies' interest to "adopt a stronger role in prevention," as well (Guinness et al., 2002). These studies both contend that including prevention methods along with treatment and care is acceptable and universally beneficial to both HIV-infected and uninfected community members.

In countries such as Botswana and South Africa, where average HIV prevalence can be higher than 30 percent, economic development and national stability could suffer serious setbacks if the lives of people living with HIV cannot be extended (Stover and Bollinger, 2001). Along with humanitarian justifications, cost-effectiveness analyses increasingly suggest that over the long term, the widespread availability of HAART in developing countries makes social, political, and economic sense.

In countries where HIV prevalence is particularly high, an increasing demand for care and high mortality among health workers can lead to a weakening of the overall health care infrastructure. A study conducted in Zimbabwe found that hospital costs for patients with HIV and AIDS were an average of 2.7 times higher than for patients with other illnesses, primarily owing to higher numbers of diagnostic tests and the prescription of prophylactic and palliative drugs (Hansen et al., 2000). The results of this study indicate that in countries where resources to support the health care system are already scarce, increased HIV prevalence will lead to a demand for care far beyond what present facilities and budgets can encompass (Hansen et al., 2000). In this context, the introduction of HAART for people with AIDS might actually help to lessen the immediate burden HIV places on hospitals in developing countries by reducing the incidence of opportunistic infections such as tuberculosis, pneumonia, meningitis, and cancers such as Kaposi's sarcoma.

In the early 1990s when only one antiretroviral drug was available to treat HIV (zidovudine, commonly known as AZT), treatment for an individual with HIV for one year in the United States was estimated to cost between US$21,000 and US$60,750 (Beck, Miners, and Tolley, 2001). Within ten years, three-drug HAART regimens were considered to be the appropriate standard of care for people with HIV and AIDS, costing between US$13,000 and US$23,000 per year in the United States (Freedberg et al., 2001). Overall, the costs of individual antiretroviral drugs have decreased and expensive hospital admissions and treatments for opportunistic infections have become less frequent, owing to patients' improved health (Beck, Miners, and Tolley, 2001). In 1991 the average cost of AIDS treatment in the United States was composed of 84 percent for zidovudine, 12 percent for clinician visits, 3 percent for laboratory tests, and 1 percent for pharmacy fees (Schulman et al., 1991). After 1996, when a range of reverse transcriptase and protease inhibitors became available in developed regions, the total cost of HIV and AIDS care (including HAART) consisted of 40 percent for antiretroviral drugs, 43 percent for hospital care, 15 percent for outpatient clinician visits, and 2 percent for emergency care costs on average (Beck, Miners, and Tolley, 2001). As the cost of antiretroviral therapy decreases and treatment reduces hospital admissions and opportunistic infections, gains in productivity and years of life come closer to balancing and overtaking the expense of HAART.

HAART first became available in wealthy nations and remains largely out of reach in most resource-scarce regions. Most data on the cost-effectiveness of triple-drug therapy for HIV and AIDS has therefore been collected in developed countries in Europe and North America (Forsythe, 1998). In the absence of comprehensive data on the costs and cost-effectiveness of HAART in developing countries, studies conducted elsewhere can still help to inform national policy by suggesting the potential benefits and drawbacks of making HIV and AIDS treatment universally available. Results from these studies rely on specific regional conditions, including medical care infrastructure, HIV prevalence, and affected populations, all of which must be considered before allocating resources to a new program.

Cost-effectiveness is quantified by dividing the cost of a medical intervention by the number of years it will extend a patient's life, based on estimates of the treatment's efficacy and a patient's risk of death without treatment (Jha, Bangoura, and Ranson,

1998). Once the basic cost-effectiveness calculation is complete, other factors such as increased productivity and decreased medical costs can be considered. For example, a 1999 study conducted in Switzerland estimated that HAART would cost approximately 45,000 Swiss francs per year of life saved. When future gains in productivity, health, and quality of life were factored in to offset the cost of treatment, however, the cost per year of life saved dropped by nearly 75 percent, bringing the price of HAART into a range comparable with other common health interventions (Sendi et al., 1999). In this way, policymakers can estimate whether the benefits of HAART and other care and prevention strategies outweigh the costs of supplying an expensive, long-term treatment.

Antiretroviral drugs will probably always cost more per person than standard prevention interventions such as condom distribution and public education campaigns, but does this mean that universal access to HAART is not feasible? Balanced against concerns that support for HAART will channel funds away from other necessary health programs are the potential long-term benefits of treating people living with HIV and AIDS. Studies in both developed and developing regions suggest that successful HAART therapy can lead to fewer and shorter hospital stays, increased productivity, and family stability for parents and children living with HIV and AIDS. Conclusive data on how long HAART therapy will extend an individual's life still do not exist, but long-term cohort studies suggest that combination antiretroviral therapy can delay the hospital visits and illness associated with advanced AIDS by five to twenty years (Forsythe, 1998).

Calculations of cost-effectiveness, when used to help make national policy decisions, must take into account not only the potential cost and efficacy of a health intervention for individuals, but also the impact the proposed intervention will have on illness and mortality in the population as a whole. A study conducted in Kampala, Uganda, examined the costs and cost-effectiveness of providing short-course nevirapine to HIV-positive pregnant women to prevent mother-to-child transmission. Of the antiretroviral drugs available to prevent mother-to-child transmission, nevirapine remains the least expensive, requiring fewer doses to mother and infant and less medical infrastructure for delivery. The Uganda study projected the costs of providing nevirapine only to HIV-infected mothers who accept therapy after voluntary testing and counseling ("targeted" model), versus providing nevirapine to all pregnant women, regardless of whether they have been tested for HIV ("universal" model) (Marseille et al., 1999). The study group measured the intervention's effectiveness in "disability adjusted life years" (DALYs), which represent years of life saved, weighted to reflect changes in quality of life and productivity.

In areas where HIV prevalence is high, antiretroviral regimens will be more cost-effective than in regions where overall prevalence remains low. In the Uganda study, the number of people who would potentially receive nevirapine therapy during birth dramatically affects the cost of therapy per DALY saved. For example, assuming local HIV prevalence to be 30 percent, targeted nevirapine delivery would cost approximately US$11 per DALY saved, whereas universal therapy would cost about US$5 per DALY saved. When HIV prevalence is estimated at 15 percent, the cost of targeted delivery rises to US$19, whereas universal delivery would cost about US$10 per DALY saved. The universal delivery strategy, providing nevirapine to all pregnant women without an HIV test, remains the most cost-effective overall, because it will always reach more women with HIV, and does not incur the additional costs associated with counseling and testing. Ethical concerns over providing antiretroviral drugs to women who are not infected with HIV could render this solution undesirable, particularly because counseling and testing have been shown to prevent some new HIV infections through education and psychological support (Marseille et al., 1999). In countries like Botswana, Lesotho, Swaziland, and Zimbabwe, where national HIV prevalence is well above 30 percent, however, antiretroviral drugs to treat and prevent HIV are likely to be cost-effective because of the sheer numbers of people whose lives could be extended, even using a targeted model of care delivery.

HIV is beginning to affect the business sector in many developing countries. Inexpensive labor and emerging consumer markets have traditionally fueled the process of economic globalization, but as HIV and AIDS decimate local populations and economies both of these incentives are in jeopardy. In countries such as Zambia and the Democratic Republic of the Congo, high HIV prevalence and corresponding employee absenteeism and mortality have led large companies to routinely hire several people to fill one position and to train all employees in multiple tasks. Elsewhere HIV and AIDS in the local workforce have led to direct costs to employers, including rising health insurance bills and the need to recruit and train more new employees. Along with these costs associated with an individual's illness, high rates of HIV in a company's workforce can have farther-reaching consequences, such as decreased efficiency and increased production time, loss of experienced workers, and low staff morale (Rosen et al., 2003).

In 2003, a group of researchers from Harvard University conducted a survey in South Africa to assess the financial impact of HIV and AIDS on six companies encompassing retail, agriculture, mining, media, utilities, and metals processing. The "AIDS tax" was calculated by determining what percentage of all employee salaries companies spent on care and treatment of HIV and AIDS in the workforce. On the individual level, the group found that the cost of a year's HIV and AIDS care was between half and three times an employee's annual salary, significantly increasing the amount of money a company could expect to spend on individual workers. At the workforce level, the AIDS tax amounted to between 0.4 and 5.9 percent of total employee salaries, representing a substantial direct cost (Rosen et al., 2003).

As in Uganda, the next phase of the Harvard group's financial analysis evaluated the cost-effectiveness of a variety of HIV prevention and care options. Company-sponsored voluntary HIV counseling and testing for employees, family members, and members of the surrounding community was estimated to cost about US$4 per person. South African companies have also conducted community outreach and education activities and created programs to treat sexually transmitted diseases among employees. This comprehensive package of prevention strategies is a low-cost option that can be implemented quickly, especially in companies with in-house medical facilities. Similar prevention programs have succeeded in reducing HIV prevalence by as much as 50 percent in one South African company (Rosen et al., 2003).

Some South African companies have already begun to offer free or subsidized HAART for HIV and AIDS to their employees, through private insurance companies, nonprofit organizations, or via in-house clinics and medical staff. Several southern African nations have negotiated significant price reductions when purchasing antiretroviral drugs from pharmaceutical companies, allowing businesses in South Africa to offer HAART to employees for as little as US$500 per person per year (Rosen et al., 2003). Assuming that HAART will extend an employee's productive life for at least five years after the regimen is initiated, the study group concluded that companies could reduce their AIDS tax by between 0.8 and 40.4 percent by providing antiretroviral therapy (Rosen et al., 2003). Rather than paying for expensive prophylactic and hospital care, companies potentially can delay the onset of the symptoms of AIDS in the workforce, thereby increasing productivity and decreasing health care costs over the long term.

From a global point of view, there are no simple answers to the question of how best to allocate scarce funds to combat HIV and AIDS effectively. Determinations of cost-effectiveness will never provide a perfect solution for all potential recipients of care, treatment, and prevention interventions focused on HIV or on other infectious diseases. This uncertainty requires that policymakers in resource-scarce regions think creatively when budgeting for public health interventions, a process that might include the formation of new public–private or international partnerships, increasing local research capacity, or encouraging all branches of government to make health a priority. When new interventions are instituted, flexibility and collaboration will allow programs to evolve along with changes in local HIV epidemics so that the most affected populations are served over the long term.

Access to Care

Access to appropriate medical care for HIV and AIDS is affected by a wide variety of social and economic factors, even in countries where antiretroviral therapy and clinical care are guaranteed to everyone who needs them. HIV is a terminal disease, often striking individuals during the most productive years of their lives, and often accompanied by intense societal stigma. These factors, along with the physical manifestations of illness experienced by people living with HIV and AIDS, require care services far beyond antiretroviral and palliative medication. People living with HIV require a range of psychosocial support, education and prevention resources, and access to medical services, including nutrition advice, obstetrical and gynecological care, and dental care, to ensure that HIV disease progression remains controlled and that further transmissions do not occur (Chequer et al., 2002). The cost and complexity of antiretroviral regimens, coupled with the barriers that the impoverished and uninsured face in accessing clinical care have led to a lack of access to optimal HIV and AIDS care since effective treatments were first developed.

The challenge of providing comprehensive HIV and AIDS care lies in the fact that communities and individuals who are most at risk for HIV infection are often the same people who have the most difficulty accessing available care and support options. Antiretroviral drugs alone do not guarantee an extended life span or improved quality of life, particularly for individuals who are unable to access other kinds of medical care and psychological support. In the United States, gaps in access to care for women, intravenous drug users, Latinos, and African Americans living with HIV were apparent in the early 1990s as soon as the first antiretroviral drugs became available (Curtis and Patrick, 1993). In Brazil where a government program to provide antiretroviral drugs was instituted in 1996, AIDS care and treatment have reduced AIDS mortality and illness dramatically, but access to these services continues to be insufficient for many women (Segurado et al., 2003). In sub-Saharan Africa, gaps in health care infrastructure along with budget shortfalls and other factors prevent most people living with HIV and AIDS from accessing any antiretroviral medications and restrict access to even the most basic forms of medical care, such as palliation and prevention services (Ramanathan, Tarantola, and Marlink, 2002). Although they have lessened over two decades in wealthier settings, these disparities in access to care for people living with HIV and AIDS in developing countries have not yet been fully addressed by the international community.

As a center for the first pharmaceutical research and development of antiretroviral drugs, as well as a developed country with strong medical infrastructure, the United States was a testing ground for improved access to medical care for people with AIDS during the 1980s and 1990s. The early detection of HIV and AIDS primarily among gay men and intravenous drug users in the United States has had an effect not only on how the virus is perceived, but also on the delivery of AIDS prevention messages, care, and medications. By 1996 when combination antiretroviral therapy including both protease inhibitors and reverse transcriptase inhibitors had become widely available, education and support networks for gay men in the country were well established, particularly in large cities on the East and West Coasts. Despite homophobia and stigma related to nonnormative sexual behavior, a study conducted between 1996 and 1998 showed that of all people with HIV and AIDS in the United States, white, gay men had the highest rates of medication, service, and care access and use (Shapiro et al., 1999). During these years, when rates of HIV transmission and disease progression were slowing among gay men, thanks to vigorous educational campaigns, HIV prevalence was rising among women and ethnic minorities (Curtis and Patrick, 1993; Marlink, Kao, and Hsieh, 2001). The same 1996–1998 study reported that women, the uninsured, African Americans, and Latinos with HIV and AIDS received "sub-optimal" medical care compared with wealthier white or male patients, including reduced access to antiretroviral drugs, prophylaxis for opportunistic infections, and psychological support (Shapiro et al., 1999).

HIV rates in the United States continue to rise most quickly among women and ethnic minorities today, particularly affecting poorer communities and those without health insurance. Gaps in access to care for these affected populations have narrowed, but HIV and AIDS care and treatment are not yet universally available. Between 1995 and 1996, the year HAART became available, AIDS mortality among men in the United States decreased by 27 percent, but mortality among women with AIDS decreased by only 14 percent. At the same time, among women and men whose survival time was increased by an antiretroviral regimen, men reported almost twice as much reduction in disease symptoms as women (Marlink, Kao, and Hsieh, 2001). In addition, a 1998 study showed that among a group of women eligible for antiretroviral therapy based on clinical symptoms and disease progression, only 49 percent were receiving antiretroviral drugs and nearly half were not receiving appropriate prophylaxis for opportunistic infections (Salomon et al., 1998).

The gap between women's need for care and the accessibility of services stems from a variety of interrelated factors. Perhaps of primary importance is the fact that until 1993, the U.S. Centers for Disease Control (CDC) did not include any conditions specific to women in its definition of AIDS. This omission left many doctors, activists, and policymakers with the mistaken impression that HIV infections remained restricted to gay men and intravenous drug users, an assumption that continues to affect women's ability to access appropriate HIV and AIDS education, care, and support (Stoller, 1998). When invasive cervical cancer was added to the list of conditions that signal the onset of clinical AIDS, the medical establishment officially acknowledged the widespread existence of HIV among U.S. women for the first time (Maiman et al., 1997). This new criteria assists physicians in identifying women with HIV during the asymptomatic period of infection (Klevens et al., 1996).

Surveys of access to and effectiveness of HIV and AIDS care among ethnic minorities in the United States suggest that African Americans and Latinos might have less access to optimal AIDS care and support compared with whites, a disparity with serious effects on disease progression and survival time. Study findings showing that ethnic minorities in the United States have less access to antiretroviral drugs, counseling services, and clinical care than whites also point to socioeconomic status as an important predictor of access to care and disease progression, regardless of race. These two factors remain closely aligned in the United States, ensuring that even if poverty or insufficient health insurance are the root causes of poor access to health care, Latinos and African Americans with HIV or AIDS will continue to be disproportionately affected (Curtis and Patrick, 1993). In 2002, AIDS-related diseases were the leading cause of death among African American men between twenty-five and forty-four years old, and the virus continues to increase quickly in minority populations even as prevalence decreases in other communities (UNAIDS, 2003).

Studies conducted among ethnic minorities in the United States after combination antiretroviral therapies became widely available continue to show disparities in access to care services and health outcomes by race and financial resources. A 2003 study of 400 people living with HIV in the United States found that African Americans and Latinos reported greater difficulties than others in accessing medical care, psychological services, transportation, and housing assistance. In addition, minority study participants were less likely to know the results and significance of laboratory tests such as HIV viral load and CD4 cell counts. This lack of knowledge suggests that among minorities communication with health care providers might be deficient, a situation that can lead to an increase in risky behaviors and faster disease progression (Reilly and Woo, 2003).

Disparities in access to health care for people with HIV and AIDS exist even in developed countries where HAART has been available to many since the first antiretroviral drugs were licensed. In South and Central America, government-sponsored AIDS care programs are currently expanding, attempting to counter social and personal factors that limit access to care and support. National programs in Brazil and Argentina ensure universal access to anti-retroviral drugs and medical care for people living with HIV and AIDS, and nine other countries in the area have made strong com-mitments to developing and supporting similar programs (Che-quer et al., 2002). Gaps between a commitment to provide free and optimal care, individuals' ability to access health care services, and individual countries' ability to finance such programs still remain, however, influenced by poverty, political instability, and women's inequitable status in society.

Brazil provides a good example of the long-term challenges and successes of a government-supported HIV and AIDS care policy that includes universal access to antiretroviral drugs. Bol-stered by a stable economy and political system, Brazil's national AIDS care program was first instituted on a national scale in 1996, the year that "combination" antiretroviral therapies became the international standard of care for people with HIV and AIDS (Segurado et al., 2003). With only about one-fifth of those eligible for treatment receiving HAART, Brazil has already seen a 50-percent nationwide decrease in AIDS mortality, along with a 75-percent decrease in length and number of hospital stays for peo-ple with HIV or AIDS. These dramatic results led to cost savings for the first time in 2001, when the estimated health expenditures avoided surpassed the total cost of providing antiretroviral ther-apy (Chequer et al., 2002).

Seven years after Brazil's national HIV and AIDS care pro-gram began, a group of researchers from universities and clinics in São Paulo State began to examine how well the universal HAART access program was working for Brazilian women. Al-though AIDS mortality in Brazil declined by 50 percent overall between 1996 and 2001, mortality among women with AIDS decreased by only 38 percent. Women reported less health bene-fit from HIV and AIDS care and treatment than men receiving the same services. After surveying 1,068 women between 1999 and 2000, the group concluded that men's and women's experiences of medical care for HIV and AIDS were different, leading to gaps in accessibility of drugs and services (Segurado, 2003).

Women's ability to take advantage of available care and treatment options in Brazil was found to be influenced primarily by their relationship to health care providers, access to psycho-logical support services, and willingness to take an initial HIV test. Among women who had taken an HIV test, a service available at anonymous HIV testing centers, maternity service centers, AIDS care clinics, blood banks, and hospitals, 64 percent felt they had received adequate counseling and support from health care workers. Almost 22 percent of women surveyed reported a negative experience related to an HIV test, however, including indifference, discrimination, and criticism from health care personnel (Segurado et al., 2003). Although psychological support is part of Brazil's HIV and AIDS care plan, women reported less access to these services than men, despite suffering from stress related to caring for family members, disclosing their HIV status to friends and loved ones, and planning for their children's futures (Segurado, 2003).

After entering the health care system, only about 45 percent of the Brazilian women with HIV and AIDS surveyed understood the significance of the CD4 count tests their primary care physicians performed, and only about 60 percent understood the importance of viral load monitoring. Women who reported a good relationship with their primary care doctor were more likely than others to understand the reasons for and results of tests associated with routine HIV monitoring. This understanding generally led women to be better able to make decisions about their own treatment, care, and support needs (Segurado, 2003). Because most women in Brazil consult a gynecologist regularly and receive much of their information about HIV transmission and prevention there, gynecologists and obstetrical services could be an important point of entry for women with HIV and AIDS seeking care and treatment. Although they are well informed on issues related to HIV transmission, the São Paulo study group suggests that Brazilian gynecologists be trained to educate women about prevention of mother-to-child transmission of HIV and the availability of antiretroviral therapies (Segurado, 2003).

The lessons learned from new and evolving national HIV and AIDS care strategies are of particular importance in resource-scarce regions where severe deficiencies in financial resources and other societal constraints limit access to even basic medical and psychological care and support. In regions such as sub-Saharan Africa, access to care is often affected by insufficient medical infrastructure, preventing people with AIDS from accessing not only costly antiretroviral regimens, but also basic palliative care, home-based care, and treatment for opportunistic infections (Ramanathan, Tarantola, and Marlink, 2002). As wealthier nations in the region such as Botswana begin to implement comprehensive, government-supported HIV and AIDS care and treatment programs, other countries are still struggling with how to make even basic services available to all. Barriers similar to those noted in the United States and South America prevent universal delivery and access to optimal care and support in sub-Saharan Africa, coupled with further financial and structural constraints.

Unreliable or insufficient health care infrastructure poses a serious problem for resource-scarce nations, but even in areas with the most limited capacity, some HIV and AIDS services can be offered to most of the population. Voluntary HIV counseling and testing services, psychosocial support, palliative care, and basic management of sexually transmitted diseases can have a major impact on rates of HIV transmission and quality of life, but require little new infrastructure before implementation. In areas with somewhat more medical care capacity, treatment and prophylaxis of opportunistic infections, delivery of antiretrovirals for prevention of mother-to-child HIV transmission, and home-based care support and referral systems can be implemented. In regions where resources are available and medical infrastructure is more extensive, HAART can be delivered in the public sector and more complex treatment of opportunistic infections and cancers is accessible (Ramanathan, Tarantola, and Marlink, 2002). At all levels of heath care infrastructure, therefore, some HIV and AIDS care is possible, if a strong government commitment and medical referral system support it.

A lack of trained staff, both doctors and nurses, in developing countries restricts access to care at any level of infrastructure. Sub-Saharan African health care systems tend to follow a "colonial" model, with health care facilities such as referral and regional hospitals concentrated in urban areas. This model has proven to be ineffective in serving the majority of people living with HIV and AIDS in the region, because an average of 70 percent of southern Africa's population lives in rural areas (Alubo, 1990). In Zimbabwe, for example, 44 percent of the government health budget is allocated to support urban health care centers that serve only 15 percent of the country's population (Sanders et al., 1998). Countries such as Botswana and Senegal are currently working to decentralize government health care facilities, both by supporting hospitals and clinics in rural areas and by encouraging local nongovernment organizations to shore up community-based support efforts (UNAIDS, 2000b; Botswana Ministry of Health, 1999).

Access to basic components of HIV and AIDS care in sub-Saharan Africa is affected by complex social and economic factors beyond the availability of health care staff and facilities. Voluntary HIV counseling and testing, an important entry point into the health care system for people living with HIV or at risk for infection, are particularly difficult to implement in rural areas. Without local laboratory facilities, HIV test kits must be shipped over long distances for analysis, which means that the delay for some people between taking an HIV test and receiving a result can be two weeks or more. Under these conditions, patient follow-up is difficult, because individuals are likely to leave the area or choose not to return to hear their results (Ramanathan, Tarantola, and Marlink, 2002). In addition, because HAART and other treatment options are not available in most sub-Saharan countries, individuals are often not motivated to seek testing, assuming that knowing their serostatus will not make any difference to the length and quality of their lives. The stigma that often surrounds HIV and AIDS reinforces this feeling of hopelessness and might discourage people from being tested, for fear of becoming ostracized within their communities (Campbell et al., 1997). Mobile testing units and the availability of rapid HIV tests have begun to overcome some of the difficulties of making voluntary counseling and testing accessible in rural areas, and education campaigns and community support programs might help to make HIV testing more acceptable in the future (Wilkinson et al., 1997).

In areas where HAART is not readily available, care for people who are ill or dying from AIDS is particularly important. Basic palliative care to treat the symptoms of opportunistic infections and alleviate pain is not prohibitively expensive, but is lacking in many regions because of inefficient distribution systems. According to the World Health Organization, in 1999 fewer than 50 percent of people in sub-Saharan Africa had access to palliative drugs, including antibiotics and pain relievers (World Health Organization, 1999). The WHO "Essential Drugs Program," which was launched in 1984, has helped raise awareness in developing nations of the need to shore up supply and distribution systems and to prioritize the delivery of basic medical care and drugs to all sectors of the population (World Health Organization, 1984). Other "essential" drugs to treat the more complex opportunistic infections associated with AIDS (pneumonia and tuberculosis, for example) remain unavailable in many regions, owing in large part to insufficient laboratory infrastructure to monitor patients' progress. In Côte d'Ivoire, for example, pilot studies prescribing the antibiotic cotrimoxazole to people with HIV and AIDS to prevent pneumonia proved the therapy to be both effective and inexpensive (Anglaret et al., 1999; Wiktor et al., 1999). Cotrimoxazole remains unavailable in many southern African countries, however, owing to a lack of trained health care providers and facilities for patient follow-up. Working with organizations like the WHO and UNICEF, many sub-Saharan African countries have developed lists of essential drugs for palliative care, taking the first steps in making consistent and effective care available to all (Ramanathan, Tarantola, and Marlink, 2002).

In regions where medical care facilities are distant, overcrowded, or unaffordable, supporting families to care for patients at home can extend medical infrastructure beyond hospitals and clinics. Home-based care eliminates costly hospital visits and reduces the costs of transportation to and from clinics, alleviating financial hardship for families. Ideally, home-based care also benefits patients by allowing them to remain within their own communities, reducing isolation from friends and family members (Ramanathan, Tarantola, and Marlink, 2002). A cost analysis of home-based care programs in developed countries such as the United States, however, shows that home-based care might not be significantly less expensive than traditional care at hospitals and clinics, when family members' expenditures of time and money are taken into account (Beck, Miners, and Tolley, 2001).

In resource-scarce regions, home-based care might not provide a workable alternative to care in medical facilities. Nurses and other health care workers who visit patients at home, particularly in rural areas, accrue significant travel costs as well as time lost during a commute. In areas where health care workers are scarce, this added drain on time and financial resources can lead to less availability of care overall (Hansen et al., 1998). Stigma and financial hardship associated with HIV and AIDS also restrict the availability of home-based care. People with HIV and AIDS are often important family income-generators, and the loss of their support along with the added costs of care can financially cripple families. In African settings with high HIV prevalence, young children are often the only members of families who remain healthy. In this context, the need to simply survive could eclipse family members' ability to care for loved ones (Ramanathan,

Tarantola, and Marlink, 2002). As in Netza, Mexico, stigma surrounding HIV and AIDS in southern Africa can affect an ill individual's ability to access care and a family's ability to give support. A desire to hide or deny the presence of an HIV-infected relative could lead to social isolation for families providing care, preventing family members from receiving the psychological support necessary to care for terminally ill loved ones (Ramanathan, Tarantola, and Marlink, 2002; Castro et al., 1998).

Access to medical and psychological care for people living with HIV and AIDS differs significantly from one individual or community to the next. Questions of when to seek an HIV test and whether or not to inform family members and loved ones of a positive result are often based on highly personal concerns and constraints. In regions where public policy actively discourages stigma and discrimination against people living with (or suspected to be living with) HIV and AIDS, individuals' reluctance to seek appropriate testing and treatment is lessened. Financial constraints remain a serious barrier to accessing HIV and AIDS care almost everywhere in the world, an issue that usually can be addressed effectively by local and national government agencies. Public health services might not be financially or physically equipped to deliver HAART, but with little additional funds or infrastructure many resource-scarce regions can potentially scale up access to palliative care, opportunistic infection prophylaxis, and prevention of mother-to-child transmission of HIV. Awareness of barriers to accessing care and available resources will help governments and caregivers in the private sector ensure that all members of society receive all available support.

Government Responses to HIV and AIDS

National governments' responses to the AIDS epidemic have the potential to profoundly affect the course of HIV and AIDS in their country and region. A continuum of positive responses have been initiated worldwide, beginning with legislation to protect the human rights of people living with HIV and AIDS and nationwide education and prevention interventions, and progressing to government-subsidized care and treatment programs that include access to highly active antiretroviral therapy. A lack of financial resources and medical infrastructure prevents many developing countries from initiating comprehensive HIV and AIDS prevention, care, and treatment initiatives, but governments on all continents have begun to develop creative ways to use available resources. As governments pioneer funding, prevention, and care delivery strategies, new kinds of partnerships have developed between public and private sectors, between government offices and nongovernmental organizations (NGO), among regions, and among governments at the international level. It is hoped that lessons learned from well-established national HIV and AIDS programs will continue to inform the strategies of newly initiated and developing government interventions.

Components that help to ensure the success of a government HIV program include organized leadership and clear implementation guidelines; functional management systems; multisectoral coordination of activities; skilled personnel; and an "enabling social, political, and economic context" (Schneider and Stein, 2001). In practical terms, this means that government leadership should be strong and organized, but must also actively seek input and leadership from nongovernmental organizations, local communities, the academic sector, businesses, and a range of government offices. HIV and AIDS interventions are most likely to succeed when they are tailored to local context and the specific needs of communities being served. Allowing states, provinces, and smaller communities to take ownership of HIV and AIDS prevention and care programs ensures that local priorities will be met, making programs more acceptable to the general population (Biswanger, 2000). Along with this decentralized and multidisciplinary approach, government programs need to consider changes in the epidemic at a national level, ensuring that interventions continue to target the communities that need them most, even as successful programs create changes in the dynamics of the epidemic (Hanenberg and Rojanapithayakorn, 1998).

Effective nationwide surveillance and quick policy development distinguish the Thai government's response to HIV and AIDS. HIV tests were available in most Thai health facilities by 1985, by which time the international community was well aware of the cause and effects of AIDS (Phanupak et al., 1985). The first nationwide sentinel survey of HIV prevalence in Thailand was conducted in 1989, a year after HIV prevalence among injecting drug users (IDUs) in the country leapt from about 1 percent to 43 percent (Weniger et al., 1991).

The Thai government's response to the AIDS epidemic evolved rapidly between 1989 and 1991. In 1989, a proposed

"AIDS Act" was presented to the government of Thailand, which would have allowed health care workers to forcibly detain and confine people infected with HIV. Amid strong lobbying from human rights groups and groups of people living with HIV and AIDS, this proposed plan was shelved, although mandatory HIV testing of people presumed to be at risk for infection (such as commercial sex workers and intravenous drug users) continued (Ungphakorn and Sittitrai, 1994). Early government-sponsored HIV prevention programs focused on HIV as a "foreign" disease that had been imported into the country from surrounding areas and international sites, barring those who tested positive for HIV infection from entering the country. This early prevention campaign increased awareness of HIV in Thailand, but also exacerbated the stigma associated with HIV infection (Ungphakorn and Sittitrai, 1994).

In 1989, in response to a significant increase in HIV prevalence among commercial sex workers, the Thai government initiated a pilot trial of the "100 percent Condom Program." The program was operationalized nationwide the following year, marking the start of the Thai government's first comprehensive HIV prevention initiative (Ungphakorn and Sittitrai, 1994). Although technically illegal since 1960, commercial sex work has been tolerated by the Thai government since the early 1980s, with new efforts aimed at regulating brothels and ensuring safer sex practices rather than attempting to discourage the industry altogether (Hanenberg and Rojanapithayakorn, 1998). The 100 percent Condom Program aims at eventually protecting 100 percent of commercial sex acts through enforced condom use in brothels and reducing the commercial sex trade overall through educational efforts. Condoms are distributed free to most Thai sex workers, who are instructed to use them with all customers or be penalized by law enforcement (Hanenberg et al., 1994). In collaboration with local police forces and government offices, the Thai government maintains a census of commercial sex establishments and the number of sex workers who staff them, tracking which brothels are in compliance with the national program and which still present a risk of STD infections (Hanenberg and Rojanapithayakorn, 1998).

As the 100 percent Condom Program expanded to a national scale, the Thai government itself was changing with the advent of a new administration in 1991. Under the leadership of Mechai Viravaidya, Thailand's new Minister of Health, the country's approach to implementing HIV and AIDS programs changed from a centralized authoritarian model to a community-based, multidisciplinary approach. This strategy focused on integrating HIV and AIDS care and treatment into every facet of government planning, encouraging all ministries to include plans to combat HIV and AIDS and mitigate their effects in new budget proposals. For the first time national AIDS policy was explicitly linked to Thailand's long-term National Plan for Social and Economic Development, integrating HIV prevention into all future funding and policy decisions (Ungphakorn and Sittitrai, 1994).

The year 1991 heralded a new "social" focus on AIDS prevention in Thailand, changing perceptions of disease transmission from a focus on high-risk groups to concentrate on factors influencing risky behaviors throughout society, such as economic hardship, peer pressure, and migratory labor. Taking into account the fact that the epidemic was rapidly spreading beyond traditionally defined risk groups, national policy continued to evolve into a holistic approach, balancing government coordination with leadership from nongovernmental organizations and people living with HIV and AIDS. The Thai government and a group of multisectoral partners continue to emphasize decentralized efforts to empower communities and people living with HIV and AIDS, to combat stigma, and to improve the social conditions that lead to increased HIV transmission risk (Phoolcharoen et al., 1998).

The Thai 100 percent Condom Program increased condom use among patrons of commercial sex workers from 14 percent in 1989 to approximately 94 percent in 1993, a change that reduced the incidence of sexually transmitted diseases such as gonorrhea and syphilis by up to 79 percent in some regions (Hanenberg et al., 1994). By 1996, STD diagnoses in government clinics were more than thirteen-fold reduced compared with 1989 when the program was initiated (Hanenberg and Rojanapithayakorn, 1998). Studies conducted among sex workers in Thailand in the late 1990s show that the number of "direct," brothel-based commercial sex workers has decreased by as much as 23 percent since the 100 percent Condom Program was instituted (Hanenberg and Rojanapithayakorn, 1998). In addition, women recently entering the sex trade might be less likely to engage in risky behaviors (Kilmarx et al., 1999). HIV surveillance among young, male military conscripts shows a steady decline in HIV prevalence from 3.7 percent in 1993 to 3.0 percent in 1994 to 2.4 percent in 1995 and 2.1 percent in 1996. This change largely reflects the adoption of safer sex practices when visiting sex workers and an overall decrease in the average number of young men's sexual partners. Among heterosexual women seeking antenatal care (a population thought to represent women who are not sex workers, but who might be at risk for HIV infection from husbands and other partners), HIV prevalence declined from 2.3 percent in 1995 to 1.8 percent in 1996 (Hanenberg and Rojanapithayakorn, 1998).

The impact of the 100 percent Condom Program on HIV transmission and prevalence of HIV and AIDS countrywide is more complex and harder to quantify. Despite clear gains in STD prevention, different sectors of the Thai population benefit from the program to varying degrees. Unlike other common STDs, such as syphilis and gonorrhea, HIV cannot be cured and will remain present in an individual's system even when antiretroviral drugs have slowed disease progression. This means that although condom use continues to reduce the chance of sexual HIV transmission in Thailand, a risk of transmission remains. Sex workers remain at a higher risk for HIV infection, because they are likely to have far more sexual partners than members of the general population (Kilmarx et al., 1999). In addition, although 100-percent condom usage remains a goal throughout the commercial sex industry, in reality rates of condom use among sex workers vary, from as high as 100 percent to as low as 69 percent (Hanenberg and Rojanapithayakorn, 1998). HIV incidence and prevalence rates have not dropped as quickly among sex workers as they have among their clients and among clients' noncommercial sexual partners, suggesting that the 100 percent Condom Program might not be protecting all sectors of society to an equal extent (Kilmarx et al., 1999).

Nationwide dissemination of the 100 percent Condom Program's messages has led to a change in sexual relationships in Thailand since 1989. Responding to prevention interventions targeting commercial sex workers and their clients, both men and women began to pursue different kinds of sexual relationships. As the numbers of "direct" brothel-based sex workers who exchange sex for money decrease, numbers of "indirect" sex workers, women who work as dancers, waitresses, and masseuses but who also might sell sex to clients on the side, are rising (Hanenberg and Rojanapithayakorn, 1998). Because these indirect and noncommercial relationships are not officially associated with the sex trade, condom use is much lower, protecting only 20 to 50 percent of all sex acts (Phoolcharoen et al., 1998). Indirect sex workers are not associated with established brothels and therefore might not enforce the use of condoms with every client, either through personal choice or because negotiating the terms of a relationship is more difficult outside of established structures (Hanenberg and Rojanapithayakorn, 1998). Thai men who have become wary of brothel-based sex workers might be more likely to seek girlfriends and other noncommercial long- or short-term sexual partners. At the same time, women who are direct sex workers might also be married or might have long-term noncommercial partners. In both these types of relationship, condom use is significantly lower than the near–100 percent rate recorded in brothels (Mills et al., 1997).

The 100 percent Condom Program in Thailand has raised national awareness about HIV transmission and AIDS, reduced STD infections among Thai men, and lowered HIV prevalence among young men and pregnant women. The program's success might stem from the fact that it presents a simple message along with an uncomplicated and easily accessible intervention, quickly targeting one of the main routes of disease transmission in the country. Over the long term, however, the program's focus on HIV transmission through commercial sex could prove to be a detriment to prevention efforts in other populations. HIV infection is now closely associated with direct sex work in the minds of many people in Thailand, which could obscure the very real risk of transmission between partners in noncommercial relationships (Mastro and Limpakarnjanarat, 1995). To ensure the continued success of prevention programs in the country, the Thai government and its private sector and NGO partners will need to continuously reinvent strategies to protect individuals who are at risk as the national epidemic evolves (UNAIDS, 2002a).

Brazil's government AIDS program has provided many other countries in the region as well as on other continents with a roadmap of how to deliver free care and support including HAART to all citizens living with HIV and AIDS. Formally initiated in 1996 (the year that triple-combination antiretroviral therapies became common), Brazil's national AIDS program is one of the largest in the developing world. The government program guarantees access to HAART for all people living with HIV and AIDS, along with a spectrum of HIV prevention options, related medical care, and specialist consultations (Segurado et al., 2003). Antiretroviral therapy is affordable on a wide scale in Brazil because Brazilian law stipulates that government laboratories may break drug patents to produce low-cost generic versions of essential medications in times of national emergency. This law allowed the Brazilian government to supply antiretroviral drugs to 115,000 people in 2002 at a far lower price than what was paid by wealthier countries (Anonymous, 2002a).

Brazil's first case of AIDS was diagnosed in 1980, and until 1985 the national epidemic progressed slowly. Until the mid-1980s nearly all cases of HIV and AIDS in Brazil were in people living in the capital cities of São Paulo and Rio de Janeiro States (regions that remain severely affected by HIV). Between 1985 and 1988, HIV incidence and prevalence began to increase more quickly, and by the end of 1988, HIV infections had been diagnosed in all twenty-seven Brazilian states. HIV prevalence increased quickly and steadily after 1986, until the number of people living with AIDS peaked between 1996 and 1997 and then began to decrease almost as quickly as it initially rose with the initiation of the country's national program (Meira, 2002). In 2002, 610,000 adults and children were living with HIV and AIDS in Brazil, with average prevalence ranging from 1.25 percent in major cities to 0.22 percent in rural areas (UNAIDS, 2002a).

Nationwide HIV incidence (the number of new HIV infections) in Brazil has remained nearly constant between 1996 and 2002, ranging from a high of 24,017 new infections in 1994 to 15,013 in 2002, the lowest number of new infections since 1992 (UNAIDS, 2002a). The Brazilian government responded quickly to the epidemic, even during the years that HIV infections remained comparatively uncommon and were confined only to specific regions. Between 1980 and 1988 the National Program on AIDS was established and began a series of prevention efforts, including male and female condom distribution, screening of donated blood, and prevention of mother-to-child transmission. The Ministry of Health first made zidovudine (AZT) monotherapy available to people with HIV then quickly approved the use of double-drug combination therapy after it was recommended at the Tenth International AIDS Conference in 1994 (Meira, 2002). Two years later, in response to international research studies and the development of new antiretroviral drugs, the Ministry of Health drafted a "National Consensus on Antiretroviral Therapy," declaring a three-drug HAART regimen to be the approved standard of care for people with HIV and AIDS. At the end of 1996, this three-drug therapy was approved for free distribution to all eligible people with HIV and AIDS in Brazil, and a countrywide system of laboratory monitoring was developed to track individuals' disease progression and viral resistance mutations (Meira, 2002). In addition to decreasing the incidence of new HIV infections, these efforts resulted in a 17.4 percent decrease in AIDS deaths between 2000 and 2001, and a 50 percent decrease in AIDS mortality over all (Meira, 2002; Chequer et al., 2002).

By September 2001, the Brazilian government program was providing HAART to almost 20 percent of people living with HIV and AIDS in the country. This figure represents about twenty-three times as many people as were receiving HAART at the end of 1997 (Chequer et al., 2002). Although HAART access in Brazil has still not expanded to universal availability, significant progress continues to be made. Rollout of Brazil's national program has been significantly faster and more consistent than the expansion of similar initiatives in less-affluent countries in the region, such as Cuba, Peru, and Chile. A strong health care infrastructure, particularly nationwide laboratory monitoring capacity, has greatly facilitated the expansion of Brazil's national HAART program (Chequer et al., 2002). Less-developed countries in South America, Africa, and elsewhere could face greater challenges in increasing both funding and drug distribution and monitoring systems when seeking to implement similar programs on a national scale.

Brazil is in a unique position to advise other developing countries on strategies for and challenges of implementing national AIDS care programs, particularly those that include a HAART provision component. In addition, Brazil's experience will help to shed light on the long-term implications of significantly improving length and quality of life for people living with HIV. Of particular interest in recent years is the effect of access to HAART on children and young adults infected with HIV, particularly because young people remain disproportionately affected by the epidemic worldwide. In 2001, 130,000 children who had lost one or both parents to AIDS were living in Brazil, and 13,000 HIV-positive children were living in the country (UNAIDS, 2002b). This generation of children is growing up with access not only to potent antiretroviral drugs, but also to psychological support, family counseling, and educational services. New research must now be conducted to assess the continuing psychological and educational needs of adolescents and young adults living with HIV (Abadía-Barrero, 2002).

The dynamics of the AIDS epidemic have changed in Brazil since the 1980s, and national policy will need to evolve to better serve different groups of people. Most new HIV infections in Brazil now occur through heterosexual contact, which means that the epidemic's effect on women is increasing. During the early years of the epidemic, HIV transmission took place primarily via homosexual contacts between men: In 1985 the ratio of men to women living with HIV was 24:1. This ratio has changed in recent years such that the proportion of men to women living with HIV and AIDS was only 2:1 in 2002 (Meira, 2002). Every year women make up a greater percentage of people who require AIDS care and support, and national policy must adapt to ensure that they are adequately served (Segurado et al., 2003). Brazil is one of the first developing countries to face these challenges brought on by a stable, accessible health care program for people living with HIV and AIDS. The flexibility of the Brazilian National AIDS Program could potentially provide a model for similar efforts worldwide in the future.

In 2000, UNAIDS approved a Global Strategy Framework on HIV/AIDS, laying out a rubric for successful national responses to the epidemic. Along with an emphasis on the involvement of local stakeholders and people living with HIV and AIDS, the framework states that a key element of successful national AIDS programs is coordination and involvement from central government (Piot and Coll Seck, 2001). Commitment from communities, health care workers, and local government offices can significantly impact the course of AIDS at the regional level, but centralized political leadership lends an important consistency and impetus to these efforts (Biswanger, 2000). In countries where central government is either unstable because of international or civil war, or unreceptive to particular HIV and AIDS care, prevention, and support interventions, the lack of a coordinated response can adversely affect efforts to control the epidemic's spread and impact.

Countries such as Senegal and Nigeria that have instituted comprehensive HIV and AIDS care and prevention initiatives despite limited financial and physical resources often choose to begin a national program via pilot studies. These efforts deliver HIV and AIDS treatment and support to small cohorts of individuals, often initially seeking to include those who are able to partially fund their own care. Results from pilot studies allow policymakers to judge the capacity, educational efforts, and financial resources necessary to scale up programs to the national level, ensuring that they will be cost-effective and locally appropriate (Laurent et al., 2002; Kaiser Family Foundation, 2001b).

In Senegal, the pilot phase of a national AIDS treatment program was initiated in 1998. This program was one of the earliest in Africa to offer HAART to AIDS patients through the public sector, providing researchers with an opportunity to study the feasibility and effectiveness of delivering HAART to African populations. After reaching agreements for antiretroviral drug price reductions with pharmaceutical companies and generic drug makers, the Senegalese government arranged to subsidize just over 95 percent of the costs of patient care, with each program participant paying about US$34 per year. After eighteen months of medical follow-up, patients' adherence to multidrug HAART regimes was high and comparable to rates of adherence recorded in clinical trials in developed countries. A steady drug supply and good individual adherence to drug regimens ensured both that participants' health remained stable and that little viral resistance to antiretrovirals developed. The Senegalese government's commitment to ensuring and regulating a supply of low-cost, high-quality drugs for AIDS treatment had an important impact on this pilot program, suggesting that similar coordination at a national level can lead to the success of a nationwide AIDS care delivery program (Laurent et al., 2002). Medical infrastructure for other elements of HIV and AIDS care remains a concern in Senegal, however, despite the efficacy of antiretroviral drugs. Laboratory and diagnostic services for identification and treatment of opportunistic infections such as pneumonia are not yet optimal even at medical facilities in the capital city of Dakar, and could be more seriously lacking in rural areas. This gap in the continuum of care services that people living with HIV and AIDS require will continue to lead to unnecessary illness and mortality until medical infrastructure is improved nationwide, a task in many ways more costly and time-consuming than simply supplying antiretroviral therapies (Laurent et al., 2002).

Nigeria, the most populous country in Africa, has experienced severe political turmoil and civil war since 1960, when the country declared independence from Britain. After Nigerian independence was formally achieved in 1963, a democratically elected government ruled for only three years before an attempted military coup led to the installation of a military government. Nigeria remained under military rule for the next thirty-six years, although short-lived civilian regimes were elected in 1979 and 1993. The country's democratic election of its current president, retired general Oluscgun Obasanjo, took place in January 1999, after years of intense domestic and international pressure, including suspension of aid from the United States (Washington Post Company, 2003).

Accurate statistics on HIV prevalence and incidence in Nigeria are scanty, because of continual breakdowns and shortages in medical care and government infrastructure. National HIV prevalence is estimated at about 5 percent, meaning that the country is home to more than 2.5 million people living with HIV and AIDS (UNAIDS, 2000a). Estimates from NGOs and community leaders suggest that among some groups, HIV prevalence might be as high as 30 percent, but systematic surveillance is challenging. Nigeria is one of the largest producers and exporters of oil in the world, but little of the income from this industry benefits local communities. In 2002, 70 percent of Nigerians were living in extreme poverty, and nationwide unemployment remains significant (Hargreaves, 2002). In the past, the Nigerian government committed very few resources to public health care delivery and infrastructure, allocating just 2 percent of the government's yearly budget to health care, or an average of US$8 per person per year (Hargreaves, 2002; United Nations Development Programme, 2002). This shortfall means that almost three-quarters of all health care is delivered on a fee-for-services basis in the private sector, ranging from private doctors and clinics to traditional and faith healers to unlicensed pharmacists dealing in drugs purchased on the black market (Hargreaves, 2002).

The election of President Obasanjo in 1999 and the ensuing return of some political stability in Nigeria have allowed national government to make public health a new priority. With government support, the National Action Committee on HIV/AIDS in Nigeria formed to develop strategies for repairing and creating medical infrastructure, and delivering affordable care and support (Hargreaves, 2002). On April 26, 2001, President Obasanjo announced that Nigeria had reached an agreement with Indian generic drug maker Cipla to supply 10,000 people with HAART for US$350 per person per year (Donnelly, 2001b). Of this US$350, the Nigerian government will pay for about 90 percent, and the remaining US$8–9 will be paid by patients (Hargreaves, 2002). This price reduction represents a significant discount from the average US$600 per person per year that Cipla charges in developing countries, signaling that if resource-scarce countries demonstrate strong leadership in the fight against HIV and AIDS, important financial concessions can be negotiated (Donnelly, 2001b).

Nigeria's pilot rollout of HAART delivery to 10,000 people with AIDS officially began in September of 2001, despite the fact that elements of necessary medication tracking and disease monitoring had not yet been operationalized (Kaiser Family Foundation, 2001b). Although bringing hope to Nigeria's public sector, and increasing the demand for HIV testing and prevention materials among the general population, the future of Nigeria's national AIDS treatment program remains doubtful. Nigerian health care providers are now faced with difficult choices, as AIDS treatments become available to only a small fraction of their patients. For many Nigerians, even US$9 per year is too much to spend for medical care, putting this treatment out of reach of many affected communities (Donnelly, 2001a). As demonstrated in Brazil and Thailand, appropriate care and support for people living with HIV and AIDS includes many more services than the delivery of antiretroviral drugs. The need for comprehensive care presents a long-term challenge for Nigeria, where limited or nonexistent medical and social infrastructure prevent the government and other partners from scaling up voluntary counseling and testing sites, condom promotions, psychological support services, and facilities for opportunistic infection prophylaxis, diagnosis, and treatment (Hargreaves, 2002).

As African countries such as Senegal, Botswana, and Nigeria begin to broaden their national response to HIV and AIDS, countries such as South Africa struggle to define national government's priorities related to HIV treatment and prevention and the scope of efforts that will be feasible. South Africa's first democratic elections were held in 1994, and the African National Congress (ANC) has since controlled the government, first lead by President Nelson Mandela and then by President Thabo Mbeki. The ANC began to address the growing problem of HIV and AIDS in South Africa even before the end of Apartheid, collaborating with the government to organize the first South African AIDS Conference in 1992. This conference led to the creation of the National AIDS Committee of South Africa (NACOSA) during the same year (Schneider and Stein, 2001).

NACOSA drafted a National AIDS Plan for South Africa to be put into effect after the 1994 elections. Working from a grassroots political and human rights framework, the 1994 National AIDS Plan emphasized multidisciplinary collaboration coordinated by central government, human rights protections for people living with HIV and AIDS, and promotion of women's sexual rights. After the ANC was elected in 1994, President Nelson Mandela prioritized AIDS as an important public health and security issue. Despite this commitment, implementation of the National AIDS Plan began via provincial health ministries only, without the multidisciplinary and nongovernmental components originally envisioned by NACOSA (Schneider and Stein, 2001).

The 1994 National AIDS Plan was never fully implemented in South Africa, perhaps because its goals and philosophies assumed a higher level of infrastructure and more cooperation among disparate public health workers than was feasible during the years of post-Apartheid political reorganization. Deficiencies in South African health infrastructure at the national and provincial levels have prevented new HIV and AIDS prevention and care programs from delivering their services widely. This delay in turn has prevented organizations from spending funds allocated to HIV and AIDS by central government and international donors (Schneider and Stein, 2001).

Politicians and others who are concerned about HIV and AIDS in South Africa continue to seek solutions to improving care and prevention services, but the magnitude of the epidemic in South Africa has led many to seek "quick fix" solutions. In 1997, for example, the South African Cabinet announced that a new drug called "Virodene" had been developed as a promising treatment for AIDS. Independent review of the drug (a biological solvent) showed that it was not effective in any animal or biological models. Two ethics committees turned down requests for authorization of clinical trials of Virodene in humans, sparking a public outcry and allegations from the government that the medical establishment was withholding a life-saving therapy. HIV/AIDS has become a way for the South African public to demand accountability from government officials on issues related to health and human rights. This activism has quickly garnered international attention, bringing the debate over the South African government's role in proving HIV and AIDS prevention, care, and treatment services into a global arena (Schneider and Stein, 2001).

The South African government's future commitment to providing HIV and AIDS care remains unclear, as activists demand expanded access to HAART, universal delivery of antiretroviral drugs to prevent mother-to-child transmission, and low-cost treatment options for opportunistic infections. Building off of South Africa's long and successful history of grassroots political activism, groups such as the National Association of People Living with AIDS (NAPWA) and the Treatment Action Campaign (TAC) have thrown their energy into ensuring that HIV and AIDS care and prevention services become available to all. The TAC was founded in 1998 as a multisectoral forum for people living with HIV and AIDS, nongovernmental organizations, health care workers, researchers, and others to demand that the South African government make AIDS treatments available to all who need them. In addition, the TAC works to lobby international pharmaceutical companies to reduce the prices of antiretroviral drugs and treatments for opportunistic infections, to make these therapies accessible in developing countries (Treatment Action Campaign: An Overview, n.d.).

Spurred by the formation of the TAC, the fight for AIDS care in South Africa continues as a grassroots political movement. Between 1999 and 2000, South African President Thabo Mbeki began to consult with a group of "AIDS dissidents," scientists and doctors who contend that AIDS is not caused by HIV, but instead arises as a result of malnutrition, malaria, poverty, drug abuse, and poor hygiene. In light of this theory, Mbeki and members of the South African Department of Health suggested in 1999 that international pharmaceutical companies had greatly exaggerated concerns over AIDS in order to profit off of drug sales in developing countries (Epstein, 2000). Although Mbeki stated in 2000 that the South African government's actions on HIV and AIDS would in the future be based on the "thesis" that HIV causes AIDS, government support for care and prevention interventions involving antiretroviral drugs remained weak (Hartley, 2000).

In October 1998, the South African government closed down a series of pilot studies investigating the safety and feasibility of distributing AZT to pregnant women to prevent mother-to-child transmission of HIV. This decision was primarily based on concerns over the expense of providing antiretroviral drugs and the government's philosophy of guaranteeing that no group would be "privileged" above another in terms of health care spending (Knox, 1998). The TAC began a series of protests and legal actions beginning with a multiprovince petition in 1998 (Treatment Action

Campaign: An Overview, n.d.). This series of actions culminated with the TAC, the Children's Rights Center, and Dr. Haroon Saloojee of the University of the Witwatersrand filing suit against the South African Department of Health to force the government to provide nevirapine to all HIV-infected pregnant women (Treatment Action Campaign, 2001). Judge Chris Botha of the Pretoria High Court ruled against the government on December 14, 2001, stipulating that the government must draft and implement a national plan to prevent mother-to-child HIV transmission as quickly as possible (*Agence France Presse,* 2001). Although this court decision has been upheld through an appeal by the government in 2002, universal mother-to-child transmission prevention programs have not yet been scaled up nationwide (Constitutional Court of South Africa, 2002).

Local government responses to HIV and AIDS in South Africa differ strikingly from central government policy in some regions. KwaZulu-Natal Province, the region hardest-hit by HIV and AIDS and also one of the poorest provinces in the country, chose to override the government's policy against providing nevirapine to prevent mother-to-child HIV transmission in early 2001. Western Cape Province took the same step in 2000, leaving seven provinces without pubic support for mother-to-child transmission prevention (Kaiser Family Foundation, 2001a). In April 2002, KwaZulu-Natal Province submitted a successful funding proposal to the Global Fund to Fight AIDS, Tuberculosis, and Malaria, an international fund established by the secretary general of the United Nations to combat the three diseases in developing countries. The KwaZulu-Natal program, entitled the "Enhancing Care Initiative," was awarded US$27 million over five years to increase access to voluntary counseling and testing services, treat opportunistic infections, provide nevirapine to prevent mother-to-child transmission, and treat HIV-infected health care workers with HAART. The South African government has delayed disbursement of these funds to KwaZulu-Natal, preferring that support from the Global Fund benefit all provinces equally and be administered centrally according to national AIDS policy (*Agence France Presse,* 2002). An agreement for disbursal of the Global Fund's grant was not reached until August 2003 (UN Integrated Regional Information Networks, 2003).

In a 2001 article on AIDS policy in the post-Apartheid era, two South African researchers from the University of the Witwatersrand note: "The presence of individuals and groups, both inside and outside government willing to challenge and provide a critical mirror to government and society, is key to the medium and long term success of AIDS policy implementation" (Schneider and Stein, 2001, 729). This philosophy in many ways has informed past political struggles in South Africa as well as current policy debates, ensuring that local stakeholders will continue to make their voices heard. Although serious constraints to accessing sufficient HIV and AIDS care and support still exacerbate the effects of HIV and AIDS in South Africa, groups like the TAC have made significant and concrete legal, medical, and policy advances since the late 1990s.

HIV Vaccine Design and the Ethics of International Clinical Trials

"In the history of medicine the only things that have really worked to stop diseases in the third world have been vaccines. Drugs won't work for us. Prevention has obviously failed. Education is almost impossible. Without a vaccine we are going to keep on losing and we are going to lose a lot" (Specter, 1998). Dr. Peter Mugenyi of the Uganda Joint Clinical Research Center made this statement in 1998 to a reporter for the *New York Times* almost four years after the first preparations were made in Uganda to host a clinical trial of an experimental AIDS vaccine (Mugenyi, 2002). Researchers, educators, and activists have addressed the need for an HIV vaccine to varying degrees since the worldwide AIDS epidemic began, so far without concrete medical success, but with an ever-growing awareness of the complexity of HIV itself and its effects on global society.

In 1793 Dr. Edward Jenner found that people who had been infected with the benign cowpox virus became immune to deadly smallpox infection. Jenner's discovery resulted in the first successful vaccine in medical history, changing the way that researchers approached the problem of eliminating serious infectious diseases, such as polio, measles, influenza, and hepatitis (Klein and Ho, 2000). As of 2002, the U.S. Food and Drug Administration licensed twenty-six vaccines for use in humans, fourteen to prevent bacterial diseases, and twelve to prevent viral infections. Some of these vaccines, including those preventing polio, measles, mumps, and rubella, have been widely distributed in developing countries by international health organizations such as UNICEF (Hilleman, 2002). Other vaccines are too costly for developing country governments to afford, remaining available only in wealthy regions with strong medical infrastructure. This group includes a Hepatitis B vaccine, which was developed in the 1980s through clinical trials based in Senegal and the Gambia, but which is now too expensive for most African nations to provide (Specter, 1998; Whittle, Lamb, and Ryder, 1987).

The process of developing a new vaccine can be time-consuming, particularly when the physical and genetic makeup of the target virus or bacterium is complex. Although the influenza and measles vaccines were developed less than ten years after these diseases were identified (in 1933 and 1954, respectively), the average amount of time between disease characterization and the development of an effective vaccine has been close to three decades. The vaccine for rabies was not developed until almost seventy years after the disease was first identified (Klein and Ho, 2000). The HIV virus was identified in the mid-1980s, and even after almost twenty years of study a successful vaccine remains elusive. As the epidemic's impact increases and more regions are affected, the need for a vaccine in the fight against HIV and AIDS is increasing, leading to the creation and expansion of international partnerships between scientists, philanthropists, governments, educators, and communities.

For some of the same reasons that HIV is a difficult virus to treat, the development of an HIV vaccine is a challenging process. The HIV virus mutates quickly and randomly because of errors during the reverse transcription process (when HIV's RNA is "transcribed" within a host cell to form viral DNA and the building blocks of new virions). This tendency to mutate allows HIV to adapt to the presence of antiviral agents quickly, creating new strains of the virus that are resistant to antiretroviral drugs and ensuring that a vaccine targeting only a single strain of HIV will not provide significant protection (Bolognesi, 1990). In addition, the HIV virus attacks the human immune system, which means that host immune response can potentially increase viral activity and allow HIV virions to replicate more quickly within the body (Fust, 1997). The human immune system can successfully fight off HIV for a time, until viral factors that cause immune suppression become high enough to cause illness and AIDS. For the majority of people who are infected with HIV, however, immune response provides only temporary protection from illness. A successful

HIV vaccine could enhance the human body's successful attack on HIV without allowing the virus to overwhelm the immune system (Bolognesi, 1990).

Human immune response to the presence of disease antigens involves the mobilization of B- and T-immune cells that control two different but interconnected components of strategies for preventing infection. When a virus enters the body, B cells release antibodies that bind to the viral envelope, or coating, to prevent the virus from infecting host cells. Antibodies are highly specialized, keyed to recognize specific details of viral structure. T cells are responsible for the development of "cell mediated immunity," recognizing and eliminating host cells that have become infected by a virus. CD8+ T cells destroy or disable infected cells, while CD4+ "helper" T cells alert the body to the presence of a virus, and "recruit" B cells and CD8+ T cells to the site of infection (Tizard, 1995). HIV's primary targets are CD4+ T cells, which allow the virus to circumvent many of the body's natural protections by attacking the cells that direct the immune system itself. A successful HIV vaccine would bolster the body's antibody response, but because HIV mutates so quickly, antibody protection will not remain effective for long. Many researchers argue that an HIV vaccine also needs to stimulate cell-mediated immunity (Klein and Ho, 2000).

Vaccines to prevent viruses trigger the body's immune response by providing B and T cells with "copies" of the characteristics of the target disease. Vaccines can be made up of an "attenuated" strain of the virus, a "killed" or inactivated version, or specific "subunits" of viral DNA and structure genetically attached to a harmless carrier virus. "Attenuated" viruses are weakened by altering a live virus so that it will be incapable of causing infection or illness, and "killed" vaccines are created by exposing the virus to formaldehyde or another agent. Advances in genetics and bioengineering have allowed scientists to isolate characteristic sections of viral DNA and portions of virion structure, which can then be grafted onto a harmless virus that will carry these portions of a more dangerous virus into the body. This sensitization allows B and T cells to recognize exposure to the virus itself in the future. HIV's life cycle involves incorporation of its genetic material into the host's own DNA. This "genetically dangerous" situation, in addition to HIV's ability to mutate renders the use of an attenuated HIV vaccine too risky, as the possibility exists for "harmless" modified HIV virions to revert to infectious "wild type" strains in the body (Haynes, Putman, and Weinberg, 1996). Subunit vaccines, although successful in preventing diseases such as hepatitis B, could be impractical for HIV prevention, because they provoke only an antibody response from the immune system, rather than the necessary combination of antibodies and cell-mediated immunity (Hilleman, 1996). Hopefully the future genetics and bioengineering will lead to a better understanding of human immune response and how to use that knowledge to build an effective vaccine.

As new vaccine candidates emerge, the question of where and how to conduct vaccine trials has become immediate and contentious. Almost 90 percent of all HIV infections occur in developing and resource-scarce countries, regions where the need for a vaccine is particularly critical because antiretroviral therapies and complex medical care remain prohibitively expensive. At the same time, the majority of clinical research on HIV and AIDS, including vaccinology, originates in wealthy developed countries such as the United States. When the time comes to test a new vaccine candidate, clinical trials may take place through a partnership between stakeholders in developing countries and foreign investigators. International and local governments, ethicists, scientists, universities, and others must work to ensure not only that these trials are carried out in observance of the highest ethical standards, but also that trial design, location, and procedure account for and accommodate local needs and realities (Angell, 1997; Specter, 2003).

For forty years, between 1932 and 1972, the U.S. Public Health Service sponsored a clinical trail at Tuskegee University to study the progression of untreated syphilis infection. Although penicillin became available during the course of the study and was shown elsewhere to be an effective cure for syphilis, the 412 African American men participating in the study were never offered any treatment for their illness. When articles in New York and Washington newspapers alerted the public to the fact that study participants were being denied appropriate medical care at Tuskegee, the Nixon administration ended the project. Study investigators justified their research strategy by arguing that poor African American men in the region were unlikely to be able to afford syphilis treatment, so the Tuskegee study examined only what would have taken place anyway without any medical intervention (Reverby, 2000).

The Tuskegee trial is a permanent reminder of the importance of ensuring that the human rights of participants in clinical trials are respected and that study aims and the pursuit of medical knowledge do not overshadow safety and individual well-being. In 1989 the World Health Organization issued the "Declaration of Helsinki," which stated, "In any study, every patient—including those of a control group, if any—should be assured of the best proven diagnostic and therapeutic method." Ethicists and medical researchers have traditionally interpreted this statement as referring to the best care worldwide, which is usually the standard of care available in the wealthiest developed nations. This interpretation was reinforced by the "International Ethical Guidelines for Biomedical Research Involving Human Subjects" developed in 1993 by the World Health Organization and the Council for International Organizations of Medical Sciences. These guidelines state that when clinical trials are conducted internationally, study participants must be guaranteed care equivalent to the standard of care in the sponsoring country (Angell, 1997).

HIV and AIDS have highlighted the disparity between the medical care available in developed and developing countries. Along with financial constraints, lack of strong medical infrastructure prevents access to optimal medical care in developing countries. This means that even in areas where financial support from international researchers and donors is available, physically delivering state-of-the-art care services might be difficult or even impossible. Traditionally, new vaccines have been developed and tested in wealthy countries where a medical safety net is available to study participants who become infected with the disease a vaccine would prevent. HIV prevalence remains low in developed countries compared with nations in southern Africa, Southeast Asia, and Eastern Europe, where a vaccine is most needed, but developing countries with high HIV prevalence often do not have the funds or infrastructure to adequately care for people with HIV and AIDS. The question remains for researchers from developed countries and HIV-ravaged communities in resource-scarce regions, of how to bring experimental vaccines to the populations that need them most without harming or exploiting volunteers in clinical trials (Specter, 1998).

By the early 1980s, scientists and health care workers in Uganda had begun to anticipate the first clinical trials of a candidate HIV vaccine. Shortly after the first cases of HIV in Rakai

District indicated the seriousness of the Ugandan AIDS epidemic, representatives of the World Health Organization met with Ugandan researchers and doctors to develop guidelines for carrying out safe, ethical vaccine studies in the country. In 1994 the World Health Organization returned to conduct Uganda's first "vaccine preparedness study" in conjunction with a second study carried out by the U. S. National Institutes of Health. These studies followed groups of volunteers for two years to assess whether Ugandan communities were ready to host an HIV vaccine trial. Studies focused on the question of whether Ugandan health care workers could educate study participants so that those who received a candidate vaccine would not develop a false sense of protection leading to risky behaviors. After two years, both studies showed that participants were willing to accept an HIV vaccine and that risky sexual behavior among study participants declined after intensive education and outreach efforts (Mugyenyi, 2002).

After the success of the two preparedness trials, the Ugandan Joint Clinical Research Center began to investigate the possibility of conducting a local vaccine trial. At the time, no vaccine candidates had been developed to prevent HIV-1 subtypes A and D, which are most common in Uganda, so researchers from Uganda and the United States decided to test ALVAC-HIV vCP205, a candidate vaccine against HIV-1 subtype B, which had previously been tested in France. The aim of the study was to determine whether a vaccine designed for one subtype could provide "cross-clade" protection against others, a finding that could increase the likelihood of discovering a vaccine that would be effective worldwide (Mugyenyi, 2002).

Before any trial could begin in Uganda, issues of medical and technical infrastructure as well as political support and community education had to be addressed. Over the course of two years, Ugandan research staff were trained locally in data management skills, laboratory techniques, and research practices, while others traveled abroad to earn advanced degrees in epidemiology, immunology, public health, and counseling. During this time, in collaboration with the U.S. hospitals and universities overseeing the clinical trial, a new laboratory building was constructed at the study site and equipped with state-of-the-art HIV diagnostic and monitoring equipment. In the public sector, Ugandan Cabinet and Parliament members held debates on issues related to the upcoming trial, and media outlets invited commentary from researchers and others involved in the preparation process. The study group also formed a community advisory board made up of local stakeholders, including health care workers, nongovernmental organizations, and community and religious leaders. The advisory board worked as a liaison between the study staff and investigators and the communities where the study would take place, spearheading educational efforts, ensuring that the study was carried out according to established ethics and safety guidelines, and encouraging trial volunteers to act as "ambassadors and witnesses." Uganda's fist HIV vaccine trial began with forty HIV-negative volunteers in January 1999. If the vaccine is found to be safe, future trials will recruit hundreds more volunteers to test whether it is effective in an African population (Mugyenyi, 2002).

Four years after Uganda's phase 1 vaccine trial began, Dr. Mugyenyi and others in and outside of Uganda are still pondering the ethical implications of holding clinical trials in a country where universal access to optimal AIDS care and treatment has never been available. These reflections are timely, as early safety tests of vaccines conclude and subsequent tests of efficacy requiring thousands of volunteers are planned for the future. Vaccine efficacy studies (phases 2 and 3 of three-part vaccine trials) are most useful if they are conducted in regions where HIV incidence and prevalence are high, ensuring that a vaccine's protective qualities will be sufficiently tested. HIV prevalence in developed countries such as in Europe and North America are too low to give quick, definitive results, whereas high-prevalence African and Asian countries provide a testing ground that is in many ways ideal. Balanced against contentions that no clinical trial can be in compliance with ethical guidelines without offering optimal AIDS treatment to participants, is the very real desperation of many developing countries where millions of citizens are ill or dying from AIDS (Mugyenyi, 2002).

Uganda, after consultations with individual communities, universities, researchers, doctors, and religious leaders, chose to pursue HIV vaccine trials despite a lack of health care options and infrastructure. Scientists at the Uganda Virus Research Institute and the Joint Clinical Research Center are currently collaborating with a wide range of international organizations, including the International AIDS Vaccine Initiative, the British Medical Research Council, and the U.S. Centers for Disease Control on vaccine studies. Vaccine studies have not delivered highly active antiretroviral therapy to all Ugandans living with HIV and AIDS or enhanced national medical care to a level found in developing countries, but the process of preparing for vaccine research has created extensive new scientific and laboratory infrastructure. In addition, vaccine trials have significantly increased nationwide awareness of HIV, access to information on disease prevention, and understanding of scientific studies (Specter, 2003; Mugyenyi, 2002).

No final resolution has been brought to the debate over the ethics of international clinical research sponsored by developed countries and carried out in resource-scarce regions. The Tuskegee study remains a haunting testament to the rationalizations that can justify exploitation of research participants in the name of medical progress. The reality of HIV and AIDS in sub-Saharan African and other developing regions demands that new solutions be found soon, so that the gap between health care in wealthy and resource-scarce countries will not further delay access to potentially lifesaving scientific advances. Uganda's experience with vaccine trials might be an example of how developing countries can enter the international research community and make the debate over medical ethics relevant to their own specific needs and situations. The AIDS epidemic takes a different form in every region of the world, and research science must therefore be able to adapt to local contexts, capacities, and priorities.

References

Abadía-Barrero, C. E. 2002. Growing up in a world with AIDS: Social advantages of having AIDS in Brazil. *AIDS Care* 14(3): 417–423.

Agence France Presse. SAfrica-AIDS: South Africa accepts UN AIDS grant, but sets own terms. *Agence France Presse,* 16 July 2002.

———. SAfrica-AIDS: S. African court orders government to provide AIDS drug. *Agence France Presse,* 14 December, 2001.

Aggleton, P., and M. Maluwa. 2000. *Comparative Analysis: Research Studies from India and Uganda HIV and AIDS-Related Discrimination, Stigmatization, and Denial.* Geneva: UNAIDS.

Alubo, S. O. 1990. Debt crisis, health, and health services in Africa. *Social Science and Medicine* 31: 639–648.

Angell, M. 1997. The ethics of clinical research in the third world. *NEJM* 337(12): 847–849.

Anglaret, X., G. Chene, A. Attia, et al. 1999. Early chemoprophylaxis with trimethoprim-sulphamethoxazole for HIV-1 infected adults in Abidjan, Cöte 'dIvoire: A randomized trial. *Lancet* 353: 1463–1468.

Anonymous. 2002a. Brazil shares blueprint of successful battle against HIV/AIDS. *AIDS Policy and Law* 17(16): 1.

Anonymous. 2002b. HIV on Sesame Street [editorial]. *The Boston Herald*, 13 July 2002, 1–16.

Associated Press. 2002. South Africa's Sesame Street gets HIV+ Muppet [press release]. Published September 17, 2002. Accessed April 17, 2002. Available at: http;//www.muppetcentral.com/news/2002/091702.s html.

Beck, E. J., A. H. Miners, and K. Tolley. 2001. The cost of HIV treatment and care: A global review. *Pharmacoeconomics* 19(1): 13–39.

Biswanger, H. P. 2000. Scaling up HIV/AIDS programs to national coverage. *Science* 288: 2173–2176.

Bolognesi, D. P. 1990. Approaches to HIV vaccine design. *Trends in Biotechnology* 8(2): 40–45.

Botswana Ministry of Health. 1999. *Sentinel Surveillance Report.* Gaborone: Botswana Ministry of Health.

Campbell, C. H., M. E. Marum, M. Alwano-Edyegu, et al. 1997. The role of HIV counseling and testing in the developing world. *AIDS Education and Prevention* 9: 92–104.

Castle, C. J., S. Solomon, S. Swarnalakshmi, S. Thomas, S. Priya, and C. Costello-Daly. 2002. Strengthening HIV/AIDS care and support also improves prevention services. Presented at: the XIV International AIDS Conference, July 7–12, Barcelona, Spain.

Castro, R., E. Orozco, P. Aggleton, et al. 1998. Family responses to HIV/AIDS in Mexico. *Soc Sci Med* 47(10): 1473–1484.

Chequer, P., P. Cuchi, R. Mazin, and J. M. G. Calleja. 2002. Access to anti-retroviral treatment in Latin American countries and the Caribbean. *AIDS* 16(suppl. 3): S50–S57.

Constitutional Court of South Africa. 2002. Case CCT 8/02. Available at: http://www.tac.org.za/Documents/MTCTCourtCase/ConCourt JudgmentOrderingMTCTP-5July2002.pdf. Accessed: March 13, 2004.

Creese, A., K. Floyd, A. Alban, and L. Guinness. 2002. Cost-effectiveness of HIV/AIDS interventions in Africa: A systematic review of the evidence. *Lancet* 359: 1635–1642.

Curtis, J. R., and D. L. Patrick. 1993. Race and survival time with AIDS: A synthesis of the literature. *American Journal of Public Health* 83(10): 1425–1428.

D'Amelio, R., E. Tuerlings, O. Perito, et al. 2001. A global review of legislation on HIV/AIDS: The issue of HIV testing. *JAIDS* 28: 173–179.

Donnelly, J. H. 2001a. Despair drive[s] AIDS fight in Nigeria. *Boston Globe*, 13 May 2001, A-1.

———. 2001b. Nigeria reaches deal with Indian firm to buy AIDS drugs. *Boston Globe*, 26 April 2001, A-22.

Epstein, H. 2000. The mystery of AIDS in South Africa. *New York Review* 47(12): 50–56.

Forsythe, S. 1998. The affordability of antiretroviral therapy in developing countries: What policymakers need to know. *AIDS* 12(suppl. 2): S11–S18.

Freedberg, K. A., E. Losina, M. C. Weinstein, et al. 2001. The cost effectiveness of combination antiretroviral therapy for HIV disease. *NEJM* 344(11): 824–831.

Fust, G. 1997. Enhancing antibodies in HIV infection. *Parasitology* 115(suppl. 1): S127–S140.

Gilmore, N., M. A. Somerville. 1994. Stigmatization, scapegoating, and discrimination in sexually transmitted diseases: Overcoming "them" and "us." *Soc Sci Med* 39(9): 1339–1358.

Goemaere, E., N. Ford, and S. R. Benatar. 2002. HIV/AIDS prevention and treatment [correspondence]. *Lancet* 360(9326): 86–87.

Gonsalves, G. 2002. HIV/AIDS prevention and treatment [correspondence]. *Lancet* 360(9326): 87–88.

Gordon, C. M., A. D. Forsyth, T. J. Coates, M. H. Merson, and P. A. Volberding. 2002. HIV prevention in treatment settings: U.S. and international research priorities. Presented at: the XIV International AIDS Conference, July 7–12, Barcelona, Spain. Abstract number MoPeG4206.

Guinness, L., D. Walker, P. Ndubanii, J. Jama, and M. P. Kelly. 2002. Impact of HIV/AIDS and priorities for treatment and prevention strategies in selected companies in Zambia. Presented at: the XIV International AIDS Conference, July 7–12, Barcelona, Spain. Abstract number TuPeE5150.

Hanenberg, R., and W. Rojanapithayakorn. 1998. Changes in prostitution and the AIDS epidemic in Thailand. *AIDS Care* 10(1): 69–79.

Hanenberg, R. S., W. Rojanapithayakorn, P. Kunasol, and D. S. Sokal. 1994. Impact of Thailand's HIV-control programme as indicated by the decline of sexually transmitted diseases. *Lancet* 344: 243–245.

Hansen, K., G. Chapman, I. Chitsike, et al. 2000. The costs of HIV/AIDS care at government hospitals in Zimbabwe. *Health Policy and Planning* 15(4): 432–440.

Hansen, K., G. Woelk, H. Jackson, et al. 1998. The cost of home-based care for HIV/AIDS patients in Zimbabwe. *AIDS Care* 10: 751–759.

Hargreaves, S. 2002. Time to right the wrongs: Improving basic health care in Nigeria. *Lancet* 359: 2030–2035.

Hartley, W. Mbeki spells out government's AIDS stance. *Business Day* (South Africa), 21 September 2000, 1.

Havanon, N., A. Bennett, and J. Knodel. 1993. Sexual networking in provincial Thailand. *Studies in Family Planning* 24(1): 1–17.

Haynes, B. F., S. B. Putman, and J. B. Weinberg. 1996. Update on the issues of HIV vaccine development. *Annals of Medicine* 28(1): 39–41.

Herek, G. M., and J. P. Capitanio. 1993. Public reactions to AIDS in the United States: A second decade of stigma. *Am J Pub Health* 83(4): 574–577.

Hilleman, M. R. 1996. Strategies for the achievement of prophylactic vaccination against HIV. *Antibiotics and Chemotherapy* 48: 161–172.

———. 2002. Overview of the needs and realities for developing new and improved vaccines in the 21st century. *Intervirology* 45: 199–211.

Jacobson, M., N. L. Peter, and J. Laiser. 2002. Nevirapine therapy for prevention of maternal to child transmission of HIV. Presented at: Second National Multisectoral AIDS Conference in Tanzania, December 16–20, Arusha, Tanzania. Abstract number O42.

Jha, P., O. Bangoura, and K. Ranson. 1998. The cost-effectiveness of forty health interventions in Guinea. *Health Policy and Planning* 13(3): 249–262.

Kaiser Family Foundation. 2001a. KwaZulu-Natal officials "override" national government, make AIDS drug available at public hospitals for HIV-positive pregnant women. *Kaisernetwork.org Daily HIV/AIDS Report*, 22 January. Available at: http://www.kff.org. Accessed: May 27, 2003.

Kaiser Family Foundation. 2001b. Nigeria begins AIDS drug program after delay. *Kaiser Family Foundation Daily HIV/AIDS Report*, 11 September. Available at: http://www.kff.org. Accessed: May 19, 2003.

Kaiser Family Foundation. 2002. Treatment Action Campaign asks high court to force South Africa to follow Nevirapine Ruling despite government appeal. *Kaisernetwork.org Daily HIV/AIDS Report*, 1 February. Available at: http://www.kff.org. Accessed: May 27, 2003.

Kilmarx, P. H., K. Palanuvej, A. Chitvarakorn, et al. 1999. Seroprevalence of HIV among female sex workers in Bangkok: Evidence of ongoing infection risk after the "100 percent Condom Program" was implemented. *JAIDS* 21: 313–316.

Klein, E., and R. J. Y. Ho. 2000. Challenges in the development of an effective HIV vaccine: Current approaches and future directions. *Clinical Therapeutics* 22(3): 295–314.

Klepp, K. I., S. S. Ndeki, M. T. Leshabari, et al. 1997. AIDS education in Tanzania: promoting risk reduction among primary school children. *American Journal of Public Health* 87(12): 1931–1936.

Klevens, R. M., P. L. Fleming, M. A. Mays, et al. 1996. Characteristics of women with AIDS and invasive cervical cancer. *Obstetrical Gynecology* 88(2): 269–273.

Knox, R. A. Despite epidemic, South Africa cuts AZT project. *Boston Globe,* 1 December 1998, A17.

Laurent, C., N. Diakhaté, N. F. N. Gueye, et al. 2002. The Senegalese government's highly active antiretroviral therapy initiative: An 18 month follow-up study. *AIDS* 16: 1363–1370.

Maiman, M., R. G. Fruchter, M. Clark, et al. 1997. Cervical cancer as an AIDS defining illness. *Obstetrical Gynecology* 89(1): 76–80.

Manuel, C., P. Enel, J. Charrel, et al. 1990. The ethical approach to AIDS: a bibliographical review. *Journal of Medical Ethics* 16: 14–27.

Marlink, R., H. Kao, and E. Hsieh. 2001. Clinical care issues for women living with HIV and AIDS in the United States. *AIDS Research and Human Retroviruses* 17(1): 1–33.

Marseille, E., P. B. Hofmann, and J. G. Kahn. 2002. HIV Prevention before HAART in sub-Saharan Africa. *Lancet* 359: 1851–1856.

Marseille, E., J. G. Kahn, F. Mmiro, et al. 1999. Cost-effectiveness of single-dose nevirapine regimen for mothers and babies to decrease vertical HIV-1 transmission in sub-Saharan Africa. *Lancet* 354: 803–809.

Mastro, T. D., and K. Limpakarnjanarat. 1995. Condom use in Thailand: How much is it slowing the HIV/AIDS epidemic? *AIDS* 9: 523–525.

Meira, D. A. 2002. Acquired immunodeficiency syndrome in Brazil. *Croatian Medical Journal* 43(4): 475–479.

Mills, S., P. Benjarattanaporn, A. Bennett, et al. 1997. HIV risk behavioral surveillance in Bangkok, Thailand: Sexual behavior trends among eight population groups. *AIDS* 11(suppl. 1): S43–S51.

Mugyenyi, P. N. 2002. HIV vaccines: The Uganda experience. *Vaccine* 20: 1905–1908.

Parker, R., P. Aggleton, K. Attawell, J. Pulerwitz, and L. Brown. 2002. HIV/AIDS-related stigma and discrimination: A conceptual framework and an agenda for action. Washington, DC: Horizon Program.

Phanuphak, P., C. Locharernkul, W. Panmuong, and H. Wilde. 1985. A report of three cases of AIDS in Thailand. *Asian Pacific Journal of Allergy and Infections and Immunology* 3: 195–199.

Phoolcharoen, W., K. Ungchusak, W. Sittitrai, and T. Brown. 1998. Thailand: Lessons from a strong national response to HIV/AIDS. *AIDS* 12(suppl. B): S123–S135.

Piot, P., and A. M. Coll Seck. 2001. International response to the HIV/AIDS epidemic: planning for success. *Bulletin of the World Health Organization* 79(12): 1106–1112.

Piot, P., D. Zewdie, and T. Türmen. 2002. HIV/AIDS prevention and treatment [correspondence]. *Lancet* 360(9326): 86–88.

Ramanathan, K., D. Tarantola, and R. Marlink. 2002. "Access to HIV and AIDS Care." In *AIDS in Africa, 2nd Edition,* edited by M. Essex, S. Mboup, P. Kanki, R. Marlink, and S. Tlou. New York: Kluwer Academic/Plenum Publishers, pp. 436–457.

Reilly, T., and G. Woo. 2003. Access to services and maintenance of safer sex practices among people living with HIV/AIDS. *Social Work in Health Care* 36(2): 81–95.

Reverby, S. M., ed. 2000. *Tuskegee's Truths: Rethinking the Tuskegee Syphilis Study.* Chapel Hill: University of North Carolina Press.

Rosen, S., J. Simon, J. R. Vincent, et al. 2003. AIDS is your business. *Harvard Business Review* 81(1): 5–11.

Salomon, L., M. Stein, C. Flynn, et al. 1998. Health services use by urban women with or at risk for HIV-1 infection: The HIV epidemiology research study (HERS). *Journal of Acquired Immunodeficiency Syndromes and Human Retrovirology* 17(3): 253–261.

Sanders, D., J. Kravitz, S. Lewin, et al. 1998. Zimbabwe's hospital referral system: Does it work? *Health Policy and Planning* 13: 359–370.

Schneider, H., and J. Stein. 2001. Implementing AIDS policy in post-Apartheid South Africa. *Social Science and Medicine* 52: 723–731.

Schulman, K.A., L. A. Lynn, H. A. Glick, and J. M. Eisenberg. 1991. Cost effectiveness of low-dose zidovudine therapy for asymptomatic patients with human immunodeficiency virus (HIV) infection. *Annals of Internal Medicine* 114: 798–802.

Segurado, A.C., S. D. Miranda, M. D. R. D. O. LaTorre, et al. 2003. Evaluation of the care of women living with HIV/AIDS in São Paulo, Brazil. *AIDS Patient Care and STDs* 17(2): 85–93.

Sendi, P. P., H. C. Bucher, T. Harr, et al. 1999. Cost effectiveness of highly active antiretroviral therapy in HIV-infected patients. *AIDS* 13: 1115–1122.

Shapiro, M. F., S. C. Morton, D. F. McCaffrey, et al. 1999. Variations in the care of HIV-infected adults in the United States: Results from the HIV Cost and Services Utilization Study. *JAMA* 281(24): 2305–2315.

Specter, M. Urgency tempers ethics concerns in Uganda trial of AIDS vaccine. *New York Times*, 1 October 1998, A1.

———. 2003. The vaccine. *The New Yorker*, February 3: 54–65.

Stoller, N. E. 1998. *Lessons from the Damned: Queers, Whores, and Junkies Respond to AIDS*. New York: Routledge.

Stover, J., and L. Bollinger, for The Futures Group International. 2001. The economic impact of AIDS. Available at: http://www.tfgi.com. Accessed: May 8, 2001.

Tauzin, W. J., F. Upton, C. Stearns, et al. 2002. Energy and Commerce Members Question Sesame Character Introduction. Available at: http://energycommerce.house.gov/107/letters/07122002_667print.htm. Accessed: March 9, 2004.

Tizard, I. R. 1995. *Immunology: An introduction*. Philadelphia, PA: W. B. Saunders College Publications.

Treatment Action Campaign. n.d. Treatment Action Campaign: An overview. Available at: http://www.tac.org.za. Accessed: May 27, 2003.

Treatment Action Campaign, H. Saloojee, Children's Rights Center, et al. 2001. Founding affidavit in the high court of South Africa Transvaal provincial division. Available at: http://www.tac.org.za/Documents/MTCTCourtCase/ccmfound.rtf. Accessed: March 13, 2004.

UNAIDS. 2000a. Epidemiological fact sheets on HIV/AIDS and sexually transmitted infections: Nigeria, 2000 update. Available at: http://www.unaids.org. Accessed: May 21, 2003.

UNAIDS. 2000b. UNAIDS regional fact sheets: Senegal, June 2000 update. Available at: http://www.unaids.org. Accessed: May 25, 2003.

UNAIDS. 2002a. AIDS Epidemic Update December 2002. Available at: http://www.unaids.org. Accessed: February 3, 2003.

UNAIDS. 2002b. Epidemiological fact sheets on HIV/AIDS and sexually transmitted infections: Brazil, 2002 update. Available at: http://www.unaids.org. Accessed: May 21, 2003.

UNAIDS. 2003. AIDS Epidemic Update 2003. Available at: http://www.unaids.org. Accessed: June 16, 2004.

Ungphakorn, J., and W. Sittitrai. 1994. The Thai response to the HIV/AIDS epidemic. *AIDS* 8(suppl. 2): S155–S163.

UN Integrated Regional Information Networks. 2003. Johannesburg: Global Fund money becomes available. *UN Integrated Regional Information Networks*, 7 August.

United Nations Development Programme. 2002. Human development report. Available at: http://www.hdr.undp.org/default.cfm. Accessed: May 22, 2003.

Warwick, I., S. Bharat, R. Castro, et al. 1998. Household and community responses to HIV and AIDS in developing countries. *Critical Public Health* 8(4): 311–328.

Washington Post Company. Time line: Nigeria's history of turmoil. Available at: http://www.washingtonpost.com/wp-srv/inatl/longterm/nigeria/timeline.htm. Accessed: May 22, 2003.

Weniger, B. G., K. Limpakarnjanarat, K. Ungchusak, et al. 1991. The epidemiology of HIV infection and AIDS in Thailand. *AIDS* (suppl. 2): S71–S85.

Whittle, H. C., W. H. Lamb, and R. W. Ryder. 1987. Trials of intradermal hepatitis B vaccines in Gambian children. *Annals of Tropical Pediatrics* 7(1): 6–9.

Wiktor, S. Z., M. Sassan-Morokro, A. D. Grat, et al. 1999. Efficacy of trimethoprim-sulphamethoxazole prophylaxis to decrease morbidity and mortality in HIV-1 infected patients with tuberculosis in Abidjan, Côte d'Ivoire: A randomized controlled trial. *Lancet* 353: 1469–1475.

Wilkinson, D., N. Wilkinson, C. Lombard, et al. 1997. On-site HIV testing in resource-poor settings: Is one rapid test enough? *AIDS* 11: 377–381.

World Health Organization. 1984. Report of a WHO meeting on drug policies and management: procurement and financing of essential drugs. Geneva: World Health Organization.

World Health Organization. 1999. Removing Obstacles to Health Development: *Report on Infectious Diseases*. Geneva: World Health Organization.

World Summit of Ministers of Health on Programmes for HIV Prevention. 1988. London declaration on AIDS prevention. *International Nursing Review* 35(4): 119.

3

Chronology

The history of the human immunodeficiency virus (HIV) epidemic, even before the virus was detected on every continent, is best examined from a global perspective. Retrospective studies and epidemiological investigations conducted since the early 1980s show that the human immunodeficiency virus was present in Africa possibly decades before it was first detected and named in the United States. More recent government and community-based responses in Africa, Asia, and South America have affected global perceptions of the HIV epidemic as well as international research, trade, and funding priorities. As international and in-country transportation and communication become more accessible, the HIV epidemic is becoming both more visible and harder to combat. In the future, international partnerships such as the Global Fund to Fight AIDS, Tuberculosis, and Malaria and Doctors without Borders might provide the key to delivering HIV and AIDS prevention, care, and treatment programs in regions that are resource-scarce or lacking sufficient health care infrastructure.

Scientific Discovery

Advances in HIV and AIDS medicine, prevention, surveillance, and virology can have far-reaching social impact, although they often take place in academic or commercial contexts. In some instances, cultural and political factors influence the design and application of medical advances, in other cases international standards of health care and human rights influence the application of new discoveries. In designing and supporting HIV prevention interventions for underserved groups such as refugees, sex workers, and intravenous drug users, new information from laboratories and clinical trials must be adapted to local needs and resources. Antiretroviral therapy and mother-to-child HIV transmission prevention programs rely on scientific advances to inform drug choices and treatment practices, but social factors continue to influence the success of such programs on the ground. These influences and relationships highlight the possibility for both tension and synergy between scientific exploration and the cultural and political context of the human immunodeficiency virus.

Global and Regional Responses to HIV and AIDS

This chronology tracks the evolution of international, governmental, and community-level responses to the HIV epidemic, focusing on countries that have pursued either a uniquely comprehensive and effective HIV and AIDS policy, or nations whose present response does not yet reflect the true severity of the national epidemic. In many countries, particularly large nations with decentralized health care infrastructure such as India, local and provincial responses to HIV and AIDS by government and nongovernmental organizations constitute important components of the national response to HIV. In other nations where health care infrastructure is weak or government support insufficient, the activities of nongovernmental organizations represent the most effective and visible efforts to combat HIV and AIDS in the country. In Thailand and Botswana, two countries with stable health infrastructure, early commitment to universal access to optimal HIV and AIDS care or prevention services has begun to affect the course of the epidemic. From a global perspective, a single country's groundbreaking response, such as Brazil's decision to manufacture and distribute generic versions of antiretroviral drugs, has worldwide policy and health implications.

1959   A single blood sample collected in 1959 in Kinshasa, Zaire (now the Democratic Republic of the Congo), tests positive for the presence of HIV in 1986. Researchers from Atlanta, Durham, Seattle, and Boston test the sample multiple times to ensure that this result is not a false-positive one, which is common when blood samples are tested for HIV many years after they are collected. The Kinshasa sample remains positive for HIV antibodies through all tests, suggesting that the 1959 sample and contemporary stains of HIV share common ancestors (Nahmias et al., 1986).

1971   Brazil's Industrial Property Code states that pharmaceuticals and chemical products cannot be patented in the country (Brazilian Industrial Property Office, n.d.).

1975   The Indian government's "Hathi Committee Report" states India's policy of seeking "self-sufficiency" in pharmaceutical production and pricing, paving the way for later production of generic antiretroviral drugs and other medicines (National Pharmaceutical Pricing Authority [India], 1986).

1976   India's first "Drugs (Prices Control) Order" is instituted, emphasizing the importance of simplifying the national drug pricing system to ensure that medications are affordable to poor or marginalized sectors of society (National Pharmaceutical Pricing Authority [India], 1986).

1977   A Danish surgeon working in Zaire (now the Democratic Republic of the Congo) since 1972 dies after several years of illness. Between 1976 and 1977, she was hospitalized with severe diarrhea, oral candidiasis, Pneumocystis carinii pneumonia, and other symptoms of a compromised immune system. Tests during this period show that her T cell count is unusually low. In 1976, HIV and AIDS have not been defined, preventing a definitive diagnosis, but in retrospect the surgeon's many illnesses are similar to the opportunistic infections common among African AIDS patients. The case is reported in *The Lancet* in 1983 (Bygbjerg, 1983).

1980   Retrospective studies estimate that 100,000 people are living with HIV and AIDS globally (Mann, Tarantola, and Netter, 1992).

1981   Prevalence of cryptococcal meningitis, a common opportunistic infection among individuals living with AIDS in Africa, begins to increase sharply. Although only fifteen cases of cryptococcal meningitis were reported throughout Zaire from 1953 to 1967, between 1981 and 1982, fifteen cases are reported in a single hospital in Kinshasa (Renoirte et al., 1967; Lamey, 1982).

June 5   The U.S. Centers for Disease Control publish a case report on five gay men diagnosed with Pneumocystis carinii pneumonia in Los Angeles between October 1980 and April 1981. Of the five men, two died within two months of their first hospital admission. All individuals were diagnosed with a variety of opportunistic infections in addition to Pneumocystis pneumonia, including oral and esophageal candidiasis and severe cytomegalovirus infection. In addition, most of the men had experienced recurring fevers for two to five months before pneumonia was diagnosed. This article is one of the first reports of AIDS cases in the United States, published before the human immunodeficiency virus was isolated (U.S. Centers for Disease Control, 1981).

A retrospective study conducted in 1987 shows that in 1981 approximately 3 percent of men attending sexually transmitted disease clinics in Nairobi, Kenya, were infected with HIV (Piot et al., 1987). By 1990, this figure increased to 23 percent (Tyndall, Odhiambo, and Ronald, 1991).

1982   September Seven Japanese scientists from the Kochi Medical School and the Kyoto University Primate Institute report that they have detected a form of "adult T cell leukemia virus" (later termed HTLV) infection in a group of captive Japanese monkeys. Out of twenty monkeys, eighteen are antibody positive for T cell leukemia virus, and cells infected with the virus have been isolated in two individuals. The effect of viral infection on the Japanese monkeys is not yet clear. The study team ends its report with a question: "are monkeys the natural reservoir of ATLV (adult T cell leukemia viruses)?" (Miyoshi et al., 1982).

1983   A study conducted in Zambia documents the appearance of a new "atypical aggressive" form of Kaposi's sarcoma (Bayley, 1984). Two years later, another study conducted in Uganda and Zambia shows that about 90 percent of individuals with this new form of "aggressive" Kaposi's sarcoma also test positive for HIV antibodies (Bayley, 1985).

April   Responding to previous letters, a British physician writes to *The Lancet* to report on the case of a patient from Zaire who immigrated to England in 1977 seeking medical care for her daughter. The three-month-old baby had been ill with oral thrush since birth, and tests conducted in London showed that she had a depressed immune system. Although the three-month-old responded well to treatment, her mother became ill in 1977 with oral thrush, fever, weight loss, and other symptoms. After a series of bacterial infections during the following months, she became infected with cryptococcal meningitis. She died shortly after returning to Zaire in 1978. This case, although not formally diagnosed as AIDS, meets many of the clinical criteria, prompting the British correspondent to suggest in 1983 that cryptococcal meningitis might be indicative of HIV infection in Zaire (Vandepitte, Verwilghen, and Zachee, 1983).

May 20   Scientists from France isolate a new retrovirus from the blood of an individual with AIDS. Laboratory analysis shows that the virus is related to the previously characterized human T cell leukemia viruses (HTLV) I and II. The group concludes that the new variant of HTLV is transmitted among humans and is related to the development of clinical AIDS (Barré-Sinoussi et al., 1983).

October   A group of researchers from Belgium, the United States, and Zaire collaborate with the government

1983 of Zaire to begin AIDS surveillance in the capital city Kin-
cont. shasa (Mann et al., 1986).

1984 Thailand's first government survey of HIV prevalence is
completed in Bangkok clinics for male STD patients.
None of the 100 individuals tested for HIV antibodies are
infected. Surveys are conducted yearly after 1985
(Weniger et al., 1991). During the same year, Thailand's
minister of public health forms the National Coordinating Committee on AIDS. Leadership of the committee
shifts in 1991 to include the Prime Minister's Office,
emphasizing the importance of including HIV and AIDS
interventions in all facets of national policymaking (Ungphakorn and Sittitrai, 1994).

January   Scientists determine that CD4+ T lymphocytes
are an essential "receptor" site for HIV during infection.
Lymphocytes that express the CD4 antigen act to induce
and strengthen the body's immune response to an infection (Dalgleish et al., 1984).

March   In a letter to *The Lancet*, a group of Dutch physicians report that they have been treating five patients
originally from Zaire and Chad presenting with AIDS-
like symptoms, including fever and severe weight loss.
The research group notes that their findings "suggest
that black Africans, immigrants or not, may be another
group predisposed to AIDS" (Clumeck et al., 1983). This
letter marks the first record of likely AIDS cases among
African individuals who report none of the "risk factors"
common to those living with AIDS in the United States
(Katlama et al., 1984).

April 15–17   The First International AIDS Conference is
held in Atlanta, Georgia. The conference is sponsored by
the World Health Organization and a variety of U.S. government offices, including the Food and Drug Administration, the Alcohol, Drug Abuse, and Mental Health
Administration, and the Health Resources and Services
Administration (U.S. Centers for Disease Control and
Prevention, 1984).

May 4   A group of U.S. researchers report on the isolation of a retrovirus from the blood of multiple individuals with AIDS. Because this virus is related to human T cell leukemia viruses I and II, the researchers name the new virus "HTLV-III." Later testing reveals that this virus is likely the same one that was detected by French scientists in 1984 (Gallo et al., 1984).

October   A month-long study is conducted in Kigali, Rwanda, to survey the prevalence of AIDS in the city's Centre Hospitalier. In four weeks, twenty-six cases of AIDS are diagnosed. Among women living with AIDS, nearly half report that they are sex workers (Van de Perre et al., 1984).

A study is published that documents eighteen patients from Zaire, Chad, and Burundi who received treatment in a Belgian hospital between 1979 and 1983. Patients were hospitalized with a variety of opportunistic infections common to individuals living with AIDS, including Pneumocystis carinii pneumonia, cryptococcal meningitis, Kaposi's sarcoma, and frequent bacterial infections. Physicians recorded abnormally low T cell counts in most patients, 55 percent of whom died within the four-year period (Clumeck et al., 1984).

1985   The World Health Organization founds its "Special Programme on AIDS," which begins to function worldwide within a year. The programme aims to slow the spread of HIV and AIDS globally and to mitigate the impact of AIDS in high-prevalence regions (Tarantola, 2001).

Results from an eight-month study of AIDS prevalence in Kinshasa, Zaire, show that the number of recorded cases of AIDS has increased 61 percent between January and February 1985. At the end of the study, 295 AIDS cases have been documented. Researchers note that cases are evenly divided between men and women, unlike the results of surveillance conducted in the United States. The earliest symptoms of illness among study participants took place in 1978 (Mann et al., 1986).

1985 March   Test kits to detect the presence of HIV-1 anti-
cont. bodies become commercially available after a yearlong
research and development phase sponsored by the U.S.
Public Health Service, the National Cancer Institute, and
five pharmaceutical companies. During the early phases
of test development, the U.S. Public Health Service recommends that U.S. blood banks prepare to begin testing
all donated blood and plasma for HIV antibodies as soon
as test kits become available (Petricciani, 1985).

May   A group of researchers from Zaire, the United
States, and Europe conduct a survey of HIV prevalence
among 250 hospital outpatients in Katana in eastern
Zaire. Although none of the individuals surveyed show
signs of progression to clinical AIDS, just over 12 percent
test positive for HIV antibodies. The research group concludes that HIV is not "new" in Zaire, because HIV infection has become common even among isolated, rural
populations. Additionally, the group's analysis suggests
that this rural population might have begun to "adapt"
to HIV, living longer with the virus before becoming ill
than individuals in more recently exposed communities
(Biggar et al., 1985).

June   Researchers working at the New England Regional
Primate Research Center isolate samples of a virus from a
group of rhesus macaques suffering from opportunistic
infections associated with immune deficiency. Previous
studies characterized a simian virus similar to HTLV-1,
but the monkeys in this study are experiencing a wider
range of symptoms, including candidiasis, cytomegalovirus, and brain lesions. Noting "striking similarities to
the human AIDS virus" after a series of protein and antibody analyses, the New England group concludes that the
virus sampled from the macaques is closely related to
HTLV-III (later known as HIV), the virus that causes
AIDS. The new monkey virus is named STLV-III (simian
T-lymphotropic virus III, later shortened to SIV) (Daniel et
al., 1985; Kanki et al., 1985b).

October   Ugandan and British physicians report on the
emergence of a "new disease" in Uganda's Rakai district.

"Slim disease" is characterized by extreme weight loss, chronic diarrhea, fever, and bacterial infections. Most patients living with slim disease test positive for HIV antibodies, although opportunistic infections such as Kaposi's sarcoma are less common in this group than among people living with HIV and AIDS in the United States. These findings suggest that the opportunistic infections associated with AIDS in Africa might differ from those observed in North American settings (Serwadda et al., 1985). These findings are strengthened by reports of other cases of slim disease elsewhere in Uganda that state that this "new" disease is "simply identical with AIDS as seen in Africa" (Kamradt, Niese, and Vogel, 1985, 145).

November The New England Primate Research Center group tests sixty-seven healthy African Green monkeys living in the wild for antibodies to STLV-III (SIV). Of those surveyed, 40 percent test positive for SIV antibodies, and samples of the same virus that was characterized in October are isolated from seven monkeys. None of the infected monkeys show any signs of disease or immunosuppression. African Green monkeys are common in sub-Saharan Africa and in the past have transmitted viruses such as Ebola, yellow fever, and Marburg disease to humans (Kanki, Alroy, and Essex, 1985a).

December Senegalese, French, and U.S. investigators report on a study of 289 female sex workers in Dakar, Senegal. Of the women, 6.9 percent test positive for HIV antibodies, but further tests show that the Senegalese form of the HIV virus is more closely related to STLV-III than to previously characterized strains of HIV (Barin et al., 1985).

1986 The U.S. Centers for Disease Control estimate that 750,000 people are currently living with HIV and AIDS in the United States (Karon et al., 1990).

March 15 The results of a six-week clinical trial of "3'-azido–3'-deoxythymidine," later known as zidovudine, or AZT, are announced. Individuals living with HIV and

1986
cont. AIDS who participated in the trial demonstrated measurable health gains over six weeks, including weight gain, decrease in the symptoms of opportunistic infections, and a decrease in viral load (Yarchoan et al., 1986). AZT, the first antiretroviral drug, targets reverse transcriptase, the protein responsible for converting HIV's viral RNA to DNA in host cells. The Food and Drug Administration approves AZT for use in adults in 1987, but the drug is not approved until May 1990 for use in children (U.S. Food and Drug Administration, Antiretroviral HIV Drug Approvals).

April   Three new genes are sequenced from HIV, two of which have not been observed in any other retrovirus. The three genes are designated "3' orf" (3' open reading frame), "sor" (short open reading frame), and "tat." The "tat" gene is responsible for activating HIV's viral transcription process (Arya and Gallo, 1986). The "sor" gene is partly responsible for virus transmission and replication (Fisher et al., 1987).

July   The new HIV discovered in Senegal in December 1985 is isolated from two study participants. Genetic tests support earlier conclusions that this virus is more closely related to an SIV found among sooty mangabey monkeys than to HIV-1. These two investigations present further evidence of the existence of a second human immunodeficiency virus, later dubbed HIV-2 (Clavel et al., 1986).

November   Rising global HIV prevalence places AIDS as the "most serious epidemic of the past 50 years," according to a group of researchers from the U.S. Centers for Disease Control and the World Health Organization. As of late 1986, HIV has been detected in seventy-four countries worldwide (Quinn et al., 1986).

1987 The first cases of HIV and AIDS are diagnosed in Russia and Ukraine (Shargorodsky, 2000). The first HIV-2 infection in the United States is diagnosed in a woman who recently emigrated from West Africa. By 1991, seventeen cases of HIV-2 have been diagnosed in the United States, seven of which have progressed to AIDS (O'Brien, George, and Holmberg, 1992).

The Global Network of People Living with HIV and AIDS is founded (Global Network of People Living with HIV and AIDS, n.d.).

1988   One hundred forty delegates to the World Summit of Ministers of Health on AIDS in January agree unanimously to designate December 1 as World AIDS Day. Later in 1988 the United Nations General Assembly declares support for World AIDS Day as a way for governments, nongovernmental organizations, and others to show solidarity in the fight against AIDS (UNAIDS, 2000a).

January   Results from the first clinical trial of zalcitabine (ddC) show that the antiretroviral drug successfully increases T cell counts in participants with HIV and AIDS, but also leads to more frequent drug-related toxicities than AZT (Yarchoan et al., 1988). The drug ddC is approved for use in adults in 1992, but is never licensed for use in children (U.S. Food and Drug Administration, Antiretroviral HIV Drug Approvals).

June   The United States Presidential Commission on the Human Immunodeficiency Virus Epidemic publishes its first report to U.S. President Ronald Reagan. The Report states, "The HIV epidemic will be a challenging factor in American life for years to come and should be a concern to all Americans." The Presidential Commission estimates that 1.5 million Americans are currently living with HIV, and 500,000 people with HIV and AIDS in the United States will have died by 1992 (Watkins et al., 1988).

Brazil begins to distribute free care and medications to treat opportunistic infections in people with HIV and AIDS via the country's newly implemented Unified Health System (Glavão, 2002).

September   HIV's "vpu" gene, which is responsible for viral replication and the assembly of new virions, is char-

1988
cont.
acterized through genetic sequencing (Strebel, Klimkait, and Martin, 1988).

October   Thailand institutes a national requirement that all donated blood and blood products be screened for the presence of HIV (Ungphakorn and Sittitrai, 1994).

1989
The Thai government puts its Medium Term Plan for AIDS Prevention and Control into effect. This plan, covering the period from 1989 to 1991, emphasizes integrating HIV prevention and education into all aspects of medical care, calling for nondiscrimination toward people living with HIV and AIDS. The plan focuses on prevention interventions, including condom distribution, educational activities, and training in HIV and AIDS care for medical personnel (Ungphakorn and Sittitrai, 1994).

June 1   The World Health Organization's Global Program on AIDS estimates that 480,000 people are living with HIV and AIDS in the world. Of this total, 56 percent are living in Africa and 36 percent live in North, South, and Central America (Mann, 1989).

July   The working group that discovered AZT publishes a report on a clinical trial of didanosine (ddI), a new antiretroviral drug. After forty-two weeks of treatment, participants taking didanosine have higher T cell counts and decreased viral loads (Yarchoan et al., 1989). The Food and Drug Administration approves didanosine in October 1991 for use in both adult and pediatric patients (U.S. Food and Drug Administration, Antiretroviral HIV Drug Approvals).

November   The Thai 100 percent Condom Program is put into effect in Ratchaburi Province and is adopted by an additional thirteen provinces during the next year. Through condom distribution and a nationwide advertising campaign, the 100 percent Condom Program seeks to protect 100 percent of commercial sex acts in Thailand, to prevent the transmission of HIV between sex workers and their clients (Rojanapithayakorn and Hanenberg, 1996).

December   The number of HIV-2 infections in Europe has increased twenty-fold since December 1987. The total number of HIV-2 infections in fourteen European countries is now estimated at 452 (Smallman-Raynor and Cliff, 1991).

The World Health Organization estimates that 5 to 10 million people are living with HIV and AIDS worldwide. Only between 1 and 3 percent of these cases of HIV have been reported (World Health Organization Global Programme on AIDS, 1989).

1990   The International Council of AIDS Service Organizations (ICASO) is founded to support communities and community-based organizations worldwide in the fight against AIDS. ICASO also seeks to promote human rights protection for people and communities affected by HIV and AIDS, and to encourage people living with HIV and AIDS to become more involved in community responses to the epidemic (ICASO, n.d.).

South Africa's first national HIV prevalence survey is completed, showing an average HIV prevalence of 0.8 percent among women attending antenatal clinics. By 1991, prevalence among this group is 1.5 percent (Schneider and Stein, 2001).

HIV prevalence among Thai military conscripts has increased almost six-fold since 1989 to 2.9 percent (Weniger et al., 1991).

In São Paulo, Brazil, HIV prevalence among pregnant women visiting antenatal clinics has risen from 0.2 percent in 1987 to 1.3 percent (one in every seventy-five women) (Duarte et al., 1991). The Brazilian Ministry of Health begins to distribute free zidovudine to people living with HIV and AIDS. Delivery of antiretroviral "monotherapy" (treatment with only one antiretroviral drug) through the public health system is a component of Brazil's National Program of Sexually Transmitted Diseases and AIDS (Meira, 2002).

1990   April   The identification of DNA sequences specific to
cont.   HIV-2 allows clinicians to distinguish between HIV-1
and HIV-2 infection using existing HIV test kits (Zuber et
al., 1990).

September   The World Health Organization reports that
301,517 people are living with AIDS globally, and 8 to 10
million people are infected with HIV. Of the total reported AIDS cases, about 60 percent are in North, South,
and Central America, 24 percent are in Africa, and 13
percent are in Europe (VI International Conference on
AIDS, 1991).

1991   Mechai Viraviadya directs the design of Thailand's
1992–1996 National AIDS Prevention and Control Plan.
The new plan focuses on the integration of HIV and
AIDS care and prevention with plans to strengthen the
country's social and economic development (Ungphakorn and Sittitrai, 1994).

HIV is removed from Thailand's list of reportable diseases, allowing the Thai Red Cross to create the country's
first anonymous HIV testing and counseling site (Ungphakorn and Sittitrai, 1994). At the same time, forty new
STD and AIDS treatment centers are established throughout Thailand. By the end of 1994, the Thai government has
set up 349 additional STD clinics (Rojanapithayakorn and
Hanenberg, 1996).

January   Four years after the first cases of HIV-1 were
diagnosed in India, twenty-two serum samples from
HIV-infected individuals in Bombay are sent to Frank-
furt for analysis. The results of these tests show that five
of the twenty-two individuals are infected either with
both HIV-1 and HIV-2, or with HIV-2 alone. This is the
first report of HIV-2 infections in India, but the relatively
high prevalence among twenty-two randomly selected
samples suggests that HIV-2 has been present in the population for some time. HIV-1 and HIV-2 are both likely to
be more widespread in India than previously reported
(Rübsamen-Waigmann et al., 1991a).

April   Laboratory tests show that an antiretroviral compound called Ro 31–8959 blocks HIV's protease enzyme, which is required for viral replication (Jacobsen et al., 1992). Ro 31–8959 appears to be effective against HIV-1, HIV-2, and a common strain of SIV. These findings mark the early development of the first antiretroviral drug to effectively target protease (Martin et al., 1991).

August   The Thai National AIDS Committee approves the nationwide implementation of the 100 percent Condom Program. By April 1992 the 100 percent Condom Program is in effect in all provinces in Thailand, supported by local police forces and governors (Rojanapithayakorn and Hanenberg, 1996).

In Bombay, India, a study of patients attending STD clinics finds that 32.1 percent are infected with HIV (Rübsamen-Waigmann et al., 1991b). During the previous year, HIV prevalence among injection drug users in Manipur Province was 54 percent (Ramachandran, 1991), and 1.35 percent of pregnant women surveyed in Madras were living with HIV (Sankari et al., 1991).

At the end of 1991, 2.9 million people are living with AIDS worldwide. Sixty-eight percent of all people with HIV or AIDS are living in sub-Saharan Africa. North America, the second most affected region, accounts for 9.2 percent of the global total. Of all people living with HIV and AIDS, 8.1 percent are in South and Central America, and Western Europe and Southeast Asia account for more than 10 percent. Forty percent of all people living with HIV and AIDS globally are women (Mann, Tarantola, and Netter 1992).

1992   A Phase I/II trial in September of stavudine (D4T), the fourth reverse-transcriptase inhibitor, concludes that the drug is safe for use in humans (Dudley et al., 1992). Development of D4T, originally known as 3'-deoxythymidin-2'-ene, began in 1987 (Lin, Schinazi, and Prusoff, 1987), but trials *in vivo* in humans did not begin until nearly five years later. The Food and Drug Administration approves

1992
cont. D4T for use in adults in 1994, and for use in children in 1996 (U.S. Food and Drug Administration, Antiretroviral HIV Drug Approvals).

October   The South African Department of Health and the African National Congress convene a conference on HIV and AIDS that is attended by more than 450 people. The National AIDS Committee of South Africa forms out of the conference and is delegated to draft South Africa's first National AIDS Plan (Schneider and Stein, 2001).

December   A Phase I study of the reverse transcriptase inhibitor lamivudine (3TC) in a group of twenty participants living with HIV shows that the antiretroviral is safe for use in adults (Van Leeuwen et al., 1992). 3TC is licensed for adult and pediatric use in November 1995 (U.S. Food and Drug Administration, Antiretroviral HIV Drug Approvals).

1993 A Phase I study of nevirapine, a new reverse transcriptase inhibitor, shows that the drug is safe for use in humans (Cheeseman et al., 1993). Earlier studies of nevirapine conducted in 1991 on blood and cell samples suggest that nevirapine might be effective in individuals with HIV and AIDS who have developed viral resistance to other reverse transcriptase inhibitors (Richman et al., 1991). Nevirapine is approved for use in adults in 1996, and for use in children two years later (U.S. Food and Drug Administration, Antiretroviral HIV Drug Approvals).

March   A study of sixty-six patients in various stages of HIV progression shows that high viral loads are common among all people living with HIV, regardless of disease stage or severity. The study also shows that measurement of viral load provides a reliable prediction of disease stage and CD4 T cell decline, allowing clinicians to better monitor the efficacy of antiretroviral therapy (Piatak et al., 1993). A study conducted in 1996 shows that viral load measurements might be the most effective predictor of HIV disease progression, giving a more accurate prognosis than CD4 T cell counts (Mellors et al., 1996).

1994   The South African government begins to implement the National AIDS Plan developed by the National AIDS Committee, hiring a National AIDS Program director to coordinate the country's response from within the Department of Health (Schneider and Stein, 2001).

A comprehensive study of the genetics of HIV-2 shows that five subtypes of the virus currently exist (designated subtypes A through E). Like HIV-1, HIV-2 subtypes show a high level of genetic diversity and an ability to form recombinant strains (Gao et al., 1994).

April 15   Members of the World Trade Organization (WTO) ratify the Agreement on Trade-Related Aspects of Intellectual Property Rights (TRIPS). TRIPS provides a framework to regulate intellectual property rights internationally, ensuring that patent protections are applied consistently worldwide. The TRIPS declaration, while requiring all countries to recognize and protect intellectual property rights, states in Article 8: "Members may, in formulating or amending their laws and regulations [regarding protection of intellectual property rights], adopt measures necessary to protect public health and nutrition." In addition, TRIPS states in Article 31 that national governments may waive patent protections without authorization from the patent's holder, "In the case of a national emergency or other circumstances of extreme urgency, or in cases of public, non-commercial use" (World Trade Organization, 1994).

October   Genetic sequencing of a strain of HIV from a Brazilian woman reveals that the virus is a recombinant of HIV subtypes B and F, proving that HIV can form recombinant strains in regions where multiple subtypes are prevalent. In addition, the same recombinant B/F virus is isolated from the woman's most recent sexual partner, proving that recombinant strains can be transmitted sexually (Sabino et al., 1994).

November   Results from a three-year trial show that zidovudine therapy reduces HIV transmission from

1994
cont.
mothers to infants during pregnancy and birth by 67.5 percent. In this trial, mothers receive zidovudine before and during birth and infants receive the antiretroviral for six weeks postpartum (Connor et al., 1994).

November   The genetic diversity of HIV has led to the emergence of viral strains that are resistant to reverse-transcriptase inhibiting antiretroviral drugs such as AZT, ddC, and d4T. These resistant strains are also found in individuals who have never been treated with a reverse-transcriptase inhibitor (Najera et al., 1994).

The Monitoring the AIDS Pandemic (MAP) Network reports that 11 million people with HIV and AIDS are currently living in sub-Saharan Africa, representing about 65 percent of all people with HIV and AIDS world-wide. Nineteen southern and central African countries account for 90 percent of the continent's HIV and AIDS cases. In Kenya, Malawi, Botswana, Rwanda, Tanzania, Uganda, Zambia, and Zimbabwe 10–30 percent of women attending antenatal clinics are living with HIV (Monitoring the AIDS Pandemic, 1995).

1995
India's second "Drugs (Prices Control) Order" is put into effect, allowing the Indian government to fix the retail prices of drugs produced by manufacturers in the country, to fix "ceiling prices" of drugs, and to revise the price of bulk drugs and formulations (Government of India, 1995).

March   Continuing previous investigations of HIV-1's ability to form recombinant strains from multiple sub-types, a group of English researchers shows that even highly genetically divergent subtypes of HIV have the ability to form recombinants (Robertson, Hahn, and Sharp, 1995).

April   A Phase I/II trial of saquinavir, the first protease inhibitor, determines the drug to be safe and effective in individuals who have not received any previous anti-retroviral therapy (Kitchen et al., 1995). The Food and

Drug Administration approves saquinavir for adults only in December 1996, more than five years after Ro 31–8959 was first tested in laboratories (U.S. Food and Drug Administration, Antiretroviral HIV Drug Approvals). Approval comes two years after three European trials in France, England, and Italy demonstrated the drug's safety and effectiveness (Vella, 1994). Within three months, the Food and Drug Administration approves two more protease inhibitors: ritonavir and indinavir. Ritonavir is the only protease inhibitor of the three that is licensed for use in children (U.S. Food and Drug Administration, Antiretroviral HIV Drug Approvals).

Agouron Pharmaceuticals announces that the first human trial of the protease inhibitor nelfinavir in eight individuals has shown the drug to be safe (James, 1995). After the release of these favorable findings, a larger Phase II pilot study of nelfinavir is initiated during the same year (Chapman, 1995). Nelfinavir is approved by the Food and Drug Administration in March 1997 for use in both adults and children with HIV and AIDS (U.S. Food and Drug Administration, Antiretroviral HIV Drug Approvals).

December   Investigators identify three antibodies produced by human CD8+ T cells to combat HIV (Cocchi et al., 1995).

Thirteen million people are currently living with HIV or AIDS in sub-Saharan Africa. The United Nations estimated that by 2000, 30–40 million people would be living with HIV and AIDS worldwide (UNAIDS, 1996b).

1996   The Joint United Nations Programme on AIDS (UNAIDS) is founded to be "the main advocate for global action on the epidemic." UNAIDS is cosponsored by the United Nations Children's Fund, the United Nations Development Programme, the United Nations Population Fund, the United Nations Educational, Scientific and Cultural Organization, the World Health Organization, the World Bank, the United Nations Office on Drugs and Crime, and the International Labor Organization (UNAIDS, 2003).

1996
cont.
May   Dutch scientists conduct a study of the human CCR-5 gene, a cell receptor site for HIV infection. A group of Caucasian individuals exhibits a genetic mutation in the CCR-5 gene that prevents HIV-1 from binding to the surface of host cells. The mutation is not present in study participants from Africa and Asia. Individuals who have inherited the mutant CCR-5 from both parents are apparently resistant to HIV infection, whereas those who inherited the mutant CCR-5 from only one parent show slower disease progression (Samson et al., 1996). A study conducted in the United States at the same time shows definitively that individuals who have inherited the CCR-5 mutation from both parents are protected from sexual transmission of HIV-1. The same study suggests that as many as 20 percent of individuals in Caucasian populations have inherited this mutation from at least one parent. These findings could have important implications for HIV vaccine design and AIDS treatment in the future (Liu et al., 1996).

May 14   Brazilian President Fernando Henrique Cardoso approves Law Number 9,279/96, which stipulates that as of May 1997 chemicals and pharmaceuticals can be patented in Brazil. Reversing the country's 1971 Industrial Property Code, Law 9,279/96 brings Brazil into compliance with the terms of the TRIPS agreement. Any pharmaceutical products developed before 1997 are exempt from the new law, allowing the Brazilian government to legally produce generic versions of most antiretroviral drugs (Tang, 1996).

July   Data from a Phase I/II trial of the reverse transcriptase inhibitor delavirdine show that the drug is safe and effective, particularly when administered as part of a three-drug antiretroviral regimen (Davey et al., 1996). Delavirdine is approved for use in adults less than a year later by the Food and Drug Administration, but has not been licensed for use in children (U.S. Food and Drug Administration, Antiretroviral HIV Drug Approvals).

December   The Brazilian government operationalizes a nationwide antiretroviral drug distribution system. The government's AIDS care program also includes prevention components, such as educational outreach, blood screening, and prevention of mother-to-child transmission of HIV (Meira, 2002). In June 1996, the Ministry of Health initiates an HIV education and condom distribution program specifically aimed at adolescents and young adults (*Reuters*, 11 June 1996).

UNAIDS reports that 22.6 million people are living with HIV and AIDS worldwide at the end of 1996, 3.1 million of whom were infected with HIV during the past year. Only about half of the world's HIV infections have been officially reported, owing to stigma, inadequate medical infrastructure, and other factors. Fourteen million people with HIV and AIDS live in sub-Saharan Africa, 5.2 million in southern Asia, 2.6 million in North America, South America, and Europe, 270,000 in the Caribbean, and 250,000 in central Europe, north Africa, and the Pacific (UNAIDS, 1996b).

1997 Brazil's National Network of Viral Burden Determination is implemented, coordinating a series of state-of-the-art laboratories across the country to measure CD4 cell counts, viral load, and HIV progression among individuals receiving health care in the public sector (Meira, 2002).

September A forty-eight-week Phase II trial of the reverse transcriptase inhibitor efavirenz shows that the drug is effective in reducing viral load when prescribed in combination with indinavir (Anonymous, 1997a). Efavirenz is approved in September 1998 for use in children and adults (U.S. Food and Drug Administration, Antiretroviral HIV Drug Approvals). Also in September pharmaceutical company Glaxo-Wellcome (now Glaxo-SmithKline) releases the results of the first human trial of abacavir. The company announces that the reverse transcriptase inhibitor is effective, but only in individuals who have not previously developed viral resistance to AZT or 3TC (Anonymous, 1997b). Abacavir is licensed for use in adults and children in December 1998 (U.S. Food and Drug Administration, Antiretroviral HIV Drug Approvals).

1997
cont.
Results from a clinical trial comparing an antiretroviral regimen made up of two reverse transcriptase inhibitors and a protease inhibitor with a regimen of two reverse transcriptase inhibitors alone, show that triple-combination therapy is most effective in slowing disease progression to AIDS or death. The three drug regimen (indinavir, zidovudine, and lamivudine) lowered mortality to 1.4 percent (compared with 3.1 percent in the two-drug group) and progression to AIDS to 6 percent (compared with 11 percent in the two-drug group) (Hammer et al., 1997). After other investigators publish similar results, triple-combination antiretroviral therapy (known as "highly active antiretroviral therapy" or HAART) is supported as the standard of care for people living with HIV and AIDS (Hirsch et al., 1997).

November   Investigators discover that CD4 T lymphocytes hold a "reservoir" of HIV virions indefinitely, even when an HIV-infected individual is receiving antiretroviral therapy. A longer period of time on antiretroviral therapy does not lead to a decrease in these latent HIV reservoirs, suggesting that an interruption in therapy will cause the HIV virions to reactivate. Once an individual is infected with HIV, the virus can never be fully removed from his or her system. This means that antiretroviral therapy must continue for life (Finzi, 1997).

1998
February 18   Forty-two pharmaceutical companies file a lawsuit against the government of South Africa. The suit's applicants argue that South Africa's 1997 Medicines and Related Substances Control Amendment Act is illegal and unconstitutional because it allows the South African government to either import or locally manufacture generic versions of patented drugs (Pharmaceutical Company Lawsuit, 1998).

April   The U.S. Centers for Disease Control and the National Institutes of Health (NIH) publish the first "Report of the NIH Panel to Define Principles of Therapy of HIV Infection and Guidelines for the Use of Antiretroviral Agents in HIV-Infected Adults and Adolescents." The guidelines recommend that clinicians treating people with HIV and AIDS prescribe only combination anti-retroviral regimens made up of three drugs (including two reverse transcriptase inhibitors and one protease inhibitor). "Monotherapy" should be avoided, because this approach will quickly lead to the emergence of drug-resistant viral strains. The guidelines also confirm that even when antiretroviral therapy had decreased an individual's viral load below detectable levels, reservoirs of latent HIV virions still exist within the body, with the potential to resume replication and infection when antiretroviral therapy is interrupted or halted (U.S. Centers for Disease Control and Prevention, 1998).

July   Indian newspapers report on an HIV and STD sentinel survey in Tamil Nadu Province. The survey, conducted by six government and academic research institutions, found that 2.4 million people are infected with an STD in Tamil Nadu Province, and nearly half a million people are living with HIV. HIV prevalence is highest in rural areas and among adults aged between forty and forty-five. These findings suggest a need to expand local AIDS prevention strategies, which until now have primarily targeted individuals in urban areas between the ages of fifteen and nineteen (FT Asia Intelligence Wire, July 16, 1998).

July 21   The Russian military releases statistics that show a four-fold increase in HIV infections among service personnel over the last year. One hundred twenty-eight cases of HIV were diagnosed during 1997 in the Russian armed forces, whereas only thirty-two were noted from 1993 to 1996. A high rate of injection drug use among soldiers has contributed to the increased incidence of HIV (Arnold, 1998).

September 14   India's National AIDS Program Director J. V. R. Prasad Rao announces a significant "upgrade" in the national estimate of HIV prevalence in India. Although earlier estimates suggested that India was home to about 67,000 people living with HIV and AIDS (PLWHA), Rao announces that there are actually between 3 and 5 million PLWHA in the country, bringing

1998
cont.
national prevalence to between 0.3 and 0.5 percent. In the five worst affected provinces (Andhra Pradesh, Tamil Nadu, Maharashtra, Karnataka, and Manipur) HIV prevalence might be as high as 1 percent. Rao warns that the Indian government and people must act quickly to prevent "an Africa-like situation" in India (*Agence France Presse*, 14 September 1998).

November   Results of a small clinical trial conducted in Birmingham, Alabama, show that T-20, the first drug in the new class of "fusion inhibitors," is effective and safe for use in humans. T-20 prevents HIV replication and lowers patient viral loads by blocking HIV virions from attaching to host cells (Kilby et al., 1998).

Manipur Province in India embarks on a new "harm reduction" program to prevent HIV transmission among injection drug users (IDUs). The program, coordinated by Manipur's AIDS Control Society in collaboration with twelve nongovernmental organizations and a network of peer educators, provides IDUs with clean needles for injection at several "drop-in centers" in the province's most affected regions. IDUs account for 72 percent of new HIV infections in Manipur, far surpassing heterosexual transmission, which until now had been the sole focus of government HIV prevention efforts (Kumar, 1998).

December   In response to a reduction in government subsidies for antiretroviral drugs, a group of people living with HIV and AIDS in Chiang Mai Province, Thailand, found the "New Life Friends Centre." The centre administers a privately funded antiretroviral "medicine bank" to ensure that no individual's antiretroviral dosage is interrupted (Outlook Reporters, 1998).

The Russian government announces that nearly 2,000 people have been infected with HIV between May and November. More than 60 percent of all people living with HIV and AIDS in Russia were infected between 1997 and 1998 (*Agence France Presse*, 3 November 1998).

1999   March   A trial conducted in Bangkok, Thailand, shows that HIV transmission from mothers to infants is decreased by about 50 percent among mothers who receive only a "short course" of zidovudine, taking the antiretroviral twice per day after thirty-six weeks of pregnancy. No zidovudine is delivered to babies. The results of this trial are important for women living with HIV in developing countries where the cost of zidovudine treatment often renders the drug inaccessible (Shaffer et al., 1999).

June 17   The World Bank announces a credit of US$161 million to the Indian government to fight HIV and AIDS. World Bank support will finance about 80 percent of the cost of India's National AIDS Control Program for five years. The program will include peer counseling to individuals engaging in high-risk activities such as sex work and injection drug use, voluntary counseling and testing services, sexually transmitted disease control, blood bank safety, and home- and community-based care coordinated through hospitals and local clinics (*Asia Pulse*, 17 June 1999).

August 1   The first condom vending machine in the country is installed in Delhi, India. Condoms will cost one rupee each (about three cents). If "the Delhi experiment" proves successful in increasing condom usage in the area, similar vending machines could be installed in up to 250 more locations throughout the city (Srinath, 1 August 1999).

September   The Brazilian Ministry of Health releases the results of a nationwide survey on HIV risk in the general population. The survey's results show that although AIDS mortality has declined as a result of accessible antiretroviral therapies, the incidence of unsafe sex remains high, with only 24 percent of those surveyed reporting that they always used a condom during sex in the past year. In addition, 32 percent of women and 47 percent of men surveyed became sexually active before the age of fifteen, indicating the importance of

1999   additional prevention interventions focused on adoles-
cont.   cents (BBC News, 1999).

A Ugandan trial shows that nevirapine is as effective as zidovudine in preventing HIV transmission from mother to infant during pregnancy and birth. Only two doses of nevirapine, one to the mother during delivery and one to the newborn, reduce the risk of mother-to-infant transmission to 8.2 percent. Nevirapine therapy is the simplest, most effective, and least costly method of preventing mother-to-child HIV transmission developed to date (Guay et al., 1999).

September 10   The forty-two pharmaceutical companies that filed a notice of motion against the government of South Africa in 1997 to prevent manufacture or importation of generic antiretroviral drugs suspend the lawsuit indefinitely (Lewis, 1999).

October 20   Chinese government officials and medical experts hold a public symposium on HIV prevention and education in Beijing. Representatives from the Ministry of Health emphasize the importance of education and communication to prevent HIV transmission. At the same time, reporters attending the symposium complain that interviewing people living with AIDS can be difficult, as local governments in China are often reluctant to publicize the presence of HIV in their regions (Global News Wire, 21 October 1999).

November 3   South African President Thabo Mbeki questions the safety of zidovudine (AZT), an antiretroviral drug used to treat HIV and AIDS and to prevent mother-to-child transmission of the virus. Citing court cases brought in the United States, England, and South Africa over drug-related illness, Mbeki states that zidovudine is "a danger to health." Although South African and international drug monitors have declared zidovudine to be safe for use in humans, the Ministry of Health will oversee an investigation of the drug's safety before it is endorsed for use by the government (Wakin, 1999).

November 30 Russia's deputy health minister announces that 12,000 new cases of HIV have been reported in Russia since January 1999, bringing the total number of people living with HIV or AIDS to about 23,500. Most new HIV infections take place via illegal intravenous drug injection in prisons, the military, and in the general population, but 200 children have also been infected via mother-to-child transmission. Although the Health Ministry acknowledges that HIV is reaching epidemic proportions in Russia, Deputy Minister Gennady Onishchenko describes the situation as "still not as dramatic as Africa or Asia." The Russian government has only allocated about US$800,000 for HIV and AIDS care and prevention in 1999, focusing research efforts on creating and manufacturing new antiretroviral therapies (Yablokova, 1999, 91).

November 30–December 3   The World Trade Organization (WTO) meets in Seattle, Washington, amid violent and peaceful protest from U.S. and African nongovernmental organizations. Protesters demand better representation for developing countries at WTO sessions and increased access to affordable drugs (including antiretrovirals and drugs to treat tuberculosis and malaria) for resource-scarce nations (Fleshman, 1999).

2000   January 10   In its first meeting of the year, the United Nations Security Council holds a "Debate on Impact of AIDS on Peace and Security in Africa." Representatives from UNAIDS, the United Nations Development Programme, and the World Health Organization speak to the council, along with African heads of state, United Nations Secretary-General Kofi Annan, and U.S. Vice President Al Gore. This meeting is the first time in more than fifty years that the Security Council has met to discuss a public health issue (United Nations, 2000).

February   A study of 220 people taking triple-combination antiretroviral therapy including a protease inhibitor shows that individuals on this type of antiretroviral are likely to develop severe and potentially chronic drug-related side effects and toxicities during the course of

2000
cont.
treatment. Drug-related syndromes include lipodystrophy (redistribution of body fat leading to wasting in
some areas and increased fat deposits in others); lactic
acidosis (a buildup of lactic acid in the bloodstream,
leading to difficulty breathing, muscular weakness in the
legs and arms, and nausea); and loss of liver function.
Although "highly active antiretroviral therapy" (a three-
drug combination including a protease inhibitor) can
inhibit viral replication over the long-term, it is likely
that most individuals will experience serious health consequences as a result of exposure to antiretroviral drugs
(Carr et al., 2000).

March   The first African trial of a candidate HIV-1 vaccine is completed in Uganda, testing a vaccine designed
to protect against HIV-1 subtype B in forty volunteers.
The vaccine does not provoke a strong immune response
among recipients and is not considered likely to confer
protection against multiple HIV-1 subtypes (Cao et al.,
2000).

The South African president's office announces that President Mbeki will consult with two U.S. "AIDS dissidents" to gain further information on the transmission
and treatment of HIV and AIDS. Biochemist David Ras-
nick and African history scholar Charles Geshekter have
both stated that HIV does not cause AIDS, a stance dis-
puted by the WHO, UNAIDS, and clinicians worldwide
(Swarns, 2000). Mbeki's spokesman publishes an article
in Johannesburg's *Business Day* accusing drug companies
of "enriching" themselves at the expense of patients in
developing countries. The article states that pharmaceutical manufacturers "propagate fear" about HIV and
AIDS to increase their profits, bolstering the South
African government's assertion that antiretroviral drugs
are too costly and unsafe to be provided through the
public health system (Selsky, 2000).

May 11   In a speech to attendees at a medical education
conference in Bihar Province, Dr. Ajay Kumar, president
of the Indian Medical Association, announces that none
of the province's blood banks conform to the WHO

guidelines for transfusion and blood collection safety. Nationwide, only forty Indian blood banks conform to these international guidelines, producing only about half the amount of blood required in the country (Jha, 2000).

UNAIDS announces that pharmaceutical companies Boehringer Ingelheim, Bristol-Myers Squibb, Glaxo Wellcome (now GlaxoSmithKline), Merck, and F. Hoffmann-La Roche have formed a coalition (the "Accelerating Access" initiative) to improve the affordability and accessibility of AIDS treatments. Drug companies participating in these negotiations are expected to significantly discount their patented antiretroviral medications in resource-scarce countries (UNAIDS, 2000c). This formal announcement comes three days after UNAIDS and the five drug companies issued a "Joint Statement of Intent" to explore future partnerships and strategies to increase the availability of AIDS care in developing countries (UNAIDS, 2000b).

May 17 The Brazilian government requests that the World Health Organization create a database of all available formulations of antiretroviral drugs worldwide. The database would allow developing countries to "shop around" for low-priced antiretroviral drugs, including generic versions manufactured in Brazil, Thailand, and India. The Brazilian proposal gains broad support from delegates to the 2000 World Health Assembly (McNeil, 2000).

May 25 In a news conference Vadim Pokrovsky, head of the Russian Federal AIDS Prevention Center, states that Russia could have as many as 400,000 cases of HIV and AIDS by the end of 2000 and up to 1 million by 2005 if the national epidemic is not addressed. Although intravenous drug users account for most cases of HIV in Russia, the virus is beginning to spread via sexual contact, particularly among young people. According to Pokrovsky, Moscow's city government can provide care and treatment for residents living with HIV, but the rest of the country lacks the necessary funds to mount an effective treatment campaign (Isachenkov, 2000).

2000 June 12–14 Forty-five African researchers and clini-
cont. cians meet in Nairobi, Kenya, to discuss HIV vaccine
development in Africa. The "Nairobi Declaration: An
Appeal for an AIDS Vaccine" published at the close of
this meeting calls on African scientists to develop and
test new candidate HIV vaccines and urges international
funders and research organizations to increase support
for vaccine trials and clinical research in Africa (Nairobi
Declaration Signatories, 2000). The declaration's signatories are the first members of the African AIDS Vaccine
Program, an international, cooperative research network
dedicated to the development of HIV vaccines in Africa
to benefit African populations (AAVP, 2003).

June 16 Brazilian Catholic bishops issue a statement
that "the Church has not changed its position" against
the use of condoms to prevent sexual transmission of
HIV (Olmos, 2000b). Several days earlier, a small group
of Brazilian bishops suggested that Catholics in Brazil
should be allowed to use condoms when engaging in
"high risk" sex, such as between men, or with sex workers. The June 16 statement reaffirms the Vatican's 1968
ban on all birth control methods, including condoms
(Olmos, 2000a).

July 9–14 The XIII International AIDS Conference is
convened in Durban, South Africa. This is the first time
the conference is held in a developing country (U.S. Centers for Disease Control, 2000).

July The scientific journal *Nature* publishes "The Durban Declaration," a document produced at the end of the
XIII International AIDS Conference. Responding to the
"AIDS dissidents" appointed to the South African government's HIV and AIDS research task force, the declaration states that "The evidence that AIDS is caused by
HIV-1 or HIV-2 is clear cut, exhaustive, and unambiguous, meeting the highest standards of science." More
than 5,000 physicians, scientists, researchers, and advocates sign the declaration, which was drafted by an organizing committee of 250 members from more than fifty
countries (Durban Declaration Signatories, 2000).

July 18   The United Nations Security Council meets to discuss global HIV and AIDS for the first time. The Security Council resolves to encourage member governments to take a more active role in AIDS treatment and prevention efforts and commits to further support for UNAIDS and other United Nations-sponsored efforts to mitigate the impact of HIV globally (U.S. Department of State, 2000).

July 19   The Thai government announces a comprehensive sex-education program that will be implemented starting "in nursery schools." The new program aims to reduce teenage pregnancies and to slow the spread of HIV among young people in the country through education programs coordinated by the Ministry of Public Health's family planning unit (*Reuters*, 19 July 2000).

August   Australian investigators isolate and characterize a viral sample from an individual infected with two genetically distinct strains of HIV-1 subtype B. These data confirm that individuals can be simultaneously "coinfected" with multiple subtype strains. In addition, the two B subtype strains exhibit differing preferences for infection sites and differing pathogenic effects. For the first time scientists show that coinfection with multiple HIV-1 strains can lead to viral "synergy," which can render each HIV strain more harmful to its host than it would have been alone (Wang et al., 2000).

The Group of Eight (G-8) nations (Canada, France, Germany, Italy, Japan, Russia, the United Kingdom, and the United States) endorses a set of "International Development Targets." Targets include "A 24% reduction in HIV infection rates among 15–24 year olds in the worst affected countries by 2005 and globally by 2015" along with a reduction in tuberculosis mortality and child mortality in developing countries. Four months later, the European Commission issues a policy document on international development that includes increased commitment to a "coordinated global response" to HIV and AIDS, particularly focused on microbicide and vaccine development (Richards, 2000).

2000
cont.

September   Results from a World Bank report on Thailand show that although the country's HIV prevention efforts have slowed the spread of the epidemic, recent budget cuts to condom promotion and AIDS education programs have resulted in a decline in condom use among young men visiting sex workers. The World Bank states that this kind of national program must be supported over the long term to ensure lasting behavior change (*Deutsche Presse-Agentur,* 17 September 2000).

September 11   South Africa's ruling political party, the African National Congress, issues a confidential document to President Thabo Mbeki and Health Minister Manto Tshabalala-Msimang, calling on the president to acknowledge that HIV causes AIDS (*Agence FrancePresse,* 14 September 2000).

September 29   The Accelerating Access Initiative's multisectoral Contact Group meets for the first time to discuss how international health organizations, nongovernmental organizations, pharmaceutical manufacturers, and governments can work together to increase access to HIV and AIDS care and support. As of this meeting, Botswana, Burkina Faso, Burundi, Central African Republic, Chile, Côte d'Ivoire, Gabon, Swaziland, Uganda, and Ukraine have expressed interest in receiving this technical support. Cameroon, Nigeria, Senegal, and Zimbabwe join this group in October (UNAIDS, 2000b).

October   The World Medical Association meets in Scotland to amend the "Declaration of Helsinki on Ethical Principles for Medical Research Involving Human Subjects." The amended document states, "the benefits, risks, burdens and effectiveness of a new method should be tested against those of the best current prophylactic, diagnostic, and therapeutic methods." This addendum aims to ensure that more tests of antiretroviral treatment for people living with HIV and AIDS and mother-to-child transmission prevention compare new treatments with established therapies rather than a placebo (World Medical Association, 2000, C-29).

October 11 Russia's National Center for the Fight Against AIDS launches a nationwide advertising campaign aimed at preventing new HIV infections through sexual contact and intravenous drug use. This educational campaign was initiated in response to new government statistics stating that more new HIV infections occurred in 2000 alone than between 1987 and 1999 (*Agence France Presse*, 11 October 2000).

October 15 South African President Thabo Mbeki states his intention to "withdraw" from the debate over HIV and AIDS transmission, progression, and treatment. Acknowledging that his controversial views on the relationship between HIV and AIDS have caused "confusion" in South Africa, Mbeki announces that the government's policies will now operate under the "thesis" that HIV causes AIDS (*Agence France Presse*, 15 October). A week later, the South African Ministry of Health issues guidelines on AIDS treatment that state that HIV causes AIDS, but makes no reference to the efficacy of antiretroviral therapies in preventing mother-to-child transmission of the virus. The South African Health Ministry will neither endorse nor provide antiretroviral drugs to prevent mother-to-child transmission, on the grounds that such therapy is too expensive and has not yet been proved to be effective (Nessman, 2000).

October 23 After a week of meetings mediated by UNAIDS, the Senegalese government announces that it has reached agreements with Bristol-Myers Squibb, Merck, and GlaxoSmithKline to purchase discounted antiretroviral drugs, including stavudine, didanosine, indinavir, efavirenz, zidovudine, and lamivudine. Senegal is the first African country to take advantage of drug companies' offers to reduce the prices of antiretroviral medication. Triple-combination antiretroviral therapy is expected to cost between US$950 and US$1850 per person per year in Senegal (Schoofs and Waldholz, 2000).

October 27 South Africa's opposition party, the Democratic Alliance, announces that it will purchase discounted

2000
cont.

antiretroviral drugs to prevent mother-to-child transmission of HIV and to provide postexposure prophylaxis to rape survivors. Drugs will be delivered in KwaZulu-Natal, the one South African province the Alliance controls (Cohen, 2000).

October 31   The Chinese government announces that the number of people living with HIV in the country has increased by 37 percent over the last year to about 20,700 individuals (Xinhua News Agency, 2000).

November   A series of articles in Chinese newspapers and magazines expose the role of unsafe blood collection techniques in the spread of HIV in rural provinces (Rosenthal, 2000). The articles are spurred by the publication of a document titled "Revealing the 'blood wound' of the spread of HIV/AIDS in Henan Province—written on the eve of the first AIDS day of the new millennium." Composed under the pseudonym "He Aifang," the article alleges that HIV and AIDS have been a serious problem in Henan Province since 1995 because of commercial blood collection. He suggests that local government repressed all information about the numbers of people living with HIV and AIDS in Henan until national surveillance forced a full disclosure in 2000 (He, 2000). The U.S. Embassy in China labels He's article "a poison pen attack on the director of the Henan Province Health Department," but also states that He's statistics and estimates have been confirmed by other Chinese AIDS researchers (U.S. Embassy in China, 2000). Further articles are published in Guangdong Province's Communist newspaper, *Southern Weekend,* and *The People's Daily,* the Communist Party's national newspaper (Rosenthal, 2000).

November 21   Indian generic drug company Cipla offers to donate a generic version of nevirapine to the Indian government to prevent mother-to-child transmission of HIV (Hamied, 2000).

December 13   At the second meeting of the Accelerating Access Initiative's Contact Group, the WHO reports that thirty-four pharmaceutical manufacturers have expressed interest in collaborating with the initiative to make HIV and AIDS care more available in resource-scarce regions. Twenty-five of the companies manufacture generic versions of drugs and diagnostics (UNAIDS, 2000e).

The number of people living with HIV and AIDS in Ukraine rises to 31,360, a nearly eighty-fold increase since 1994. By the end of 2000 Russia and Ukraine have roughly comparable numbers of individuals living with HIV nationally, although Russia's total population is approximately three times that of Ukraine. The first wave of HIV transmissions in Ukraine took place primarily through intravenous drug use, but recent prevalence surveys indicate that transmission via sexual contact in the general population is becoming increasingly common (Shargorodsky, 2000).

2001　A survey of HIV-2 prevalence among immigrants from west Africa is conducted in Brescia, Italy, between 1999 and 2001. Over the three-year study period, nineteen cases of HIV-2 are detected in individuals originally from Benin, Ghana, Côte d'Ivoire, Burkina Faso, and Nigeria. These nineteen cases represent the first diagnoses of HIV-2 in Italy (Quiros-Roldan et al., 2001).

January 1　In an editorial in the *Washington Post,* Indian author and health policy analyst Siddharth Dube states: "The [AIDS prevention] programs in place today [in India] would possibly have been sufficient to curb the epidemic a decade ago; today they serve only to mask the fact that it is all but unchecked" (Dube, 2001).

February 1　South African clinicians and AIDS advocates announce that the government will provide HIV-infected pregnant women and their babies with a short course of nevirapine to prevent mother-to-child transmission of HIV. The program will begin in several pilot sites in March 2001 and will eventually be expanded to national coverage. Boehringer-Ingelheim will donate nevirapine to the South African government for five years (Jeter, 2001).

2001
cont.
February 9   The World Health Organization issues a statement "welcoming" reports that generic drug companies such as Cipla will begin to manufacture antiretroviral drugs. The WHO statement stresses that although the organization will continue to work with governments, commercial pharmaceutical companies, generic drug makers, and others to reduce the costs of AIDS treatment, increased public and private funding to improve health care and infrastructure will be vital in developing countries (World Health Organization, 2001).

February 23   Cipla and Mèdcins Sans Frontieres (MSF, Doctors without Borders) issue a joint release stating that Cipla will make triple-combination antiretroviral therapy available to developing country governments for US$600 per patient per year. In addition, Cipla will sell antiretroviral drugs to MSF at a discounted "humanitarian price" of US$350 per patient per year to support existing pilot programs (Mèdcins Sans Frontieres and Cipla Pharmaceuticals, 2001).

March 4   The lawsuit brought by forty-two pharmaceutical companies against the South African government returns to court, despite some companies' concerns over public relations with customers in Africa and elsewhere (Cooper, 2001).

March 7   The director of Cipla sends a letter to South Africa's registrar of patents in the Department of Trade and Industry, requesting compulsory patent licenses for nevirapine, lamivudine, zidovudine, stavudine, didanosine, efavirenz, indinavir, and abacavir in order to sell generic versions of these drugs in South Africa. Citing studies carried out in Brazil and materials from the Treatment Action Campaign, Cipla suggests that a more competitive drug market will decrease the costs of both generic and patented antiretroviral drugs in South Africa (Hamied, 2001).

March 14   Bristol-Myers Squibb announces that it will significantly reduce the prices of stavudine and didanosine in Africa to a combined price of US$1 per patient per day, stating that "We seek no profits on AIDS drugs in Africa, and we will not let our patents be an obstacle." In addition, Bristol-Myers Squibb will allow other manufacturers to sell a generic version of stavudine in African countries, although the company has not withdrawn from the lawsuit filed in South Africa to prevent manufacture and import of generic versions of antiretroviral drugs (Petersen and McNeil, 2001, A1).

South African President Thabo Mbeki refuses to declare a state of public health emergency in the country. During a state of emergency the World Trade Organization would allow the South African government to authorize the production of generic versions of antiretroviral drugs to treat HIV and AIDS. Although the South African "Medicines and Related Substances Control Act" of 1997 would allow manufacture of generic drugs during a public health emergency, the lawsuit brought by a group of pharmaceutical companies against the South African government currently prevents this course of action (Cohen, 2001a).

March 21   Indian news sources report that the Union Ministry of Health and Family Welfare and the Indian Council for Medical Research have signed a memorandum of understanding with the international AIDS Vaccine Initiative (IAVI) to develop and test an HIV vaccine in India. IAVI will provide US$3 million to support the Indian government's vaccine development efforts, with the goal of initiating a phase-I vaccine trial by mid-2002. The new vaccine would target HIV-1 subtype C, the subtype most common in India and Africa (Global News Wire, 21 March 2001).

March 22   Representatives from the World Health Organization, UNICEF, UNAIDS, and the European Commission meet with staff from Cipla to discuss issues related to making antiretroviral therapies accessible in developing countries. The United Nations has identified thirty-four manufacturers of HIV and AIDS-related drugs and diagnostic materials worldwide, including twenty-nine suppliers of generic products. This list, which includes Cipla, will be made available to developing countries to

2001
cont.
assist in resource allocation and price comparisons (UNAIDS and WHO, 2001).

March 27   Abbott Laboratories announces that it will sell its antiretroviral drugs lopinavir and ritonavir "at no profit" in African countries. Abbott will also sell a rapid HIV test at no profit in Africa, noting that this diagnostic test is designed for use in regions with limited laboratory infrastructure (Abbott Laboratories, 2001).

South African President Thabo Mbeki and Cuban President Fidel Castro sign an agreement to seek and develop inexpensive AIDS treatment options, including generic versions of patented antiretroviral drugs. After supporting the African National Congress during the struggle against Apartheid, Cuba has remained in partnership with South Africa, with 400 Cuban doctors working in South Africa's public health system and 200 South African medical students studying in Cuba during 2001 (Sanz, 2001).

April 11   World Health Organization director Gro Harlem Brundtland states on a Norwegian public radio broadcast, "A number of drug companies are contributing and reduced [AIDS drug] prices fairly considerably, but they have to go further." During this week the World Trade Organization convenes the first meeting of a multisectoral group of international experts and officials to consider issues related to HIV and AIDS care, antiretroviral drug access, and pricing (*Reuters,* 11 April 2001).

April 19   After a six-week recess, the group of pharmaceutical companies suing the South African government over potential patent violations drops its case, acknowledging that South Africa can legally import or manufacture generic versions of antiretroviral drugs (McGreal, 2001).

April 24–27   The Organization for African Unity (OAU) holds a summit in Abuja, Nigeria, dedicated to issues related to HIV and AIDS. The OAU publishes the "Abuja Declaration on HIV/AIDS, Tuberculosis and Other

Related Infectious Diseases," which calls for the creation of a "global AIDS fund" of US$5–10 billion (Organization for African Unity, 2001). The proposed fund would support multisectoral initiatives and programs to "enhance" national AIDS "action plans." This idea provides the basis for the Global Fund to Fight AIDS, Tuberculosis, and Malaria, proposed in the same month by United Nations Secretary-General Kofi Annan. The fund will support developing countries' efforts to treat, prevent, and mitigate the impact of the three diseases through internationally funded public–private partnerships, research, and interventions (Global Fund to Fight AIDS, Tuberculosis, and Malaria, 2003a).

April 25   Cipla Pharmaceuticals begins to negotiate bulk antiretroviral drug purchases with the governments of Cameroon, Côte d'Ivoire, and Algeria (Donnelly, 2001).

April 26   President Olesegun Obasanjo announces that Nigeria will buy enough antiretroviral medication to treat 10,000 Nigerians living with AIDS (approximately 0.4 percent of all Nigerians living with HIV and AIDS in 2001). The Nigerian government signed a deal with Cipla Pharmaceuticals to purchase generic versions of stavudine, lamivudine, and nevirapine at a total cost of US$350 per person per year, a significant reduction from Cipla's earlier US$600 offer (Donnelly, 2001).

May   Chengdu, the capital of Sichuan Province in China, enacts a series of laws that will prevent people living with HIV and AIDS from marrying or working as surgeons or preschool teachers. In addition, the laws require that sex workers and drug users apprehended by the police be tested for HIV and that HIV-infected prisoners be isolated in separate facilities. Sichuan residents who have traveled abroad for more than a year are subject to mandatory HIV testing. The new laws are sharply criticized by UNAIDS, local newspapers, and Chinese AIDS officials as a violation of human rights and a spur to stigma and misinformation about HIV (Pomfret, 2001). Similar laws are proposed in Beijing, Shenyang,

2001
cont. and other regions, despite the central Chinese government's policy of ensuring human rights protections for all people living with HIV and AIDS (Chang, 2001a).

May 7   As of the third meeting of the Accelerating Access Initiative Contact Group, thirty-six countries are working with the initiative to expand access to HIV and AIDS care and support. Twenty countries are in Africa, eleven in Latin America and the Caribbean, three in Europe, and two in Asia. Burkina Faso, Burundi, Cameroon, Côte d'Ivoire, Gabon, Mali, Morocco, Rwanda, Senegal, and Uganda have reached a final agreement with pharmaceutical companies to purchase AIDS-related drugs and diagnostics at significantly reduced prices. Barbados, Benin, the Central African Republic, Chile, Ethiopia, Kenya, Mexico, Romania, Swaziland, Thailand, Venezuela, and Vietnam are close to completing national strategies for addressing HIV and AIDS after consultation with the United Nations (UNAIDS, 2001a).

June 5   President Festus Mogae announces that the government of Botswana will begin to implement a national program to give free antiretroviral therapy to all people living with HIV and AIDS in the country (Pan African News Agency, 2001a). Botswana's national program aims to treat 20,000 people with HIV and AIDS with triple-combination antiretroviral therapy annually. In addition, the government program will provide tuberculosis prophylaxis and drugs to prevent mother-to-child HIV transmission to people living with HIV and AIDS (Pan African News Agency, 2001b).

June 6   The pharmaceutical company Pfizer announces that it will donate diflucan to fifty developing countries to treat people living with HIV and AIDS. Diflucan is an antifungal medication used to treat cryptococcal meningitis and esophageal candidiasis, two common opportunistic infections associated with AIDS in Africa (Crossette, 2001a).

June 10   GlaxoSmithKline Pharmaceuticals announces that it will reduce the prices of abacavir and amprenavir, along with a reduction in the price of Trizivir (a combination of abacavir, zidovudine, and lamivudine) in sixty-three developing countries. Discounts will range from 53 percent for amprenavir to 76 percent for Trizivir (Zimmerman, 2001).

June 26 On the first day of a United Nations General Assembly meeting, the United States announces it will withdraw a suit against the government of Brazil aimed at protecting pharmaceutical companies' patents on antiretroviral drugs. The Brazilian government agrees to give the United States ten days notice before initiating the process of manufacturing a generic version of a patented drug (Crosette, 2001b). Brazil and the United States will form a task force to address future issues of patent protection and drug access (World Trade Organization, 2001a).

June 27 The United Nations convenes a special session on HIV and AIDS. At the conclusion of this international meeting, delegates and heads of state issue the "Declaration of Commitment on HIV/AIDS." The declaration states that AIDS "constitutes a global emergency and one of the most formidable challenges to human life and dignity, as well as to the effective enjoyment of human rights, which undermines social and economic development throughout the world and affects all levels of society—national, community, family and individual" (United Nations, 2001, 1).

June 29 The Australian federal government will form an agreement with Australia-based drug manufacturers to reduce the cost of antiretroviral drugs in the Asia-Pacific region. This move will reduce the cost of treating people living with HIV and AIDS by up to 95 percent, bringing drug prices to about US$500 per person per year. Countries affected will include Fiji, Papua New Guinea, and Thailand (Riley, 2001).

July The Group of Eight (G-8) nations commit to a joint donation of US$1.3 billion to the Global Fund to Fight AIDS, Tuberculosis, and Malaria at a meeting in Genoa,

2001
cont.
Italy. The Global Fund's Transitional Working Group is also established in July. The Working Group is made up of representatives from developing countries, donor countries, nongovernmental organizations, and members of United Nations agencies (G-8, 2001).

July 18 Senior management at Bristol-Myers Squibb sends a fax to South African generic drug manufacturer Aspen Pharmacare stating that Bristol-Myers Squibb will not prosecute Aspen for breaking antiretroviral drug patents. The suggested "immunity from suit" would last for five years and applies only to Aspen Pharmacare (Zimmerman, Block, and Pearl, 2001).

August 3 Following official reports of rising HIV prevalence in China and new reports on the impact of unsafe blood collection techniques on rural HIV incidence, the Chinese government announces a new US$235 million "AIDS Prevention and Control Fund." Over five years, the fund will support community-based care for people living with HIV and AIDS, and will establish 250 "improved" blood collection stations to ensure that China's blood supply is free of HIV and that blood collection takes place safely (*Agence France Presse*, 3 August 2001).

August 21 In South Africa, the Treatment Action Campaign, the Children's Rights Centre, and a pediatrician representing 450 colleagues file a lawsuit against the South African government in the Pretoria High Court. The suit aims to force the government to provide all South African, HIV-infected, pregnant women with nevirapine to prevent mother-to-child transmission of HIV. The lawsuit also requires that the government present a national policy on the prevention of mother-to-child HIV transmission, including the provision of nevirapine, counseling services, and baby formula to prevent transmission via breast milk (*Agence France Presse*, 21 August 2001). The South African government's refusal to make nevirapine universally available constitutes a violation of women and children's constitutional rights to medical care, according to the doctors and activists who file the suit (Nessman, 2001).

August 30   The Ugandan government and the International AIDS Vaccine Initiative (IAVI) formalize a partnership to support and accelerate the development of HIV vaccines in Uganda, Africa, and worldwide. IAVI will partner with the Uganda Virus Research Initiative to increase national scientific and research capacity and clinical trial infrastructure (*PR Newswire*, 2001).

August 31   Thailand's Ministry of Public Health announces that AIDS is now the leading cause of death in the country, causing more fatalities than cancer, accidents, and heart disease (*Agence France Presse*, 31 August 2001).

September 1   One week after the Brazilian government threatens to issue a compulsory license to produce a generic version of Roche Holding's antiretroviral drug nelfinavir, Roche agrees to reduce the drug's price by an additional 40 percent (Rich, 2001). This agreement prevents Brazil from becoming the first developing country to issue a compulsory license to create a generic antiretroviral drug without the patent-holder's permission (Rich and Petersen, 2001).

September 5   The governments of Cambodia, China, Laos, Thailand, and Vietnam sign a joint memorandum of understanding in Phnom Penh, pledging to work together to slow the spread of HIV in Southeast Asia. The partnership's prevention efforts will focus on mobile populations such as truck drivers, migrant workers, and sex workers (*Agence France Presse*, 5 September 2001).

September 12   Doctors without Borders and the Brazilian government announce that they have signed a cooperative letter of intent. Brazil and Doctors without Borders will collaborate to provide developing countries with technical assistance in exporting, producing, prescribing, and distributing antiretroviral drugs, using Brazil's

2001
cont.
national AIDS care program as a model (*Reuters*, 13 September 2001).

October 24   South African President Thabo Mbeki announces that the government has no immediate plans to change or increase spending on HIV and AIDS prevention and care. The announcement comes after the Medical Research Council published a study on HIV and AIDS prevalence and impact in the country. The council's findings state that AIDS is now South Africa's leading killer, causing 40 percent of all adult deaths in 2000 (Cohen, 2001b). Mbeki's office had been reviewing the council's report since April (Sidley, 2001), citing concerns over discrepancies between the 2001 report and statistics released in 1995, which stated that only about 2.2 percent of deaths in South Africa were AIDS-related (Cohen, 2001b).

October 27   After several Americans die from handling mail containing anthrax, U.S. Secretary of Health and Human Services Tommy Thompson threatens to break Bayer Pharmaceuticals' patent on the antibiotic doxycycline (Cipro) if the company will not reduce the drug's price (Stevenson, 2001). Generic drug manufacturer Ivax offers to sell doxycycline to the U.S. government for about five cents per pill, leading to an agreement from Bayer to significantly reduce the price of the patented version of the drug (*Reuters*, 27 October 2001). Although the United States never breaks Bayer's patent on doxycycline, the threat of generic drug use forces a quick concession from the pharmaceutical industry.

November 12   China's first national AIDS conference takes place during this week. Although conference presenters feel comfortable discussing "sensitive" subjects such as gay rights and nondiscrimination policies, very few people living with AIDS are present during the conference proceedings (Pan, 2001).

November 14   After meeting in Doha, Qatar, the World Trade Organization adopts the "Declaration on the

TRIPS Agreement and Public Health." The "Doha Declaration" states that TRIPS must not prevent governments in developing countries from effectively addressing serious infectious diseases such as AIDS, tuberculosis, and malaria. The declaration specifically grants developing countries the right to issue "compulsory licenses" to manufacture generic drugs in a public health emergency and to determine locally when such an emergency is immanent. The issue of drug access in countries lacking sufficient infrastructure to locally manufacture generics must be resolved by World Trade Organization member states by the end of 2002 (World Trade Organization, 2001b).

November 15   Two Chinese generic drug suppliers, Shanghai Desano Biopharmaceutical Company and Northeast General Pharmaceutical Factory, apply for authorization from the Chinese government to manufacture generic versions of antiretroviral drugs, including zidovudine, didanosine, and stavudine. Because of "administrative loopholes" the manufacture of patented drugs is currently legal in China. A spokesperson from Desano estimates that generic antiretrovirals could cost as little as US$400 per patient per year in China (Chang, 2001b).

November 30   The Chinese subsidiary of Merck and Company announces that it will cut the prices of antiretrovirals crixivan and stocrin by 30 percent in China. The two drugs will now cost about US$3500 per person per year, which is still considered "too high [a price] for most ordinary patients," according to Dr. Zhang Ke, leader of AIDS clinical care at Beijing's You'an hospital (AFX-Asia, 2 December 2001).

December 5   A spokesperson for GlaxoSmithKline in China states that the company is "willing" to lower the prices of Combivir (zidovudine plus lamivudine) and lamivudine alone in China after Bristol-Myers Squibb and Merck reached similar agreements with the Chinese government in November (*AFX-Asia*, 5 December 2001).

2001   December 14   Pretoria High Court judge Chris Botha
cont.   rules that the South African government must immediately supply nevirapine to prevent mother-to-child
transmission of HIV to all HIV-infected pregnant
women, along with appropriate counseling and follow-
up care. In addition, the High Court ruling states that the
South African government must create and finalize a
national strategy for the prevention of mother-to-child
HIV transmission by March 31, 2002 (Keeton, 2001).

At the end of 2001, 40 million adults and children are living with HIV and AIDS worldwide. In sub-Saharan
Africa, 28.5 million people are living with HIV and AIDS.
In southern Asia, the world's second most affected
region, 5.6 million people are living with HIV and AIDS.
Eastern Europe, central Asia, eastern Asia, and the
Pacific region account for 2 million people living with
HIV and AIDS. In South America and the Caribbean, 1.92
million people are living with AIDS, and just under 1
million in North America. One million people are living
with AIDS in northern Africa, Western Europe, and the
Middle East. Five million people were infected with HIV
during 2001, and 3 million people died of AIDS-related
causes (UNAIDS, 2001b).

2002   On January 3, the South African province of KwaZulu-
Natal withdraws support from the national government's appeal of the Pretoria High Court's ruling on the
provision of nevirapine to prevent mother-to-child HIV
transmission. KwaZulu-Natal Premier Lionel Mtshali
lends his support to the Treatment Action Campaign and
other members of the lawsuit against the South African
government, stating that the "urgent and immediate
administration of Nevirapine (is) a moral imperative of
government" (Thom and Cullinan, 2002). Six weeks later,
Gauteng Province announces that it will voluntarily
make nevirapine available in public hospitals to prevent
mother-to-child transmission (Kraft, 2002).

January 29   Zimbabwe's Health and Child Welfare
deputy minister announces that the government of Zimbabwe will collaborate with Thailand to locally manu-

facture drugs to treat HIV and AIDS. The Thai government will donate technology and provide technical assistance, allowing Zimbabwe to produce generic versions of more than 300 drugs, including medicines used to treat tuberculosis and common opportunistic infections associated with HIV and AIDS (Xinhua News Agency, 2002a).

January 31   The Chinese government announces a US$270 million plan to upgrade blood banks and blood collection facilities nationwide to ensure that China's blood supply is uncontaminated (*Reuters*, 30 January 2002).

February 15   Russian Premier Mikhail Kasyanov and Canadian Prime Minister Jean Chretien sign more than seventy trade and investment agreements, including a three-year cooperative HIV prevention initiative aimed at reducing HIV transmission in Russia (Ingram, 2002).

March 11–April 4   The South African government appeals the Pretoria High Court's ruling that nevirapine must be made available to all HIV-infected pregnant women in the public sector, stating that national medical capacity and infrastructure are currently insufficient to scale up treatment nationwide. The High Court allows government representatives to appeal the decision to the South African Constitutional Court, but stipulates that the public health system must provide nevirapine while the appeals process takes place to avoid "unnecessary loss of life" (Cohen, 2002a). The Constitutional Court upholds the High Court's ruling during deliberations on the government's appeal. The South African government announces that it will comply with the court's order to begin to distribute nevirapine, cautioning that limited medical infrastructure will slow universal implementation (Mkhize, 2002).

March 20   The World Health Organization publishes a list of forty "quality" HIV and AIDS-related drugs to assist developing countries in identifying low-cost sources of drugs and diagnostics and in allocating

2002 resources for AIDS care. The list includes both generic
cont. and patented versions of drugs (Zimmerman, 2002).

March 22   The Thai Health Ministry announces that the
Government Pharmaceutical Organization will begin to
sell a tablet containing the antiretroviral drugs stavudine, lamivudine, and nevirapine for approximately
US$1 per day. This generic drug formulation, known in
Thailand as GPO-VIR, is now the most inexpensive antiretroviral regimen in the world, selling for less than
generic drugs produced by Cipla. GPO-VIR will reduce
medical expenses for up to 695,000 people living with
HIV and AIDS in Thailand (*Agence France Presse*, 22
March 2002).

March 26   Eighty Chinese farmers living with HIV and
AIDS from the village of Wenlou in Henan Province
protest outside local government offices, demanding
support and treatment in the first activist movement
focused on AIDS in rural China. The next day, the Chinese government announces that it will pay all community members living with HIV between 100 and 300 yuan
(US$12 and 36) per month to purchase drugs and pay for
medical care (Sui, 2002).

April   The Global Fund to Fight AIDS, Tuberculosis,
and Malaria announces its first round of grant awards
totaling approximately US$616 million over two years.
These funds will support local and multicountry efforts
in forty-three countries. Three hundred proposals were
submitted to the fund, requesting a total of more than
US$5 billion (Global Fund to Fight AIDS, Tuberculosis,
and Malaria, 2002).

The Global Fund approves a grant of US$41 million for
South Africa's KwaZulu-Natal Province, with US$11.5
million to be disbursed in 2002. The funds will be used in
the province to provide treatment for opportunistic
infections associated with AIDS, increase access to HIV
testing, provide antiretrovirals to pregnant women to
prevent mother-to-child transmission of HIV, and to provide antiretroviral treatment to health care workers liv-

ing with HIV. KwaZulu-Natal's Global Fund proposal was submitted by a multidisciplinary group of clinicians, researchers, provincial government representatives, nongovernmental organizations, and people living with HIV and AIDS brought together by the Harvard AIDS Institute's Enhancing Care Initiative (Steinglass, 2002). The initiative's goal is to bring multisectoral groups of local HIV and AIDS experts together to devise and implement novel and comprehensive approaches to HIV and AIDS care (Enhancing Care Initiative, 2000). South Africa's national government attempts to block disbursement of these funds, stating that the proposal should have been submitted via the National AIDS Committee and that the monies awarded should be shared among all provinces. The South African government did not designate the National AIDS Committee as "Country Coordinating Mechanism" for the Global Fund until after first-round proposals were due (Steinglass, 2002).

April 2   India's "National AIDS Prevention and Control Policy" is put into effect. India's Ministry of Health and Family Welfare and the National AIDS Control Organization will direct this national policy. The 2002 AIDS policy, announced in conjunction with a new National Blood Policy (Ministry of Health and Family Welfare, 2002b), will focus on involving all sectors of society in prevention and support efforts, including government ministries, nongovernmental organizations, and community leaders. The policy emphasizes the importance of a "decentralized" approach, letting each province develop and implement locally appropriate interventions that integrate HIV and AIDS care and support tuberculosis and reproductive health programs. In addition, the policy notes that "socially weak groups" such as women and children are at increased risk of HIV infection, and therefore must be provided with targeted health education, legal support, and improved financial support (Ministry of Health and Family Welfare, 2002a).

April 12   The Chinese government publishes new statistics on HIV and AIDS prevalence nationwide, estimating that approximately 850,000 people were living with

2002
cont.
HIV and AIDS in China by the end of 2001. This new estimate is 30 percent higher than previously released figures, but is more than 40 percent lower than HIV prevalence estimates for China published by the United Nations (Rosenthal, 2002).

April 17 The South African government announces that it will provide nevirapine to survivors of sexual assault as postexposure prophylaxis along with HIV testing and counseling. In addition, the government will allow public health facilities to give nevirapine to pregnant women with HIV and their babies to prevent mother-to-child transmission. A new presidential task force on AIDS will also be established to improve HIV and AIDS care and support nationwide (Cohen, 2002b).

April 18 Roche Pharmaceuticals and Trimeris, Inc. announce the results of the first phase III clinical trial of a "fusion inhibitor." After twenty-four weeks T-20 (enfuvirtide) is highly effective in reducing viral load among HIV-infected people who have developed viral resistance to other antiretroviral drugs (Roche Pharmaceuticals and Trimeris, Inc., 2002).

May After the death of a Honduran woman with AIDS who was unable to afford antiretroviral therapy, South American activists demand that the Brazilian government pledge to supply generic antiretroviral drugs to other South American countries during times of public health emergency. In addition, activists request that Brazil lobby neighboring governments to begin local production of generic antiretrovirals (Baldwin, 2002).

May 11–12 The first International Policy Makers' Conference on HIV/AIDS is convened in Delhi, India. Representatives from the governments of China, Kenya, Nepal, Nigeria, South Africa, Thailand, and Uganda participate, along with India's Prime Minister, Union Health Minister, political leaders, and state chief ministers. The "Delhi Declaration," issued after the conference, states the six governments' commitment to crafting a comprehensive response to the AIDS epidemic, including building capacity, improving access to care and treatment, promoting educational programs, and protecting the human rights of people living with HIV and AIDS. The declaration also includes a commitment to foster collaboration between government, nongovernmental organizations, people living with HIV and AIDS, the business sector, religious leaders, and others (Delhi Declaration, 2002).

May 28   By the fourth meeting of the Contact Group on Accelerating Access to HIV/AIDS-Related Care, eighty countries are collaborating with the Accelerating Access Initiative to expand access to HIV and AIDS care and support. The group includes forty-one African countries, twenty-six from Latin America and the Caribbean, five from Eastern Europe, five from Asia, and three from the Middle East. Thirty-nine countries have developed national HIV and AIDS action plans, and nineteen countries have used their national strategies to negotiate reduced prices for drugs and diagnostics. In the eleven countries where national HIV and AIDS plans were first developed, a total of 22,000 people are receiving care, a seven-fold increase since 2000 (UNAIDS, 2002a).

June 5   Brazil initiates the country's first HIV prevention campaign aimed specifically at young, gay men in response to new statistics showing that HIV rates are increasing most quickly among young people in the country. The new education campaign will focus on increasing tolerance of gay men in Brazilian society, particularly among family members and educators (Milliken, 2002).

July 5   The South African Constitutional Court rules that the government must make nevirapine available in public health facilities to prevent mother-to-child transmission of HIV and that the government may not submit any further appeals to the court's previous ruling. Health Minister Manto Tshabalala-Msimang accepts the ruling as a representative of the national government. Boehringer Ingelheim, a German pharmaceutical manufacturer, continues to offer free nevirapine to the South African government (Chege, 2002).

2002
cont.
July 10   During the XIV International AIDS Conference in Barcelona, Spain, the Brazilian government signs a letter of agreement with the International AIDS Vaccine Initiative to build local infrastructure for vaccine trials and to allocate US$2 million per year to vaccine research (Hirschler, 2002).

July 16   South African Minister of Health Manto Tshabalala-Msimang and KwaZulu-Natal Provincial Health Minister Zweli Mkhize issue a joint statement agreeing that money from the Global Fund to Fight AIDS, Tuberculosis, and Malaria will be "used in a manner that will benefit all provinces equitably." The Global Fund will not disburse the grant to support this new approach, stating that the US$41 million has been earmarked specifically to fund KwaZulu-Natal's proposal to combat HIV and AIDS (Kahn, 2002, 11).

July 31   The Brazilian government signs an agreement with the governments of the thirteen-country Portuguese-Language Community to share technology and strategies to treat and prevent HIV and AIDS. Supported by a grant from the Global Fund to Fight AIDS, Tuberculosis, and Malaria, the proposed program would assist countries in Africa, Europe, Latin America, and Asia in creating and implementing comprehensive, government-sponsored AIDS care and treatment programs modeled on Brazil's HIV and AIDS efforts (*Reuters*, 31 July 2002).

August   The Chinese government grants Northeast General Pharmaceutical Factory permission to manufacture a generic version of zidovudine (Wade, 2002).

August 25   Chinese AIDS activist Dr. Wan Yanhai is arrested and imprisoned for "revealing state secrets" shortly after publishing a confidential government report on his "AIDS Action Project" Web site. The report details HIV prevention activities taking place in Henan Province along with statistics on the number of people infected with HIV through commercial blood collection. Dr. Wan is held in custody for twenty-seven days, sparking both local and international protest and drawing attention to the role of China's blood collection industry in the current AIDS epidemic. Local and international media outlets begin to publicize the Chinese government's reluctance to reveal HIV prevalence statistics for Henan Province (Russel, 2002).

August 26   Australia, China, India, Indonesia, the Philippines, Thailand, and Vietnam embark on an international study of the causes of stigma and discrimination toward people living with AIDS. The study aims to address problems of stigma and discrimination at the local and international levels by developing new guidelines and policy instruments (Xinhua News Agency, 2002b).

August 28   The Russian State Statistics Committee announces that the official total of people living with HIV and AIDS nationwide has reached 200,000, although it is likely that many more cases have not been reported. About 3,500 new cases of HIV have been registered every month in Russia since the beginning of 2002 (Associated Press, 2002).

September 6   Qi Xiaoqui, head of China's Department of Disease Control, announces new government estimates suggesting that about 1 million people are living with HIV in China (Harmsen, 2002).

September 24   Desano Biopharmaceutical Company in Shanghai, China, announces that it has received government permission to manufacture generic versions of didanosine and stavudine. A company spokesperson states that the two antiretroviral drugs will be available to the public by the end of 2002. A representative of Bristol-Myers Squibb (the company that holds the patents to didanosine and stavudine) states that under China's existing patent laws, Desano is free to manufacture generic versions of the two drugs (Wade, 2002).

October 1   The Central Intellectual Property Court of Thailand rules that AIDS activists seeking to break Bristol-Myers Squibb's patent on the antiretroviral drug

2002
cont. didanosine may proceed with their lawsuit, which seeks to legalize generic formulation of didanosine in Thailand. In addition, the court ruling states that nongovernmental organizations may now challenge drug patents on "social grounds," including concern for public health (Noikorn, 2002).

October 16   China's first antidiscrimination legislation to protect people living with HIV and AIDS is passed in Suzhou City, Jiangsu Province. The new law forbids discrimination in education, employment, and access to medical care against people living with HIV or AIDS (*Agence France Presse*, 16 October 2002).

October 23   Merck and Company cuts the price of efavirenz by an additional 30 percent in developing countries, making the patented version of the drug less expensive than some generic formulations. Efavirenz will now cost less than US$1 per day, or just under US$350 per person per year (Zimmerman and Schoofs, 2002).

December 12   The International HIV Treatment Access Coalition is formed in Dakar and Geneva, bringing together representatives from universities, governments, nongovernmental organizations, groups of people living with HIV and AIDS, and international organizations. The coalition seeks to improve international communication around AIDS care and treatment, improve drug procurement and delivery systems, train health care workers, and increase donations to AIDS care efforts in developing countries (World Health Organization, 2002).

December 21   World Trade Organization negotiations over developing countries' right to import generic versions of patented drugs end at midnight at an impasse. Despite opposition from many developed and developing country representatives, the United States refuses to accept an agreement that does not specifically list which infectious diseases (such as AIDS, tuberculosis, and malaria) constitute a national "emergency" (Blustein, 2002). The United States remains concerned that the Doha

Declaration on TRIPS will allow developing countries to import generic drugs to treat less serious public health threats "such as asthma, obesity, and tobacco-related diseases." Developing country representatives continue to insist on autonomy in making national decisions on public health requirements and the severity of threats to public health (*Agence France Presse*, 17 December 2002).

At the end of 2002, forty-two million people are estimated to be living with HIV and AIDS worldwide. For the first time, UNAIDS reports that more than half of all people living with HIV or AIDS globally are women. In sub-Saharan Africa, 29.4 million adults and children are living with HIV and AIDS, 58 percent of whom are women. The average HIV prevalence across all of Africa is 8.8 percent, whereas average prevalence in the Caribbean, the second most affected region, is 2.4 percent. Six million people are living with HIV and AIDS in southern Asia, 1.2 million in eastern Asia, 1.2 million in Eastern Europe, and 1.5 million in South America. Australia, north Africa, North America, and Western Europe account for a total of 2.1 million people living with HIV and AIDS (UNAIDS, 2002b).

2003   Distribution of generic versions of didanosine and stavudine manufactured by Desano Biopharmaceutical Company begins on January 21 in Henan Province, China. The Chinese government funds delivery of the drugs (Associated Press, 2003).

January 28   In his State of the Union Address, U.S. President George W. Bush proposes the creation of a US$15 billion Emergency Plan for AIDS Relief for the most affected nations in Africa and the Caribbean. Bush asks Congress to approve US$15 billion over five years to "prevent seven million new AIDS infections, treat at least two million people with life-extending [antiretroviral drugs], and provide humane care for millions of people suffering from AIDS" (Bush, 2003). AIDS activists and advocates criticize the initiative for allocating only $1 billion to the Global Fund to Fight AIDS, Tuberculosis, and Malaria, which is estimated to require another US$9 billion to adequately

2003
cont.
support international AIDS programs. In addition, the Emergency Plan will not appropriate more than $2 billion in the 2004 fiscal year, phasing in support too slowly to have an immediate effect according to activists from African countries (Lobe, 2003).

February 13 Roche, a drug manufacturer based in Switzerland, announces that it will reduce the cost of the antiretroviral drug nelfinavir by approximately 73 percent in developing countries to a price of US$900 per person per year (Fuhrmans and Zimmerman, 2003).

March 13 The U.S. Food and Drug Administration grants "accelerated approval" to enfuvirtide (T-20 of "Fuzeon") after six months of phase-III testing. Clinical trials will continue to monitor enfuvirtide's long-term side effects and efficacy. Fuzeon is the first antiretroviral drug in the "fusion inhibitor" class to be approved (U.S. Food and Drug Administration, 2003).

April 11 The Global Fund to Fight AIDS, Tuberculosis, and Malaria and the South African government fail to sign an agreement to disburse the Global Fund's US$41 million grant to KwaZulu-Natal Province. The government of South Africa cites "some outstanding issues" as the cause of the delay in approval. This is the second failure within a week of negotiations and has brought the approval process to a halt (Altenroxel, 2003).

May 16 The United States Senate approves President Bush's proposed US$15 billion Emergency Plan for AIDS Relief. Under the Senate's plan, US$3 billion will be disbursed yearly to the African and Caribbean countries most impacted by HIV and AIDS. One-third of the prevention funds will support abstinence-only prevention programs, and the rest of the prevention funds will support condom distribution and other public education campaigns (Eilperin, 2003).

July 16 The United States House Appropriations Committee votes down an amendment introduced to increase disbursement of Emergency Plan for AIDS Relief funds to $3 billion in 2004. Only $2 million will be spent during the 2004 fiscal year, one-third less than the yearly contribution pledged in January (Holland, 2003).

August 7   More than a year after the original proposal was approved, the Global Fund to Fight AIDS, Tuberculosis, and Malaria and the South African government sign agreements on the fund's US$41 million grant to KwaZulu-Natal Province. The grant will support HIV and AIDS care, prevention, and support activities in KwaZulu-Natal Province and will provide funding for national prevention programs. Global Fund Executive Director Richard Feachem states, "in personally approving the proposal, President Mbeki has enabled new energy and partnership in the fight against AIDS in South Africa" (Global Fund to Fight AIDS, Tuberculosis, and Malaria, 2003b).

October 24   The William J. Clinton Presidential Foundation's HIV/AIDS Initiative announces an agreement with four generic drug manufacturers to lower the price of triple-combination antiretroviral drug regimens to less than US$140 per patient per year. The foundation will work with partner nations to develop national plans and funding for nationwide antiretroviral drug access and AIDS care. The Clinton Foundation is working with the governments of: Mozambique, Rwanda, Tanzania, South Africa, Bahamas, Dominican Republic, Haiti, and the Organization of Eastern Caribbean States (Antigua and Barbuda, Dominica, Grenada, St. Kitts and Nevis, St. Lucia, St. Vincent and the Grenadines, Anguilla, Montserrat, and British Virgin Islands) (Schoofs, 2003).

References

AAVP. The African AIDS Vaccine Programme. 2003. Available at: http://www.who.int/vaccine_research/diseases/hiv/aavp/en. Accessed: January 25, 2004.

Abbott Laboratories. Abbott Laboratories to offer AIDS drugs and rapid diagnostic test at no profit in Africa: Offer includes Abbott's protease inhibitors Kaletra and Norvir, determine test [Press Release]. March 27, 2001.

AFX-Asia. Glaxo, Bristol-Myers cannot confirm China AIDS drug prices. *AFX News Limited Company News,* 3 December 2001.

————. GlaxoSmithKline likely to cut price of AIDS drugs in China. *AFX News Limited Company News,* 5 December 2001.

Agence France Presse. India admits dramatic rise in number of HIV carriers. *Agence France Presse,* 14 September 1998.

————. 1,843 people in Russia contract AIDS virus in last six months. *Agence France Presse,* 3 November 1998.

————. South Africa's ANC calls on Mbeki to admit HIV causes AIDS. *Agence France Presse,* 14 September 2000.

————. Russian anti-AIDS campaign urges masturbation and telephone sex. *Agence France Presse,* 11 October 2000.

————. South Africa's Mbeki withdraws from HIV/AIDS debate. *Agence France Presse,* 15 October 2000.

————. China boosts AIDS funding and vows to clean up blood supply. *Agence France Presse,* 3 August 2001.

————. Lobby group sues South African government over AIDS programme. *Agence France Presse,* 21 August 2001.

————. AIDS now Thailand's number one cause of death. *Agence France Presse,* 31 August 2001.

————. Five Southeast Asian countries sign up to fight AIDS. *Agence France Presse,* 5 September 2001.

————. Thailand to launch dollar-a-day anti-AIDS cocktail. *Agence France Presse,* 22 March 2002.

————. Chinese city passes law to protect rights of AIDS patients. *Agence France Presse,* 16 October 2002.

————. US increasingly isolated at WTO talks on cheap medicines. *Agence France Presse,* 17 December 2002.

Altenroxel, L., and S. Majors. KZN's AIDS funds deal may be in jeopardy. *Cape Times* (South Africa), 11 April 2003.

Anonymous. 1997a. Efavirenz (SUSTIVA, formerly DMP-266) 48-week data announced. *AIDS Treatment News* (279): 2–3.

Anonymous. 1997b. Preliminary report on 1592. *AIDS Clinical Care* 9(9): 71.

Arnold, C. Army reports jump in HIV cases. *The Moscow Times,* 21 July 1998, sec. 1499.

Arya, S.K., and R. C. Gallo. 1986. Three novel genes of Human T-lymphotropic virus type III: Immune reactivity of their products with sera from acquired immune deficiency syndrome patients. *Proceedings of the National Academy of Science* 83(7): 2209–2213.

Asia Pulse. World Bank helps India intensify fight against HIV/AIDS. *Asia Pulse Limited,* 17 June 1999.

Associated Press. 2002. More than 3,500 new HIV cases registered every month in Russia. Associated Press, August 28, 2002.

————. 2003. Chinese Company distributing generic anti-AIDS drugs. Associated Press, January 28, 2003.

Baldwin, K. Latin American AIDS activists turn on Brazil. *Reuters,* 25 May 2002.

Barin, F., F. Denis, J. S. Allan, et al. 1985. Serological evidence for virus related to simian t-lymphotropic retrovirus III in residents of west Africa. *Lancet* 2(8469–8470): 1387–1389.

Barré-Sinoussi, F., J. C. Chermann, F. Rey, et al. 1983. Isolation of a t-lymphotropic retrovirus from a patient at risk for acquired immune deficiency syndrome (AIDS). *Science* 220: 868–871.

Bayley, A. C. 1984. Aggressive Kaposi's sarcoma in Zambia (1983). *Lancet* i: 1318–1320.

Bayley, A. C., R. Cheingsong-Popov, A. G. Dalgleish, et al. 1985. HTLV-III serology distinguishes atypical Kaposi's sarcoma in Africa. *Lancet* 1(8425): 359–361.

BBC News. 1999. AIDS success "generates sex risks." BBC News, September 22.

Biggar, R. J., M. Melbye, L. Kestens, et al. 1985. Seroepidemiology of HTLV-III antibodies in a remote population in Zaire. *British Medical Journal* 290: 808–810.

Blustein, P. Talks on low-cost drug for poor nations stall. *Washington Post,* 21 December 2002, E-01.

Brazilian Industrial Property Office. n.d. The legal system. Available at: http://www.inpi.gov.br/idiomas/conteudo/ingles.htm. Accessed: April 4, 2004.

Bush, G. W. 2003. State of the Union Address, January 28, 2003. Available at: http://www.whitehouse.gov/news/releases/2003/01/20030128-19.html. Accessed: March 30, 2004.

Bygbjerg, I. C. 1983. AIDS in a Danish surgeon (1976). *Lancet* 1(8330): 925.

Cao, H., P. Kaleebu, D. Hom, et al. 2000. Immunogenicity of a recombinant human immunodeficiency virus (HIV) canarypox vaccine in HIV-seronegative Ugandan volunteers; results of the HIV network for Prevention Trials 007 Vaccine Study. *Journal of Infectious Diseases* 187(6): 887–895.

Carr, A., J. Miller, M. Law, et al. 2000. A syndrome of lipoatrophy, lactic acidaemia and liver dysfunction associated with HIV nucleoside analogue therapy: Contribution to protease inhibitor-related lipodystrophy syndrome. *AIDS* 14(3): F25–32.

Chang, L. 2001a. Panic about AIDS hits China, leading to draconian measures. Bills curbing rights of people with HIV alarm doctors who seek better education. *Wall Street Journal,* 23 March 2001, B1.

Chang, L. 2001b. China companies may use patent law to produce cheap drugs to fight AIDS. *Wall Street Journal,* 15 November 2001, A22.

Chapman, S., J. Peterkin, B. Quart, et al. 1995. Clinical potential of a new HIV protease inhibitor. *Journal of the International Association of Physicians in AIDS Care* 1(5): 24.

Cheeseman, S. H., S. E. Hattox, M. M. McLaughlin, et al. 1993. Pharmacokinetics of nevirapine: Initial single-rising-dose study in humans. *Antimicrobial Agents and Chemotherapy* 37(2): 178–182.

Chege, W. South African court orders way cleared for AIDS drugs. *Reuters,* 5 July 2002.

Clavel, F., D. Guetard, F. Brun-Vezinet, et al. 1986. Isolation of a new human retrovirus from West African patients with AIDS. *Science* 233(4761): 343–346.

Clumeck, N., F. Mascart-Lemone, J. de Maubeuge, et al. 1983. Acquired immune deficiency syndrome in black Africans. *Lancet* 1(8325): 642.

Clumeck, N., J. Sonnet, H. Taelman, et al. 1984. Acquired immunodeficiency syndrome in African patients. *New England Journal of Medicine* 310(8): 492–497.

Cocchi, F., A. L. DeVico, A. Garzino-Demo, et al. 1995. Identification of RANTES, MIP-1 alpha, and MIP-1 beta as the major HIV-suppressive factors produced by CD8+ T cells. *Science* 270(5243): 1811–1818.

Cohen, M. 2000. Opposition party defies South African government's AIDS policy. Associated Press, October 27, 2000.

———. 2001a. No state of emergency in South Africa. Associated Press, March 14, 2001.

———. 2001b. No immediate changes planned to South Africa's AIDS policy. Associated Press, October 24, 2001.

———. 2002a. South African government granted permission to appeal court order to distribute key AIDS drug. Associated Press, March 11, 2002.

————. 2002b. South Africa shifts AIDS drug policy. Associated Press, April 17, 2002.

Connor, E. M., R. S. Sperling, R. Gelber, et al. 1994. Reduction of maternal-infant transmission of human immunodeficiency virus type 1 with zidovudine treatment. *New England Journal of Medicine* 331(18): 1173–1180.

Cooper, H., R. Zimmerman, and L. McGinley. 2001. AIDS epidemic puts drug firms in a vise: Treatment vs. profits. *Wall Street Journal*, 2 March 2001, A1.

Crossette, B. 2001a. AIDS fungus drug offered to poor nations. *New York Times*, 7 June 2001, A3.

————. 2001b. U.S. drops case over AIDS drugs in Brazil. *New York Times*, 26 June 2001, A4.

Dalgleish, A. G., P. C. Beverly, P. R. Clapham, et al. 1984. The CD4 (T4) antigen is an essential component of the receptor for the AIDS retrovirus. *Nature* 312(5996): 763–767.

Daniel, M. D., N. L. Letvin, N. W. King, et al. 1985. Isolation of T-cell tropic HTLV-III-like retrovirus from macaques. *Science* 228: 1201–1204.

Davey, R. T., Jr., D. G. Chaitt, G. F. Reed, et al. 1996. Randomized, controlled phase I/II, trial of combination therapy with delavirdine (U-90152S) and conventional nucleosides in human immunodeficiency virus type 1-infected patients. *Antimicrobial Agents and Chemotherapy* 40(7): 1657–1664.

Delhi Declaration. 2002. Parliamentarians' Commitment towards a World without AIDS. Available at: http://www.india-seminar.com/2002/520/520%20the%20delhi%20declaration.htm. Accessed: April 6, 2004.

Deutsche Presse-Agentur. World Bank criticizes Thailand's recent HIV/AIDS performance. *Deutsche Presse-Agentur,* 17 September 2000.

Donnelly, J. Nigeria reaches deal with Indian firm to buy AIDS drugs. *Boston Globe,* 26 April 2001, A22.

Durate, G., M. M. Mussi-Pinhata, M. C. C. Feres, et al. 1991. The ascendant pattern of seropositivity for HIV antibody and the risk factors associated with HIV transmission in parturients cared for at a school hospital in Brazil. Presented at: VII International Conference on AIDS, June 16-21, Florence, Italy. Abstract number W.C.3257.

Dube, S. India's AIDS explosion. *Washington Post,* 4 January 2001, A21.

Dudley, M. N., K. K. Graham, S. Kaul, et al. 1992. Pharmacokinetics of stavudine in patients with AIDS or AIDS-related complex. *Journal of Infectious Diseases* 166(3): 480–485.

Durban Declaration Signatories. 2000. The Durban Declaration. *Nature* 406: 15–16.

Eilperin, J. Senate passes $15 billion AIDS bill. *Washington Post,* 17 May 2003, A4.

Enhancing Care Initiative. 2000. Enhancing Care Initiative Web site. Available at: http://www.eci.harvard.edu. Accessed: April 6, 2004.

Finzi, D., M. Hermankova, T. Pierson, et al. 1997. Identification of a reservoir of HIV-1 in patients on highly active antiretroviral therapy. *Science* 278(5341): 1295–1300.

Fisher, A. G., B. Ensoli, L. Ivanoff, et al. 1987. The sor gene of HIV-1 is required for efficient virus transmission in vitro. *Science* 237(4817): 888–893.

Fleshman, M. 1999. WTO impasse in Seattle spotlights inequities of global trading system. *Africa Recovery Online* 13(4): Available at: http://www. un.org/ecosocdev/geninfo/afrec/vol13no4/1wto1.htm. Accessed: April 6, 2004.

FT Asia Intelligence Wire. Indian HIV infection high in state. *The Hindu* (India), 16 July 1998.

Fuhrmans, V., and R. Zimmerman. Roche to sell drug for AIDS at cost in poorer nations. *Wall Street Journal,* 13 February 2003, D3.

G-8. 2001. Genova G-8: Top Stories. Available at: http://www.genoa-g8. it/eng/attualita/primo_piano/primo_piano_13.html. Accessed: April 5, 2004.

Gallo, R. C., S. Z. Salahuddin, M. Popovic, et al. 1984. Frequent detection and isolation of cytopathic retroviruses (HTLV-III) from patients with AIDS and at risk for AIDS. *Science* 224(4648): 500–503.

Gao, F., L. Yue, D. L. Robertson, et al. 1994. Genetic diversity of human immunodeficiency virus type 2: Evidence for distinct sequence subtypes with differences in virus biology. *Journal of Virology* 68(11): 7433–7447.

Glavão, J. 2002. Access to antiretroviral drugs in Brazil. *Lancet* 360: 1862–1865.

Global Fund to Fight AIDS, Tuberculosis, and Malaria. 2002. Global Fund to Fight AIDS, Tuberculosis and Malaria announces first grants: Commits up to $616 million over two years for prevention and treatment, calls for additional resources to address world's deadliest epidemics [press release], April 25, 2002. Available at: http://www. theglobalfund.org/en/media_center/press/NY_020425.asp. Accessed: April 6, 2004.

———. 2003a. How the fund works. Available at: http://www. theglobalfund.org/en/about/how/. Accessed: April 5, 2004.

———. 2003b. South Africa grant agreements signed: Over US$40 million for treatment and prevention of HIV/AIDS and TB [press release], August 7, 2003. Available at: http://www.theglobalfund.org/en/media_center/press/pr_030807.asp. Accessed: April 6, 2004.

Global Network of People Living with HIV and AIDS (GNP+). n.d. GNP+ Web site. Available at: http://www.gnpplus.net/. Accessed: April 6, 2004.

Global News Wire. China: AIDS prevention urgent. *China Daily,* 21 October 1999, 2.

———. India to develop AIDS vaccine. *Times of India,* 21 March 2001.

Government of India. 1995. Drugs (Prices Control) Order, 1995. New Delhi: Government of India Ministry of Chemicals and Fertilizers.

Guay, L. A., P. Musoke, T. Fleming, et al. 1999. Intrapartum and neo-natal single dose nevirapine compared with zidovudine for prevention of mother-to-child transmission of HIV-1 in Kampala, Uganda: HIVNET 012 randomized trial. *Lancet* 354(9181): 795–802.

Hamied, M. K., and Cipla Pharmaceuticals. 2000. Letter from Cipla to Indian National AIDS Control Organization concerning the offer of nevi-rapine donations November 29, 2000. Available at: http://www.cptech.org/ip/health/cipla/ciplaindia11292000.html. Accessed: April 6, 2004.

———. 2001. Cipla's March 7, 2001 compulsory licensing request. Available at: http://www.cptech.org/ip/health/sa/ciplanetsh03072001.html. Accessed: April 6, 2004.

Hammer, S. M., K. E. Squires, M. D. Hughes, et al. 1997. A controlled trial of two nucleoside analogues plus indinavir in persons with human immunodeficiency virus infection and CD4 cell counts of 200 per cubic millimeter or less. *New England Journal of Medicine* 337(11): 725–733.

Harmsen, P. China has around 1 million HIV positive people. *Agence France Presse,* 6 September 2002.

He, A. 2000. Revealing the 'blood wound' of the spread of HIV/AIDS in Henan Province—written on the eve of the first AIDS day of the new millennium. Available at: http://www.usembassy-china.org.cn/sandt/henan-hiv.htm. Accessed: April 6, 2004.

Hirsch, M., R. Steigbigel, S. Staszewski, et al. 1997. A randomized controlled trial of indinavir, zidovudine, and lamivudine in adults with advanced human immunodeficiency virus type 1 infection and prior antiretroviral therapy. *Journal of Infectious Diseases* 180(3): 659–665.

Hirschler, B. Brazil ready to supply a cheap AIDS vaccine. *Reuters,* 10 July 2002.

Holland, J. J. 2003. Appropriations Committee sticks with $2 billion for AIDS in Africa funding. Associated Press, July 16, 2003.

ICASO. n.d. ICASO Web site. Available at: http://www.icaso.org. Accessed: April 6, 2004.

Ingram, J. 2002. Canadian, Russian businesses sign more than 70 deals, Prime Minister visits AIDS institute. Associated Press, February 15, 2002.

Isachenkov, V. 2000. International news: Moscow. Associated Press, May 25, 2000.

Jacobsen, H., L. Ahlborn-Laake, R. Gugel, et al. 1992. Progression of early steps of human immunodeficiency virus type 1 replication in the presence of an inhibitor of viral protease. *Journal of Virology* 66(8): 5087–5091.

James, J. S. 1995. Agouron protease inhibitor AG1343: Activity reported. *AIDS Treatment News* 222: 6.

Jeter, J. South Africa relents on maternal HIV care. *Washington Post*, 1 February 2001, A1.

Jha, A. M. Not a single blood bank in Bihar complies with WHO norms. *Times of India*, 11 May 2000.

Kahn, T. UNAIDS grant in jeopardy despite agreement. *Business Day*, 17 July 2002, 11.

Kamradt, T., D. Niese, and F. Vogel. 1985. Slim disease (AIDS). *Lancet* 2(8469–8470): 1425.

Kanki, P. J., J. Alroy, and M. Essex. 1985a. Isolation of T-lymphotropic retrovirus related to HTLV-III/LAV from wild-caught African Green monkeys. *Science* 230(4728): 951–954.

Kanki, P. J., M. F. McLane, N. W. King, et al. 1985b. Serologic identification and characterization of a macaque T-lymphotropic retrovirus closely related to HTLV-III. *Science* 228: 1199–1201.

Karon, J. M., T. J. Dondero Jr., R. Berkelman, et al. 1990. HIV prevalence estimates and AIDS case projections for the United States: Report based upon a workshop. *Morbidity and Mortality Weekly Report* 39(RR-16): 1–18.

Katlama, C., C. Leport, S. Matheron, et al. 1984. Acquired immunodeficiency syndrome (AIDS) in Africans. *Annales de la Societe Belge de Medecine Tropicale* 64: 379–389.

Keeton, C. South African court orders government to provide AIDS drug. *Agence France Presse*, 14 December 2001.

Kilby, J. M., S. Hopkins, T. Venetta, et al. 1998. Potent suppression of HIV-1 replication in humans by T-20, a peptide inhibitor of gp41-mediated virus entry. *Nature Medicine* 4(11): 1302–1307.

Kitchen, V. S., C. Skinner, K. Ariyoshi, et al. 1995. Safety and activity of saquinavir in HIV infection. *Lancet* 345(8955): 952–955.

Kraft, D. 2002. South Africa's provinces begin backlash to make key AIDS drug available to pregnant women. Associated Press, February 18, 2002.

Kumar, G. P. New plan to check spread of HIV in Manipur. *The Hindu* (India), 16 November 1998.

Lamey, B., and N. Melameka. 1982. Aspects cliniques et épidémiologiques de la cryptococcose à Kinshasa: À propos de15 cas personnels. *La Medicina Tropical* 42: 507–511.

Lewis, N. A. US industry to drop AIDS drug lawsuit against South Africa. *New York Times,* 10 September 1999, A3.

Lin, T. S., R. F. Schinazi, and W. H. Prusoff. 1987. Potent and selective in vitro activity of 3′-deoxythymidin-2′-ene (3′-deoxy-2′,3′-didehydrothymidine) against human immunodeficiency virus. *Biochemical Pharmacology* 36(17): 2713–2718.

Liu, R., W. A. Paxton, S. Choe et al. 1996. Homozygous defect in HIV-1 coreceptor accounts for resistance of some multiply-exposed individuals to HIV-1 infection. *Cell* 86(3): 367–377.

Lobe, J. 2003. World community gives Bush AIDS pledge mixed reception. Inter Press Service, January 29, 2003.

Mann, J. M. 1989. Global AIDS into the 1990s. Presented at: V International Conference on AIDS, June 4–9, Montreal, Canada. Abstract number W.C.503.M281.

Mann, J. M., H. Francis, T. Quinn, et al. 1986. Surveillance for AIDS in a central African city. *Journal of the American Medical Association* 255(23): 3255–3259.

Mann, J., D. M. Tarantola, and T. W. Netter. 1992. "The HIV pandemic: Status and trends." In *AIDS in the World,* edited by J. Mann, D. M. Tarantola, and T. W. Netter. Cambridge, MA: Harvard University Press, pp. 11–108.

Marquart, K. H., H. A. G. Müller, J. Sailer, and R. Moser. 1985. Slim disease (AIDS). *Lancet* 2(8465): 1186–1187.

Martin, J. A., M. A. Mobberley, S. Redshaw, et al. 1991. The inhibitory activity of a peptide derivative against the growth of simian immunodeficiency virus in C8166 cells. *Biochemical and Biophysical Research Communications* 176(1): 180–188.

McGreal, C. Shamed and humiliated—the drug firms back down. *The Guardian* (London), 19 April 2001, 1.

McNeil, D. G., Jr. Patent holders fight proposal on generic AIDS drugs for poor. *New York Times,* 18 May 2000, A5.

Mèdcins Sans Frontiers, and Cipla Pharmaceuticals. February 23, 2001. *Progress reported on implementation of offer for more affordable anti-AIDS drugs.* Mumbai: Cipla Pharmaceuticals.

Meira, D. A. 2002. Acquired immunodeficiency syndrome in Brazil. *Croatian Medical Journal* 43(4): 475–479.

Mellors, J. W., C. R. Rinaldo Jr., P. Gupta, et al. 1996. Prognosis in HIV-1 infection predicted by the quantity of virus in plasma. *Science* 272(5265): 1167–1170.

Milliken, M. Brazil launches first anti-AIDS campaign for gays. *Reuters,* 5 June 2002.

Ministry of Health and Family Welfare and National AIDS Control Organization. 2002a. National AIDS Prevention and Control Policy: India. New Delhi, April 2.

———. 2002b. National Blood Policy: India. New Delhi, April 2.

Miyoshi, I., S. Yoshimoto, M. Fujishita, et al. 1982. Natural adult T-cell leukemia virus infection in Japanese monkeys. *Lancet* 2(8299): 658.

Mkhize, J. South Africa government accepts court ruling on HIV drug. *Reuters,* 4 April 2002.

Monitoring the AIDS Pandemic. Workshop on the Status and Trends of the HIV/AIDS Epidemics in Africa: Final Report 1995. Available at: http://www.mapnetwork.org/docs/MAP_Kampala_1995.pdf. Accessed: April 6, 2004.

Nahmias, A., J. Weiss, X. Yao, et al. 1986. Evidence for human infection with an HTLV III/ LAV-like virus in central Africa, 1959. *Lancet* 1(8492): 1279–1280.

Nairobi Declaration Signatories. 2000. The Nairobi Declaration: An African appeal for an AIDS vaccine. Nairobi, June 14. Available at: http://www.who.int/vaccine_research/diseases/hiv/aavp/en. Accessed: January 25, 2004.

Najera, I., D. D. Richman, I. Olivares, et al. 1994. Natural occurrence of drug resistance mutations in their reverse transcriptase of human immunodeficiency virus type 1 isolates. *AIDS Research and Human Retroviruses* 10(11): 1479–1488.

National Pharmaceutical Pricing Authority (India). 1986. Drug Policy 1986: Introductory. Available at: http://www.nppaindia.nic.in/drug_pol86/txt1.html. Accessed: April 6, 2004.

Nessman, R. 2000. International news: Soweto, South Africa. Associated Press, October 24, 2000.

———. 2001. AIDS activists sue South Africa. Associated Press, August 21, 2001.

Noikorn, U. AIDS activists win court battle against US drug maker. Associated Press, October 1, 2002.

O'Brien, T., R. George, and S. D. Holmberg. 1992. Human immunodeficiency virus type 2 infection in the United States. *Journal of the American Medical Association* 267(20): 2775–2779.

Olmos, H. 2000a. Brazilian bishops propose condom use to check spread of AIDS. Associated Press, June 13, 2000.

———. 2000b. Brazil bishops condemn condom use. Associated Press, June 16, 2000.

Organization for African Unity. 2001. Abuja Declaration on HIV/AIDS, Tuberculosis and Other Related Infectious Diseases, April 24–27, 2001. Available at: http://www.un.org/ga/aids/pdf/abuja_declaration.pdf. Accessed: April 6, 2004.

Outlook Reporters. We care—show you care (HIV/AIDS medicine bank). *Bangkok Post*, 29, December 1998.

Pan African News Agency. 2001a. Botswana offers free anti-retroviral therapy. Pan African News Agency, June 5, 2001.

———. 2001b. Botswana plans HIV/AIDS anti-retroviral therapy. Pan African News Agency, October 30, 2001.

Pan, P. P. As China faces crisis, people with HIV are kept largely invisible; Beijing fears "losing control of the message." *Washington Post*, 20 November 2001, A16.

Petersen, M., and D. G. McNeil Jr. Maker yielding patent in Africa for AIDS drug. *New York Times*, 15 March 2001, A1.

Petricciani, J. C. 1985. Licensed tests for antibody to human T-lymphotropic virus type III. *Annals of Internal Medicine* 103: 726–729.

Pharmaceutical company lawsuit (forty-two applicants) against the government of South Africa (ten respondents). Case number: 4183/98. February 18, 1998.

Piatak, M., Jr., M. S. Saag, L. D. Yang, et al. 1993. High levels of HIV-1 in plasma during all stages of infection determined by competitive PCR. *Science* 259(5102): 1749–1754.

Piot, P., F. A. Plummer, M. A. Rey, et al. 1987. Retrospective seroepidemiology of AIDS virus infection in Nairobi populations. *Journal of Infectious Diseases* 133(6): 1108–1112.

Pomfret, J. Chinese city is first to enact law on AIDS; controversial rules set for infected people, high-risk groups. *Washington Post*, 15 January 2001, A16.

P. R. Newswire. 2001. Ugandan government and international AIDS

Vaccine Initiative sign agreement to accelerate testing of AIDS vaccines. *P. R. Newswire,* 30 August 2001.

Quinn, T. C., J. M. Mann, J. W. Curran, and P. Piot. 1986. AIDS in Africa: An epidemiologic paradigm. *Science* 234: 955–963.

Quiros-Roldan, E., F. Castelli, A. Pan, et al. 2001. Evidence of HIV-2 infection in northern Italy. *Infection* 29: 362–363.

Ramachandran, P. 1991. Sentinel surveillance for HIV infection. *CARC Calling* 4: 25.

Renoirte, R., J. L. Michaux, F. Gatti, et al. 1967. Nouveaux cas d'histoplasmose africaine et de cryptococcose observés en République Démocratique do Congo. *Bull Acad Roy Med Belg* 7: 465–527.

Reuters. Brazil to give teens junior-sized condoms. *Reuters,* 11 June 1996.

————. Thai kindergarten children to get sex education. *Reuters,* 19 July 2000.

————. WHO urges pharmaceutical firms to cut prices for poor. *Reuters NewMedia,* 11 April 2001.

————. Doctors group helps spread AIDS strategy. *New York Times,* 13 September 2001, B2.

————. Ivax, a generic drug maker, to supply an anthrax drug. *New York Times,* 27 October 2001, C4.

————. China, facing AIDS threat, to upgrade blood banks. *Reuters,* 30 January 2002.

————. Brazil leads Portuguese countries in AIDS fight. *Reuters,* 31 July 2002.

Rich, J. L. Roche reaches accord on drug with Brazil. *New York Times,* 1 September 2001, C1.

Rich, J. L., and M. Petersen. Brazil will defy patent on AIDS drug made by Roche. *New York Times,* 23 August 2001, C6.

Richards, T. 2000. UK defines action to tackle health in developing countries. *British Medical Journal* 321: 1434.

Richman, D., A. S. Rosenthal, M. Skoog, et al. 1991. BI-RG-587 is active against zidovudine-resistant human immunodeficiency virus type 1 and synergistic with zidovudine. *Antimicrobial Agents and Chemotherapy* 35(2): 305–308.

Riley, M. Cheap AIDS drugs on the way as Australia fights for region. *Sydney Morning Herald,* 29 June 2001, 1.

Robertson, D. L., B. H. Hahn, and P. M. Sharp. 1995. Recombination in AIDS viruses. *Journal of Molecular Evolution* 40(3): 249–259.

Roche Pharmaceuticals and Trimeris, Inc. April 18, 2002. Roche and Trimeris announce 24-week results from first phase III study of HIV fusion inhibitor T-20 [press release]. Nutley and Durham: Roche Pharmaceuticals.

Rojanapithayakorn, W., and R. Hanenberg. 1996. The 100% Condom Program in Thailand. *AIDS* 10: 1–7.

Rosenthal, E. Chinese media suddenly focus on a growing AIDS problem. *New York Times*, 17 December 2000, A6.

———. China raises HIV count in new report. *New York Times*, 12 April 2002, A10.

Rübsamen-Waigmann, H., H. V. Briesen, J. K. Maniar, et al. 1991a. Spread of HIV-2 in India. *Lancet* 337: 550–551.

Rübsamen-Waigmann, H., A. Prutzner, C. Scholz, et al. 1991b. Spread of HIV-2 in India. Presented at: VII International Conference on AIDS, June 16–21, Florence, Italy. Abstract number M.C.3291.

Russell, S. Path-breaking AIDS activist tells of detention in China. *San Francisco Chronicle*, 13 November 2002, A12.

Sabino, E. C., E. G. Shpaer, M. G. Morgado, et al. 1994. Identification of human immunodeficiency virus type 1 envelope genes recombinant between subtypes B and F in two epidemiologically linked individuals from Brazil. *Journal of Virology* 68(10): 6340–6346.

Samson, M., F. Libert, B. J. Doranz, et al. 1996. Resistance to HIV-1 infection in Caucasian individuals bearing mutant alleles of the CCR-5 chemokine receptor gene. *Nature* 382(6593): 722–725.

Sankari, S., S. Solomon, et al. 1991. Trends of HIV infection in antenatal/ infertility clinics—an ominous sign. Presented at: VII International Conference on AIDS, June 16–21, Florence, Italy. Abstract number W.C.3236.

Sanz, M. Cuban cooperation with South Africa could include patent-busting AIDS drugs. *Agence France Presse*, 28 March 2001.

Schneider, H., and J. Stein. 2001. Implementing AIDS policy in post-Apartheid South Africa. *Social Science and Medicine* 52: 723–731.

Schoofs, M. Clinton program would help poor nations get AIDS drugs. *Wall Street Journal*, 23 October 2003, B5.

Schoofs, M., and M. Waldholz. Drug companies, Senegal agree to low-cost HIV drug pact. *Wall Street Journal*, 24 October 2000, A3.

Selsky, A. 2000. South Africa lashes at drug companies. Associated Press, March 20, 2000.

Serwadda, D., N. K. Sewankambo, J. W. Carswell, et al. 1985. Slim disease: A new disease in Uganda and its association with HTLV-III infection. *Lancet* 2(8460): 849–852.

Shaffer, N., R. Chuachoowong, P. A. Mock, et al. 1999. Short-course zidovudine for perinatal HIV-1 transmission in Bangkok, Thailand: A randomized controlled trial. *Lancet* 353(9155): 773–780.

Shargorodsky, S. 2000. AIDS virus spreading in the former Soviet republics. Associated Press, July 9, 2000.

Sidley, P. Government sitting on findings. *Business Day* (South Africa), 17 September 2001, 3.

Smallman-Raynor, M., and A. Cliff. 1991. The spread of human immunodeficiency virus type 2 into Europe: A geographical analysis. *International Journal of Epidemiology* 20(2): 480–489.

Srinath, M. G. India gets condom vending machines amid concerns about population growth. *Deutsche Presse-Agentur,* 1 August 1999.

Steinglass, M. In South Africa, politics hinder AIDS treatment. *Boston Globe,* 11 June 2002, B7.

Stevenson, R. A nation challenged: the economy: Reconciling the demands of war and the market. *New York Times,* 28 October 2001, B10.

Strebel, K., T. Klimkait, and M. A. Martin. 1988. A novel gene of HIV-1, vpu, and its 16-kilodalton product. *Science* 241(4870): 1221–1223.

Sui, C. Henan AIDS sufferers win partial victory following protest. *Agence France Presse,* 27 March 2002.

Swarns, R. L. South Africa in a furor over advice about AIDS. *New York Times,* 19 March 2000, A21.

Tang, M. 1996. Brazil: New industrial property legislation. National Law Center for Inter-American Free Trade Report, 1996. Available at: http:// www.natlaw.com/pubs/spbrip1.htm. Accessed: April 7, 2004.

Tarantola, D. 2001. Facing the reality of AIDS—a 15-year process? *Bulletin of the World Health Organization* 79(12): 1095.

Thom, A., and K. Cullinan. 2002. KZN join TAC in MTCT court case against government. Health-E Online Health News Service, January 3, 2002. Available at: http://www.africamediaonline.com/showfile. asp?fileid=671. Accessed: April 7, 2004.

Tyndall, M., P. Odhiambo, and A. R. Ronald. 1991. The increasing seroprevalence of HIV-1 in males with other STDs in Nairobi, Kenya. Presented at: VII International Conference on AIDS, June 16–21, Florence, Italy. Abstract number W.C.3117.

UNAIDS, UNICEF. Epidemiology in sub-Saharan Africa: May 1996. Available at: http://www.unaids.org/en/in+focus/topic+areas/estimates +and+projections+-+epidemiology.asp?StartRow=300. Accessed: April 7, 2004.

UNAIDS. HIV/AIDS: The Global Epidemic Estimates as of December 1996. Available at: http://www.unaids.org/en/in+focus/topic+areas/estimates+and+projections+-+epidemiology.asp?StartRow=300. Accessed: April 7, 2004.

———. 2000a. History of World AIDS Day, 2000. Available at: http://www.unaids.org/wac/2000/wad00/files/history_WAD.htm. Accessed: April 7, 2004.

———. 2000b. Accelerating Access to HIV/AIDS Care, Support and Treatment Participants. 8 May 2000. Accelerating access to HIV/AIDS care and treatment in developing countries: a joint statement of intent. Geneva: UNAIDS.

———. 2000c. New Public/ Private sector effort initiated to accelerate access to HIV/AIDS care and treatment in developing countries [press release]. Geneva: UNAIDS, May 11.

———. 2000d. Report of the first meeting of the Contact Group on Accelerating Access to HIV/AIDS-Related Care. Geneva: UNAIDS, September 29.

———. 2000e. Summary of the second meeting of the Contact Group on Accelerating Access to HIV/AIDS-Related Care, Rio de Janeiro. Geneva: UNAIDS, December 13.

———. 2001a. Third meeting of the Contact Group on Accelerating Access to HIV/AIDS-Related Care: summary status. Geneva: UNAIDS, May 7.

———. 2001b. Global estimates of HIV/AIDS epidemic as of end of 2001. Available at: http://www.unaids.org/html/pub/Global-Reports/Barcelona/BRTableGlobalEstimatesEnd2001_en_pdf.htm. Accessed: April 7, 2004.

———. 2002a. Fourth meeting of the Contact Group on Accelerating Access to HIV/AIDS-Related Care. Geneva: UNAIDS, May 28.

———. 2002b. UNAIDS/WHO global and regional HIV/AIDS estimates end–2002. Available at: http://www.unaids.org/html/pub/Topics/Epidemiology/RegionalEstimates2002_en_pdf.htm. Accessed: April 7, 2004.

———. 2003. What is UNAIDS? Available at: http://www.unaids.org/en/about+unaids/what+is+unaids.asp. Accessed: October 4, 2003.

UNAIDS and WHO. 2001. Meeting with Cipla [joint press statement]. Geneva: UNAIDS, March 22.

Ungphakorn, J., and W. Sittitrai. 1994. The Thai response to the HIV/AIDS epidemic. *AIDS* 8(suppl. 2): S155–S163.

United Nations. 2000. Security council holds debate on impact of AIDS on peace and security in Africa [press release], January 10. Available at: http://www.un.org/News/Press/docs/2000/20000110.sc6781.doc.htm l. Accessed: April 7, 2004.

———. 2001. Declaration of Commitment on HIV/AIDS. Available at: http://www.un.org/ga/aids/coverage/FinalDeclarationHIVAIDS.htm l. Accessed: April 7, 2004.

U.S. Centers for Disease Control. 1981. Pneumocystis pneumonia—Los Angeles. *Morbidity and Mortality Weekly Report* 30(21): 1–3.

———. 1984. International Conference on Acquired Immunodeficiency Syndrome. *Morbidity and Mortality Weekly Report* 33(30): 444.

———. 1998. Report of the NIH Panel to Define Principles of Therapy of HIV Infection and Guidelines for the Use of Antiretroviral Agents in HIV-Infected Adults and Adolescents. *Morbidity and Mortality Weekly Report* 47(RR-5): 43–83.

———. 2000. The XIII International AIDS Conference Home Page. Available at: http://www.cdc.gov/nchstp/od/Durban/default.htm. Accessed: April 7, 2004.

U.S. Department of State. 2000. U.N. Security Council Resolution on AIDS Crisis. Available at: http://usembassy-australia.state.gov/hyper/2000/0718/epf207.htm. Accessed: April 7, 2004.

U.S. Embassy in China. 2000. Background on revealing the blood wound of the spread of HIV/AIDS in Henan Province—written on the eve of the first AIDS day if the new millennium. Available at: http://www.usembassy-china.org.cn/sandt/henan-hiv.htm. Accessed: April 5, 2004.

U.S. Food and Drug Administration. Antiretroviral HIV Drug Approvals and Pediatric Labeling Information. Available at: http://www.fda.gov/oashi/aids/pedlbl.html. Accessed: April 7, 2004.

———. FDA approves first drug in new class of HIV treatments for HIV infected adults and children with advanced disease. *FDA News,* 13 March 2003, 3–15.

Van de Perre, P., P. Lepage, P. Kestelyn, et al. 1984. Acquired immunodeficiency syndrome in Rwanda. *Lancet* 2(8394): 62–65.

Van Leeuwen, R., J. J. Lange, E. K. Hussey, et al. 1992. The safety and pharmacokinetics of a reverse transcriptase inhibitor, 3TC, in patients with HIV infection: A phase I study. *AIDS* 6(12): 1471–1475.

Vandepitte, J., R. Verwilghen, and P. Zachee. 1983. AIDS and cryptococcosis (Zaire, 1977). *Lancet* 1(8330): 925–926.

Vella, S. 1994. Update on a proteinase inhibitor. *AIDS* 8(suppl. 3): S25–S29.

VI International Conference on AIDS. 1991. AIDS 90 summary: A practical synopsis of the VI international conference, June 20–24, 1990, San Francisco. Richmond: Philadelphia Sciences Group.

Wade, C. M. 2002. China to produce generic AIDS drugs. United Press International, September 24, 2002.

Wakin, D. 1999. President's claim that AIDS drug is dangerous sets off debate. Associated Press, November 3, 1999.

Wang, B., R. B. Lal, D. Dwyer, et al. 2000. Molecular and biological interactions between two HIV-1 strains from a coinfected patient reveal the first evidence in favor of viral synergism. *Virology* 274(1): 105–119.

Watkins, J. D., C. Conway-Welch, J. J. Creedon, et al. 1988. Report of the Presidential Commission on the Human Immunodeficiency Virus Epidemic. June 1988.

Weniger, B. G., K. Limpakarnjanarat, K. Ungchusak, et al. 1991. The epidemiology of HIV infection and AIDS in Thailand. *AIDS* 5(suppl. 2): S71–S85.

World Health Organization. 2001. New offers of low-cost antiretroviral medicines: A statement from the World Health Organization [statement WHO/04]. February 9.

———. 2002. New international coalition aims to expand global access to HIV/AIDS treatment [press release].

World Health Organization Global Programme on AIDS. 1989. For delegates at the Vth International Conference on AIDS Montreal, 4 to 9 June 1989. Geneva: World Health Organization.

World Medical Association. 2000. World Medical Association Declaration of Helsinki Ethical Principles for Medical Research Involving Human Subjects. Available at: http://www.wma.net/e/policy/b3.htm. Accessed: April 7, 2004.

World Trade Organization. 1994. The final act embodying the results of the Uruguay round of multilateral trade negotiations: Annex 1C Agreement on Trade-Related Aspects of Intellectual Property Rights. Uruguay: World Trade Organization.

———. 2001a. Brazil—measures affecting patent protection: Request for the establishment of a panel by the United States. Available at: http://www.cptech.org/ip/health/c/brazil/Req4EstabPanel.html. Accessed: April 7, 2004.

———. 2001b. Declaration on the TRIPS agreement and public health WT/MIN(01)/DEC/2. Doha: World Trade Organization.

Xinhua News Agency. 2000. China has more HIV carriers. Xinhua General News Service, October 31, 2000.

————. 2002a. Zimbabwe to produce generic drugs to fight AIDS. Xinhua General News Service, January 29, 2002.

————. 2002b. Thailand to join Asian research on causes of AIDS stigma. Xinhua General News Service, August 26, 2002.

Yablokova, O. Russia says it is trying to head off AIDS epidemic. *Moscow Times*, 30 November 1999, sec. 1848.

Yarchoan, R., R. W. Klecker, K. J. Weinhold, et al. 1986. Administration of 3'-azido–3'-deoxythymidine, an inhibitor of HTLV-III/LAV replication, to patients with AIDS or AIDS-related complex. *Lancet* 1(8481): 575–580.

Yarchoan, R., H. Mitsuya, R. V. Thomas, et al. 1989. In vivo activity against HIV and favorable toxicity profile of 2¥,3¥ -Dideoxyinosine. *Science* 245(4916): 412–415.

Yarchoan, R., C. F. Perno, R. V. Thomas, et al. 1988. Phase I studies of 2',3'-dideoxycytidine in severe human immunodeficiency virus infection as a single agent and alternating with zidovudine (AZT). *Lancet* 1(8577): 76–81.

Zimmerman, R. Glaxo unveils another price cut for AIDS drugs to poor countries. *Wall Street Journal*, 11 June 2001, B7.

————. World Health Organization prepares list of quality AIDS medication. *Wall Street Journal*, 20 March 2002, B13.

Zimmerman, R., R. Block, and D. Pearl. Bristol-Myers offers not to sue firm seeking to make AIDS drugs for Africa. *Wall Street Journal*, 19 July 2001, A2.

Zimmerman, R., and M. Schoofs. Merck to cut cost of AIDS drug in poorest nations. *Wall Street Journal*, 23 October 2002, A2.

Zuber, M., K. P. Samuel, J. A. Lautenberger, et al. 1990. Bacterially produced HIV-2 env polypeptides specific for distinguishing HIV-2 from HIV-1 infections. *AIDS Research and Human Retroviruses* 6(4): 525–534.

4

Biographies

Cultural, economic, and political differences have led to significant variation in the dynamics and impact of the HIV epidemic from one nation to the next. Local and national responses to the epidemic reflect the political systems and social norms that shape a given society. Within the global "mosaic" of epidemics affecting different communities and evolving at different rates in each region, only a few individuals can have an impact on the "global" AIDS epidemic. At the local or provincial level, however, one person or organization can profoundly affect community and national responses to the epidemic and to people living with HIV and AIDS. These responses in turn can influence how the world understands the unique concerns and challenges HIV and AIDS pose to a specific region.

The following selection of biographical sketches focuses on people whose efforts to fight the AIDS epidemic locally have drawn worldwide attention to the medical, social, and political aspects of national responses. For some individuals, such as Eloan Pinheiro and Festus Mogae, action against HIV and AIDS is facilitated by support from national government, allowing for the creation of responses to HIV and AIDS that can become globally applicable models for government intervention. For others, such as Zackie Achmat, Gao Yaojie, and Wan Yanhai, active opposition of national policies on HIV and AIDS brings international attention to underserved regions and communities. People living with HIV and AIDS such as Elizabeth Glaser and Jahnabi Goswami help to put a human face on the epidemic for individuals who are not directly affected, drawing attention to underserved groups affected by the virus such as women and children.

Celebrities such as Bono and Mpule Kwelagobe have used enter-tainment and educational forums to educate the international community about HIV and AIDS, combating stigma and increas-ing awareness of the impact of HIV in underdeveloped regions. All individuals represented in this chapter have helped to shape the world's perception of the epidemic and have worked to over-come global and local disparities in access to education, care, and treatment.

Zackie Achmat (1962–)

Zackie Achmat founded South Africa's Treatment Action Cam-paign (TAC) in 1998 to protest the inaccessibility of antiretroviral medications in resource-scarce regions, particularly in sub-Saha-ran Africa. More recently, Achmat and the TAC have focused legal and grassroots activism on the South African government's lack of action to make HIV and AIDS care and treatment more affordable and available in the country (Treatment Action Cam-paign, n.d.). Achmat began his career as an equal-rights advocate in the 1970s, organizing youth protests against apartheid and coordinating antiapartheid efforts with labor and health organi-zations. After the fall of apartheid, Achmat founded the National Coalition for Gay and Lesbian Equality in South Africa to lobby for nondiscrimination in South Africa's constitution and to cam-paign for greater recognition of gay and lesbian relationships in society and in the eyes of the law. From 1994 through 1997, Achmat directed the AIDS Law Project in South Africa (H. W. Wilson Company, 2003).

Under Zackie Achmat's leadership, the Treatment Action Campaign has worked since 1998 to educate the South African government, people living with HIV and AIDS, and communities throughout the country on the availability and feasibility of free or low-cost treatment for HIV and the opportunistic infections associated with AIDS. Shortly after its formation, the Treatment Access Campaign became involved in protests against patent pro-tection for antiretroviral drugs. The campaign mobilized grass-roots support for generic drug manufacture in South Africa, pub-licizing the health and human rights repercussions of the Pharmaceutical Manufacturers Association's 1998 lawsuit against the South African government. Between 1998 and 2004, the Treat-ment Action Campaign successfully lobbied for the development of a national HIV and AIDS treatment plan and the delivery of nevirapine to all HIV-infected pregnant women to prevent mother-to-child HIV transmission (Treatment Action Campaign, n.d.). As a person living with HIV as well as an effective leader, Zackie Achmat has brought international attention to the impact of HIV and AIDS in South Africa and has energized activists worldwide to demand access to affordable HIV and AIDS support and care.

Kofi Annan (1938–)

Kofi Annan is the United Nations' seventh secretary-general. Born in Ghana, Annan studied economics and management in Ghana, Geneva, and the United States, and began work for the United Nations as an officer of the World Health Organization in 1962. He has also worked with the United Nations Economic Commission for Africa, the United Nations Emergency Force, and the Office of the United Nations High Commissioner for Refugees. Kofi Annan was appointed as UN secretary-general in 1997 and was recommended for a second term in 2001 (United Nations, 2003).

As secretary-general, Annan has created partnerships with nongovernmental organizations, businesses, and labor organizations in order to "renew" the United Nations as an ally in ensuring that the benefits of globalization are available to all constituencies within member states (United Nations, 2003). The United Nations Millennium Declaration, issued in September 2000, reflects Annan's personal priorities, including "collective responsibility to uphold the principles of human dignity, equality and equity at the global level." In addition to these general statements, the Millennium Declaration also states that United Nations Member States will "by [2015] have halted, and begun to reverse, the spread of HIV/AIDS, the scourge of malaria, and other major diseases that afflict humanity" (United Nations, 2000, sec. III: 19).

In 2001, Kofi Annan called for the development of a global fund to fight HIV and AIDS at the African Summit on HIV/AIDS, Tuberculosis, and Other Infectious Diseases in Abuja, Nigeria. Calling HIV a "continent-wide emergency," Annan estimated that US$7 to US$10 billion per year would be necessary to appropriately address HIV and AIDS along with other infectious diseases common in developing countries. This call to action led to the formation of the Global Fund to Fight AIDS, Tuberculosis, and Malaria in 2001. In Abuja, Annan also stressed that African leaders must initiate the fight against AIDS in their own regions, insisting that "only you can mobilize your citizens for this great battle [and] only you can give it the priority it deserves in your national budgets." At the end of his speech in Abuja, Annan stated: "we cannot and should not choose between prevention and treatment. We must do both," encouraging government leaders to "exploit all options to the full—including the production and importation of 'generic' drugs under license" (United Nations, 2001).

In 2001 the Norwegian Nobel Committee awarded the Nobel Peace Prize to both Kofi Annan and the United Nations. The committee's announcement states that "while clearly underlining the UN's traditional responsibility for peace and security, [Kofi Annan] has also emphasized its obligations with regard to human rights" (Associated Press, 12 October 2001).

Bono (1960–)

Bono has been the lead singer of the Irish rock band U2 since 1976. Throughout his musical career Bono has acted as a spokesman for a wide range of civil and human rights causes. In 1999, Bono embarked on the "Jubilee 2000" campaign, lobbying U.S. government officials and other members of the Group of Eight nations to forgive the debts owed by the world's poorest countries (Byrne, 1995). In 2001, Bono met with U.S. Secretary of State Colin Powell to discuss debt relief and support for HIV and AIDS care and treatment in Africa. Although this meeting was dismissed by many as a publicity stunt, Bono's encounter with the secretary of state brought nationwide attention to AIDS in Africa and the issue of debt relief for resource-scarce countries (*Agence France Presse*, 16 March 2002). A year later, Bono embarked on a two-week tour of Ghana, South Africa, Uganda, and Ethiopia with U.S. Secretary of the Treasury Paul O'Neill (*Reuters*, 30 May 2002). The trip was described as a "fact finding tour" to determine the future scale of U.S. development and humanitarian aid in the African countries hardest hit by the AIDS epidemic (*Agence France Presse*, 24 May 2002). During the course of the trip, Bono met with former South African President Nelson Mandela and visited schools, clinics, and orphanages. Through international news broadcasts, Bono challenged African governments to deliver antiretroviral medication to HIV-infected pregnant women and others living with HIV and AIDS (*Agence France Presse,* 25 May 2002). At the end of the two-week tour, Paul O'Neill pledged to "campaign" among leaders of the Group of Eight nations to increase aid for Africa, focusing on funding for clean water, primary education, and HIV and AIDS care and prevention (*Agence France Presse,* 28 May 2002).

Siddharth Dube (1961–)

A native of Calcutta, India, Dube has worked since the late 1990s to educate the Indian public about the extent of HIV's spread in the country and the low level of government support for prevention and care interventions. After publishing his first book, a novel examining economic and class disparities in India, Dube wrote *Sex, Lies, and AIDS,* a frank examination of the Indian government's response to the rapid spread of HIV in the country (Khan, 1999). Upon publication in 2000, *Sex, Lies, and AIDS* immediately became a national best-seller in India, hailed by literary critics as "A lucid, compelling and indefatigably researched attempt to stem the tide of denial, prejudice, ineptitude and bigotry that characterize Indian attitudes and policies on sex" (Khan, 1999). *Sex, Lies, and AIDS* contains an annex titled "A Kama Sutra for the Age of AIDS: How to Have Safer Sex," an informational guide considered "remarkable" (Khan, 1999) in light of the Indian government's refusal to support discussion of safer sex strategies (Dube, 2001).

In a 2001 editorial in the *Washington Post* Dube drew attention to the fact that India alone could be home to 35 million adults and children living with HIV and AIDS by 2005 if the epidemic is not immediately addressed. Calling the Indian government's response to HIV "baffling," Dube cited Tamil Nadu and West Bengal states as examples of regions with successful prevention programs. In Tamil Nadu, the state government sponsors treatment for sexually transmitted diseases, information campaigns, and sex education in schools. In West Bengal, sex workers have formed a union to protect individuals from becoming infected with HIV through exploitation or lack of appropriate information. Writing in an international forum, Dube called on the Indian government to implement such "painless" programs nationwide before the HIV epidemic spirals out of control. The editorial concludes by stating that although prevention has succeeded in some areas, "disbelief and discomfort" are likely to prevent the implementation of effective prevention measures throughout India (Dube, 2001).

Costa Gazi (1939–)

Costa Gazi became involved with the antiapartheid movement in South Africa as a member of the South African Communist Party in the 1960s and later as a member of the Pan Africanist Congress. After being arrested in 1964 for participating in "dissident activities" in South Africa, Dr. Gazi was jailed for two years then exiled to Europe until apartheid fell. Since returning to South Africa in the 1990s, Dr. Gazi has worked as a physician and professor of medicine in rural clinics and district hospitals in Eastern Cape Province and as the Pan Africanist Congress's health secretary (Helen Suzman Foundation, 2000).

In November 1999, Dr. Gazi filed a complaint with South Africa's Human Rights Commission against President Thabo Mbeki and Health Minister Manto Tshabalala-Msimang. Dr. Gazi's complaint accused the president and health minister of refusing to "ever admit that the anti-viral drugs will be affordable" and of questioning the safety and efficacy of proven antiretroviral drugs such as zidovudine and nevirapine to prevent mother-to-child transmission of HIV (*Agence France Presse*, 1 November 1999). Less than a year later, Dr. Gazi was fined for slander against South Africa's previous Health Minister Nkosazana Dlamini-Zuma after suggesting that Dlamini-Zuma be tried for manslaughter after she refused to support zidovudine distribution in public hospitals to prevent mother-to-child HIV transmission (Dickson, 2000). In the spring of 2000 Dr. Gazi announced that if the South African government would not fund distribution of antiretroviral drugs to HIV-infected pregnant women he would personally pay to provide nevirapine to twenty local clinics in Eastern Cape. Dr. Gazi estimated that close to 350 pregnant women living with HIV and AIDS were treated each month in Eastern Cape's clinics during 2000 (Dickson, 2000). Later in the year Gazi and several other officials from the Pan Africanist Congress were publicly tested for HIV infection to increase awareness about HIV prevention and testing and to combat stigma against seeking an HIV test (*Agence France Presse*, 23 May 2000). Along with the Treatment Action Campaign, Gazi has used grassroots activism to draw attention to HIV and AIDS in the region and encourage individuals to become involved in caring for and promoting the rights of people living with AIDS.

Elizabeth Glaser (1947–1994)

Elizabeth Glaser founded the Pediatric AIDS Foundation in 1988 with her friends Susan DeLaurentis and Susie Zeegan after discovering that she had been infected with HIV along with her husband, son, and daughter. In the late 1980s and early 1990s little HIV research focused on care and treatment for children living with HIV and AIDS. The Pediatric AIDS Foundation's initial mission was to identify and fund clinical research on HIV treatment and prevention among infants, children, and adolescents living with HIV and AIDS. In 1997, three years after Elizabeth Glaser's death, the organization was renamed the Elizabeth Glaser Pediatric AIDS Foundation (Elizabeth Glaser Pediatric AIDS Foundation a). The foundation is one of the first organizations of its kind to focus research support on children living with and affected by HIV and AIDS.

In September 1999 the foundation launched the Call to Action Project, an initiative focused on preventing mother-to-child HIV transmission in developing countries. The project was active in seventeen countries in Africa, Asia, Eastern Europe, and South America in 2003, aiming to serve more than 500,000 women each year. In addition to increasing access to clinical care and treatment, the Call to Action Project trains health care providers and community members in HIV prevention and care and seeks to increase women's access to confidential, voluntary counseling and HIV testing services (Elizabeth Glaser Pediatric AIDS Foundation b).

Jahnabi Goswami (1977–)

In 2002, Goswami became the first woman in India's Assam Province to publicly declare that she is living with HIV. Goswami's husband died of AIDS in 1996, and her daughter died just one year later. Ostracized by in-laws, landlords, and members of the local community, Goswami began to work for the Assam AIDS Control Society, the only government HIV and AIDS organization in the province. Through the society she formed the Assam Network of Positive People, encouraging others to tour the province with her to tell their own stories and to educate isolated communities about HIV transmission and stigma (Hussain, 2002). Goswami's outreach has helped educate the world about HIV and AIDS in India and has begun to combat the intense stigma people living with HIV and AIDS face in the region upon revealing their positive status.

Yusuf Hamied (1937–)

Hamied has owned the Indian generic drug manufacturer Cipla since before the first cases of AIDS were diagnosed in India. He inherited the company from his father, who founded Cipla in 1935 to produce medicines for India when war prevented imports from Europe (Boseley, 2003). Cipla manufactures generic versions of antibiotics, vitamins, cardiovascular drugs, antidepressants, and a range of other medications, and exports its products to 130 countries worldwide, including the United States. Cipla is legally able to produce generic copies of drugs that are patented elsewhere under the 1970 Indian Patents Act, which protects pharmaceutical patent holders' rights to production processes but not to components of drugs or to the final product (Yi, 2001).

Cipla began to manufacture generic versions of antiretroviral drugs to treat HIV and AIDS in the early 1990s, offering triple-combination antiretroviral therapy for a fraction of the $10,000–$12,000 per year it cost in the United States (Biswas, 2003). As rates of HIV infection continued to increase dramatically in India and around the world in the 1990s, Hamied focused his efforts on making HIV and AIDS treatment "a humanitarian problem, not a money problem." In September 2000, Hamied attended a European Commission meeting on poverty and infectious diseases, where he announced that Cipla would begin to sell combination antiretroviral drugs for US$800 per patient per year, about one-fourth the price of antiretroviral therapy purchased in developed countries such as the United States. At the same time, Hamied offered to donate technology and expertise to any developing countries that wanted to manufacture generic antiretrovirals locally (Boris, 2001). Less than six months later, Cipla introduced a new pricing plan for antiretroviral drugs, charging governments US$600 per patient per year and offering to sell antiretroviral drugs to nongovernmental organizations for US$350 per patient per year, or less than US$1 per day (Boris, 2001).

Reacting in part to Hamied's announcement, patent-holding pharmaceutical companies began to lower their prices for anti-retroviral drugs in resource-scarce regions to about US$600 per patient per year (Petersen and McNeil, 2001). In the same month the pharmaceutical companies suing the South African government to prevent the manufacture or import of generic drugs withdrew their case (Cooper, Zimmerman, and McGinley, 2001). In 2003, Hamied agreed to sell Cipla's triple combination antiretroviral drugs for as little as US$140 per patient per year in some circumstances. In October Hamied entered into collaboration with the William J. Clinton Presidential Foundation to produce and distribute enough antiretroviral medication to treat up to two million people in developing countries by 2008 (Biswas, 2003). Yusuf Hamied and Cipla have helped to fundamentally change the way that national governments support HIV and AIDS care, making antiretroviral medications more accessible and empowering governments to consider local production of essential drugs.

Mpule Kwelagobe (1980–)

Mpule Kwelagobe won the Miss Universe Pageant in 1999. She was the first delegate from Botswana ever to enter the competition. Since she became Miss Universe, Kwelagobe has dedicated her time to educating African youth and adolescents about HIV transmission and prevention (Face to Face International, Inc., 2001). The United Nations Population Fund (UNFPA) named Kwelagobe its goodwill ambassador for Botswana in 2000 as "a symbol of hope and optimism for the young people" (UNFPA, 2000). In 2001 Kwelagobe spoke in Senegal at a UNFPA panel cosponsored by the Senegalese government with Miss Universe delegates from India and Trinidad and Tobago on building capacity among young people for action on HIV and AIDS (Panafrican News Agency, 2001b).

In 1999, the Botswana government and DeBeers (a multinational diamond mining company) funded the creation of the Mpule Kwelagobe Children's Village, which provides care and housing for children living with and affected by HIV and AIDS. Kwelagobe has also helped to support community-based organizations in Botswana that provide home-based and hospice care for people living with HIV and AIDS (Face to Face International, Inc., 2001).

Festus Mogae (1939–)

Mogae was elected president of Botswana in 1999. At the time that he assumed office, average HIV prevalence among pregnant women in urban areas was nearly 40 percent. In 1999 Botswana initiated a mother-to-child HIV transmission prevention program, delivering zidovudine and infant formula free to women who tested positive for HIV infection (Panafrican News Agency, 2001c). Two years later, in June 2001, President Mogae announced that Botswana's public health care system would begin to distribute highly active antiretroviral therapy to all people living with HIV and AIDS in the country. This announcement marked the beginning of Africa's first comprehensive, government-sponsored HIV and AIDS care and treatment initiative (Panafrican News Agency, 2001a).

In order to afford a sufficient supply of antiretroviral drugs, Mogae negotiated price reductions with several pharmaceutical companies and increased Botswana's health budget three-fold over two years (Panafrican News Agency, 2001a). Mogae set a goal of treating 19,000 people living with AIDS in hospitals in the cities of Francistown, Gaborone, Maun, and Serowe during the program's first year of operation, expanding to treat a total of 20,000 people each year nationwide. During this phase, the country's mother-to-child transmission prevention program was expanded from its first pilot sites to serve the entire country (Panafrican News Agency, 2001c). At the end of the year, Botswana and President Mogae hosted a workshop to establish partnerships among donor agencies, government, researchers, and community members to create a network of HIV vaccine trials in sub-Saharan Africa (Panafrican News Agency, 2001d).

By the fall of 2003, about 9,000 people with HIV and AIDS were receiving antiretroviral treatment through Botswana's national program (Donnelly, 2003). This total remains significantly lower than the estimated 110,000 people in Botswana who need antiretroviral treatment and represents less than half of the number of individuals President Mogae hoped to treat within the program's first two years (UN Integrated Regional Information Networks, 2003). Attributing the national program's low enrollment to individuals' reluctance to be tested for HIV, Mogae announced in 2003 that the public health care system would begin to routinely test all patients for HIV nationwide (UN Integrated Regional Information Networks, 2003). Earlier in the year, President Mogae publicly announced that he had been tested for HIV infection following an illness with symptoms similar to AIDS. He was actually suffering from diabetes and shortly announced a negative HIV test result. This series of announcements marks the frankest discussion of HIV infection yet from an African government leader (Donnelly, 2003). Mogae continues to discuss HIV and AIDS in his state-of-the-nation addresses, seeking to decrease stigma and reluctance to be tested for HIV through public pleas for tolerance and behavior change (*Agence France Presse*, 10 November 2003). In 2003, Botswana's response to HIV and AIDS is considered to be a successful program that provides an important model for similar efforts in other developing countries worldwide (*Agence France Presse*, 10 November 2003).

Janet Museveni

Janet Museveni has been Uganda's first lady since 1986 when her husband, President Yoweri Museveni took office. In 1986 Museveni founded the Uganda Women's Effort to Save Orphans (UWESO) to assist children orphaned during Uganda's years of civil war. As Uganda's political situation stabilized, Museveni and UWESCO voted to broaden the organization's focus to encompass children orphaned by HIV and AIDS and "orphan families" made up of orphaned children caring for younger siblings. UWESCO currently provides orphans with child care, vocational training, and counseling, seeking to make children and orphan families self-sufficient and self-supporting. Owing to a shortage of funds and personnel, UWESO is not able to serve all provinces within Uganda, but government offices at the provincial level have adopted the organization's model of support and training (Uganda Women's Effort to Save Orphans, n.d.).

In 2002 Janet Museveni was awarded the first Global AIDS Leadership Award by a group of international HIV and AIDS advocacy organizations. The award recognized her support for HIV prevention measures in Uganda and her work caring for orphans (Namutebi, 2002). Since 2002, Museveni has continued to act as a vocal supporter of Uganda's HIV prevention measures focusing on the "ABC" campaign, which advocates that individuals "Abstain, Be faithful, or use Condoms." Opposed to the use of condoms outside of marriage, Museveni stresses that children and adolescents must practice "self-control" and "abstain completely from sex" before marrying (Namutebi, 2003). Museveni is a patron of the Uganda Youth Forum, which has sponsored the "Save the Next Generation from HIV/AIDS" campaign for nearly a decade (Kisambira, 2002).

Eloan Pinheiro (1948–)

Eloan Pinheiro left her research position at an international pharmaceutical company in the 1990s to become the director of Far-Manguinhos, the Brazilian pharmaceutical company responsible for developing and manufacturing the country's supply of generic medications. For nearly twenty years before HIV and AIDS were detected in Brazil, Far-Manguinhos produced generic versions of drugs for "orphan" diseases such as malaria and leprosy, which continue to affect developing regions even as they disappear from wealthier nations (Jordan, 2001). In 2002, Far-Manguinhos entered into the "Drugs for Neglected Diseases Initiative" (DNDI), a research and development partnership with Doctors without Borders, the World Health Organization, the Pasteur Institute, the Indian Council of Medical Research, and the Ministry of Health of Malaysia. DNDI seeks to create a global pharmaceutical industry focused on producing and distributing low-cost medications to treat "neglected diseases" such as malaria, chagas disease, and leishmaniasis in developing countries (Osava, 2002).

In 1998, the Brazilian government began to focus on implementing a national HIV and AIDS treatment plan, deputizing Dr. Pinheiro to analyze existing antiretroviral drugs and to use the Far-Manguinhos laboratories to create generic copies. By 2001, Far-Manguinhos had created generic versions of three-quarters of all available antiretroviral drugs under Dr. Pinheiro's leadership, producing enough medication to treat 200,000 people per year. Also in 2001 Dr. Pinheiro and Far-Manguinhos began to offer technical support to health officials from developing countries in Africa and the Caribbean who are seeking to begin local production of generic antiretroviral medications (Jordan, 2001). Thanks in part to Dr. Pinheiro's leadership, Brazil is now an international example of proactive government response to HIV and AIDS in a region where financial constraints affect access to care and treatment.

Somsak Supawitkul

Somsak Supawitkul was a community hospital director in the late 1980s and early 1990s, when HIV prevalence in the Thai village of Mae Chan began to rise. Mae Chan is located in northern Thailand near one apex of the "golden triangle" of drug trafficking between Laos, Myanmar, and other Southeast Asian nations. Early AIDS deaths in Mae Chan were highly visible in a community of fewer than 100,000 people. In 1991, as HIV prevalence among sex workers in Mae Chan rose to 50 percent and 18 percent of male military conscripts were living with HIV, Thailand began to take national action against the epidemic with the institution of the 100 percent Condom Program. At the local level, too many people with HIV and AIDS were already ill or dying, for condoms alone to have an impact on quality of life and medical support. In Mae Chan, early AIDS deaths and HIV infections, often associated with drug abuse and commercial sex work, led to families and survivors becoming ostracized and isolated from the community. At the same time, Dr. Somsak's hospital was filled to capacity with patients unable to afford antiretroviral drugs or treatment for opportunistic infections associated with AIDS.

In 1991, Dr. Somsak and his wife, Bongot, began to assemble the players who would make up the "Mae Chan Model," recruiting Buddhist monks, health care workers, community leaders, teachers, and youth to address the problem of stigma in the community and Mae Chan's overstrained health care resources. Both local and international observers find Dr. Somsak's Mae Chan project remarkable for the diversity of its group of local collaborators. Working with more than sixty Buddhist monks, Dr. Somsak set up an HIV counseling center in the community hospital and expanded this service to include "group therapy" style meetings of people living with HIV and AIDS at the hospital. During these meetings, participants prepare traditional herbal medicines under the supervision of the monks and create traditional crafts and clothing for sale to support themselves and the community. In recent years, members of the "Make Dreams New Day" youth group have organized puppet shows and plays to educate children and young people about HIV transmission and ways to combat the stigma associated with HIV infection (Hart, 2001).

As of 2001, rates of HIV infection among commercial sex workers in Mae Chan have dropped to about 20 percent, while

HIV prevalence among male military conscripts is estimated at 1.7 percent. Dr. Somsak continues to lead the Mae Chan project, focusing on community involvement and support that goes beyond prevention to address the quality of life of people living with HIV and AIDS (Hart, 2001).

Mechai Viravaidya (1941–)

Mechai became involved with family planning and rural development in Thailand in the early 1970s. He founded the Population and Community Development Association (PDA) in 1974 to educate rural communities about family planning techniques and birth control, hoping to reduce Thailand's 3.2 percent birthrate, which was nearly the highest in the world. By 1986, Thailand's average birthrate had dropped to 1.6 percent, in large part due to PDA and Mechai's distribution of condoms, numerous public appearances, and widely distributed information packets. Tackling community members' reluctance to discuss sex or condom use through humor, Mechai founded the "Cabbages and Condoms" restaurant, serving traditional Thai dishes while educating patrons on contraceptive techniques. By the time HIV and AIDS were first detected in Thailand in the late 1980s, "mechai" was Thai slang for "condom" (Wallace, 1990).

The Thai government re-formed in 1991 in the wake of a military takeover. Prime Minister Anand Panyarachun took power for a year, from 1991 to 1992, until democratic elections could be held. During this time, Mechai was appointed as a "Minister attached to the Prime Minister's Office" deputized to design and write Thailand's National AIDS Prevention and Control Program for 1992–1996. The new National Plan requires that all government ministries integrate HIV prevention activities into their proposals and budget allocations. As a result, the Thai National Plan is the first to involve all sectors of government in a country's fight against HIV and AIDS. Mechai's plan also calls for the prime minister to be directly involved with HIV prevention planning and implementation as the National AIDS Prevention and Control Committee chair (Ungphakorn and Sittitrai, 1994).

After his year as a government minister, Mechai remained active in Thai politics as a senator, continuing his public education campaigns to increase awareness of condoms and other HIV-prevention techniques in rural and urban communities through the PDA. In 1999, Mechai was appointed to the post of UNAIDS ambassador in Asia, giving him the chance to bring his message of frankness about sex and HIV prevention "across national borders" (UNAIDS, n.d.). Mechai has contributed to the international dialogue on HIV prevention and treatment from 2001 through the present, encouraging donor countries and agencies to support nongovernmental organizations in developing countries to ensure that funds have the maximum impact (*Agence France Presse*, 28 June 2001). At a 2002 World Summit on Sustainable Development in Johannesburg, South Africa, Mechai publicly criticized presidents and prime ministers of developing countries who have not sufficiently supported national HIV prevention and care measures. Mechai stated, "we've got to face the fact that unless we teach people about sexuality, proper understanding, and [that] the only lifesaver is the condom, then you can't get very far." Mechai called on all presidents and prime ministers to officially lead their national AIDS coordinating agencies to ensure that all government sectors work together (Maclennan, 2002).

Wan Yanhai (1963–)

Dr. Wan worked for the Chinese government's National Health Education Institute from 1988 to 1994. HIV prevalence began to rise dramatically across Asia during this time, and commercial blood collection in rural Chinese communities precipitated a "titanic" hidden HIV epidemic in Henan Province. Dr. Wan created China's first HIV and AIDS information and counseling hotline through the National Health Education Institute and began to conduct research on HIV risk among gay men in China. In 1992, Dr. Wan created a health education group in Beijing for gay men called "Men's World," and hosted a radio show on gay rights. Dr. Wan was fired from the Health Education Institute in 1994 for "promoting homosexuality and supporting prostitution," and "Men's World" was discontinued (Smith, 2002).

No longer working with the Chinese government, Dr. Wan's next project was to create the AIZHI (AIDS) Action Project to provide free, internet-based HIV-prevention information. In addition to this nationwide effort, Dr. Wan worked with HIV-infected farmers in Henan Province from 2000 to 2002, helping rural communities draft petitions to the Chinese government demanding "free medicine or medicine we can afford . . . [and that] the government produce copies of Western medicines as quickly as possible."

These activities brought Dr. Wan and his colleagues under close scrutiny from local and national government, who began to monitor his projects and movements in 2002 (Rosenthal, 2002, A3).

While working to gain the Chinese government's approval to make the AIZHI Action Project (renamed the Beijing AIDS Action Health Education Institute) an officially recognized non-governmental organization, Dr. Wan received an anonymous e-mail containing classified government statistics on HIV infection rates in Henan Province. The government report, marked "secret," contained details on HIV prevalence, suggesting that local government officials were well aware of the extent of HIV prevalence months or even years before the Chinese government officially acknowledged the presence of HIV in the country. In order to expose the government's lack of action to prevent the spread of HIV, Dr. Wan published the government report on his Web site, where it quickly attracted the attention of international AIDS advocacy groups as well as the Chinese government (Russell, 2002).

Dr. Wan was arrested in August 2002 and was imprisoned for a month in Beijing on charges of leaking state secrets. In the weeks following his clandestine arrest, both local and international protest from organizations including the United Nations, the United States Department of State, and Act Up brought China's HIV epidemic to international attention. The Chinese government released Dr. Wan in September after the Global Fund to Fight AIDS, Tuberculosis, and Malaria threatened to withhold China's US$90 million grant to combat AIDS as long as he was detained (Rosenthal, 2002). Later in 2002, the government announced new HIV prevalence figures for the country, bringing the official estimate of people living with HIV and AIDS to 1 million nationwide. In addition, the Chinese government began to seriously consider the manufacture of generic antiretroviral drugs to treat HIV and AIDS in hard-hit areas. The Beijing AIDS Action Health Education Institute was officially recognized two months after Dr. Wan's release from prison (Russell, 2002).

Gao Yaojie (1927–)

Dr. Gao treated her first AIDS patient in 1996 in Zhengzhou City, China. The woman, who died ten days after Dr. Gao tested her for HIV antibodies, was infected with HIV through a blood transfusion she received during surgery the previous year. Over the following months, Dr. Gao turned her attention to HIV prevention education, noticing that all HIV prevention messages in Chinese health facilities focused on intravenous drug use, heterosexual transmission, and prostitution, with no mention of the growing risk of infection via blood donation and transfusion. Dr. Gao drafted and published an HIV prevention information packet that she distributed at bus and train stations, family planning clinics, magazine stands, and through a network of acquaintances in the medical community. Between 1996 and 2001 Dr. Gao and a group of volunteers distributed more than 300,000 copies of these prevention materials (Gao, 2001).

In 1999, at the age of seventy-two, Dr. Gao began to visit rural villages in Henan Province, bringing donated medicines to treat the opportunistic infections associated with HIV and AIDS and information on HIV prevention and modes of transmission. In addition to providing medical care in isolated villages, Dr. Gao documented her visits with photographs and interviews to prove the extent of HIV transmission from blood selling in Henan and neighboring provinces. While conducting surveys of the community members she encountered on these trips, Dr. Gao noted a low level of awareness about HIV transmission, particularly in the Zhumadian and Zhoukou districts, where villagers referred to AIDS as "the strange disease" or "the nameless fever" (Gao, 2001).

In 2001, at age seventy-four, Dr. Gao was awarded the Jonathan Mann Award for Global Health and Human Rights by the United States-based Global Health Council. The Chinese government blocked Dr. Gao's application for a passport to travel to the United States in May, preventing her from receiving the award in person at the Global Health Council's 2001 conference (Pomfret, 2001). In July 2001, local government security cadres began to prevent Dr. Gao from visiting rural communities and individuals affected by AIDS, accusing Dr. Gao of trying to "embarrass" the Chinese government by publicizing the high HIV prevalence in Henan's villages (Chan, 2001). Government strictures on Dr. Gao's movements eased later in 2001 as China's national response to HIV strengthened, and the first HIV and AIDS care clinic was established in the city of Wenlou in Henan (Fackler, 2001). In 2003, Dr. Gao was awarded the prestigious Ramon Magsaysay Award, but was not allowed to travel to the Philippines to attend the awards ceremony. The Chinese government did not issue any official recognition of Dr. Gao's award, which is considered to be an

Asia-based equivalent to the Nobel Prize (Bezlova, 2003). Later in 2003 government security forces attempted to prevent Dr. Gao from attending an AIDS conference in Beijing where she was scheduled to meet with Former United States President Bill Clinton (*Agence France Presse*, 11 November 2003).

References

Agence France Presse. SAfrica-AIDS: S. African doctor takes on Mbeki over anti-AIDS drug. *Agence France Presse*, 1 November 1999.

————. SAfrica-AIDS: S. African politicians to reveal HIV status. *Agence France Presse*, 23 May 2000.

————. Australia-Asia: Aid money for Asia should go to independent NGOs: Thai senator. *Agence France Presse*, 28 June 2001.

————. US-Powell-Bono: State Department astir as US's Bono talks debt relief, AIDS with Powell. *Agence France Presse*, 16 March 2002.

————. SAfrica-US: Bono, US Treasury Secretary demand more AIDS drugs for Africa. *Agence France Presse*, 24 May 2002.

————. SAfrica-Mandela-Bono: Bono and Mandela talk about Africa. *Agence France Presse*, 25 May 2002.

————. Uganda-US: Washington to campaign for fewer loans, but more grants for Africa. *Agence France Presse*, 28 May 2002.

————. Botswana-AIDS: Botswanan president calls for nation to "change behavior." *Agence France Presse*, 10 November 2003.

————. China-AIDS-doctor: China tries to put noose on prominent AIDS activist in Beijing. *Agence France Presse*, 11 November 2003.

Associated Press. 2001. UN, Kofi Annan wins Nobel Peace Prize. Associated Press, October 12, 2001.

Bezlova, A. 2003. China: Silence on award for AIDS activist belies changed attitude. Inter Press Service, August 28, 2003.

Biswas, S. 2003. Indian drugs boss hails AIDS deal. BBC News, October 29, 2003.

Boris, J. 2001. Interview of the week: Yusuf Hamied. United Press International, February 21, 2001.

Boseley, S. Yusuf Hamied, generic drugs boss. *The Guardian* (London), 18 February 2003, 8.

Byrne, K. 1995. U2 biographies; biography: Bono. Available at: http://www.atu2.com/band/bono. Accessed: April 18, 2004.

Chan, V.P.K. AIDS crusader banned from checking on villages. *South China Morning Post*, 12 July 2001.

Cooper, H., R. Zimmerman, and L. McGinley. AIDS epidemic puts drug firms in a vise: Treatment vs. profits. *Wall Street Journal*, 2 March 2001, A1.

Dickson, P. Gazi offers to pay for HIV drugs. *Daily Mail and Guardian* (Johannesburg), 29 March 2000.

Donnelly, J. A battle line in Botswana AIDS fight; patients who reject test risk being turned away. *Boston Globe*, 24 October 2003, A8.

Dube, S. India's AIDS explosion. *Washington Post*, 4 January 2001, A21.

Elizabeth Glaser Pediatric AIDS Foundation. n.d.(a). About us: A brief history of the Foundation. Available at: http://www.pedaids.org/history.html. Accessed: April 18, 2004.

————. n.d.(b). Call to Action Project: The Foundation takes action. Available at: http://www.pedaids.org/glob_calltoaction_body.html. Accessed: April 18, 2004.

Face to Face International, Inc. 2001. Mpule Kwelagobe campaign spokesperson, Botswana. Available at: http://www.facetoface.org/sp_14.html. Accessed: April 18, 2004.

Fackler, M. 2001. AIDS activist no longer harassed. Associated Press, August 24, 2001.

Gao, Y. 2001. My "AIDS prevention" journey, 2001. Available at: http://www.usembassy-china.org.cn/sandt/gaoyaojie—aidsprevention.html. Accessed: April 18, 2004.

H. W. Wilson Company. 2003. Current Biography International Yearbook 2003—Biography: Achmat. Available at: http://www.hwwilson.com/print/cbintl2003_zachie_biography.htm. Accessed: April 18, 2004.

Hart, C. 2001. Working together in Thailand. *UNDP Choices*, December.

Helen Suzman Foundation. 2000. Interview: Dr. Costa Gazi March 2000. Available at http://www.hsf.org.za/focus17/gazifocus17.html. Accessed: April 18, 2004.

Hussain, W. 2002. Woman shines light on AIDS darkness. Associated Press, December 1, 2002.

Jordan, M. Brazil makes a name for itself pumping out cheap AIDS drugs. *Wall Street Journal*, 27 April 2001, A17.

Khan, S. Siddharth Dube: Author and development policy analyst. *The Times of India*, 18 February 1999.

Kisambira, E. First lady rallies Makerere on AIDS. *New Vision* (Kampala), 14 November 2002.

Maclennan, B. Mr. Condom lets fly at Thabo Mbeki. *Mail and Guardian* (Johannesburg), 31 August 2002.

Namutebi, J. Janet Museveni wins award. *New Vision* (Kampala), 13 May 2002.

———. Abstain from sex, Janet advises youth. *New Vision* (Kampala), 28 May 2003.

Osava, M. 2002. Developing drugs for neglected diseases that afflict poor. Inter Press Service, December 4, 2002.

Panafrican News Agency. 2001a. Botswana offers free antiretroviral treatment. Panafrican News Agency, June 5, 2001.

———. 2001b. Youth panel hopeful about battle with HIV/AIDS. Panafrican News Agency, August 7, 2001.

———. 2001c. Botswana plans HIV/AIDS antiretroviral therapy. Panafrican News Agency, October 30, 2001.

———. 2001d. Botswana has reason to celebrate on World AIDS Day. Panafrican News Agency, November 30, 2001.

Petersen, M., and D. G. McNeil Jr. 2001. Maker yielding patent in Africa for AIDS drug. *New York Times*, 15 March 2001, A1.

Pomfret, J. China blocks trip to US by AIDS award honoree. *Washington Post*, 30 May 2001, A14.

Reuters. O'Neill, Bono end Africa tour with hope, intentions. *Reuters*, 30 May 2002.

Rosenthal, E. China's top AIDS activist missing; arrest is suspected. *New York Times*, 29 August 2002, A3.

Russell, S. Path-breaking AIDS activist tells of detention in China. *San Francisco Chronicle*, 13 November 2002, A12.

Smith, R. Missing Chinese AIDS activist is longtime gay rights activist. *Washington Blade*, 6 September 2002.

Treatment Action Campaign. n.d. Overview and history of TAC's work. Available at: http://www.tac.org.za. Accessed: April 18, 2004.

Uganda Women's Effort to Save Orphans. n.d. Background and activities. Available at: http://www.uweso.org/activities.php. Accessed: April 18, 2004.

UN Integrated Regional Information Networks. 2003. Botswana: all public health facilities to offer HIV testing. UN Integrated Regional Information Networks, October 20, 2003.

UNAIDS. n.d. UNAIDS Ambassador: Biography of Mechai Viravaidya. Available at: http://www.unaids.org/html/pub/UNA-docs/BIOmechai_en_doc.htm. Accessed: April 18, 2004.

UNFPA. 2000. Miss Universe, Mpule Kwelagobe, appointed UNFPA goodwill ambassador for Botswana [press release], February 8.

Ungphakorn, J., and W. Sittitrai. 1994. The Thai response to the HIV/ AIDS epidemic. *AIDS* 8(suppl. 2): S155–S163.

United Nations. 2000. United Nations Millennium Declaration. Available at: http://www.un.org/millennium/declaration/ares552e.htm. Accessed: April 18, 2004.

———. 2001. Secretary general proposes global fund for fight against HIV/AIDS and other infectious diseases at African leaders summit [Press Release SG/SM/7779/Rev.1].

———. 2003. Biography of Kofi A. Annan. Available at: http://www.un. org/News/ossg/sg/pages/sg_biography.html. Accessed: April 18, 2004.

Wallace, C. P. Miracle man of Thailand—profile. *Los Angeles Times*, 22 January 1990, E1.

Yi, M. Compassion before profit in AIDS war. *San Francisco Chronicle*, 26 March 2001, B1.

5

Data and Statistics

The tables and figures included in this chapter provide a visual and statistical supplement to current and historical issues raised in Chapters 1, 2, 3, and 4. Drawn primarily from the results of clinical trials and international surveillance, these tables and figures present the "raw material" that researchers, policymakers, educators, and activists use to design new HIV prevention and treatment interventions, advocate for increased support, and evaluate the success of existing programs. Although much of this data is specific to a particular region of the world, a majority of the lessons learned are applicable elsewhere. For example, Figure 5.12 shows that treatment of sexually transmitted diseases in rural Tanzania can help to prevent new HIV infections in areas with limited medical infrastructure, a finding with clear importance for many other resource-scarce settings. Other figures, such as the schematic of the costs associated with HIV and AIDS treatment presented in Figure 5.20, help to illustrate the complexity of a comprehensive response to the epidemic. Figure 5.17 illustrates a dramatic increase in HIV prevalence and incidence in Eastern Europe. Along with the data on HIV infections among Romanian children presented in Table 5.6, Figure 5.17 provides evidence for a new epidemic that is growing rapidly beyond the populations who were initially most affected.

HIV and AIDS in the World Today

The data from UNAIDS in Tables 5.1 and 5.2 and Figures 5.1 and 5.2 provide a global picture of the HIV epidemic at the end of 2002.

TABLE 5.1
Global Summary of the HIV/AIDS Epidemic, December 2002

	Number of People Living with HIV/AIDS	People Newly Infected with HIV in 2002	AIDS Deaths in 2002
Total	42 million	5 million	3.1 million
Adults	38.6 million	4.2 million	2.5 million
Women	*19.2 million*	*2 million*	*1.2 million*
Children under 15 years	3.2 million	800,000	610,000

Source: UNAIDS AIDS Epidemic Update, December 2002.

TABLE 5.2
Regional HIV/AIDS Statistics and Features, End of 2002

	Epidemic Started	Adults & Children Living with HIV/AIDS	Adults & Children Newly Infected with HIV	Adult Prevalence Rate*	% of HIV-Positive Adults Who Are Women	Main Mode(s) of Transmission for Those Living with HIV/AIDS**
Sub-Saharan Africa	late '70s early '80s	29.4 million	3.5 million	8.8%	58%	Hetero
North Africa & Middle East	late '80s	550,000	83,000	0.3%	55%	Hetero, IDU
South and Southeast Asia	late '80s	6.0 million	700,000	0.6%	36%	Hetero, IDU
East Asia & Pacific	late '80s	1.2 million	270,000	0.1%	24%	IDU, Hetero, MSM
Latin America	late '70s early '80s	1.5 million	150,000	0.6%	30%	MSM, IDU, Hetero
Caribbean	late '70s early '80s	440,000	60,000	2.4%	50%	Hetero, MSM
Eastern Europe & Central Asia	early '90s	1.2 million	250,000	0.6%	27%	IDU
Western Europe	late '70s early '80s	570,000	30,000	0.3%	25%	MSM, IDU
North America	late '70s early '80s	980,000	45,000	0.6%	20%	MSM, IDU, Hetero
Australia & New Zealand	late '70s early '80s	15,000	500	0.1%	7%	MSM
TOTAL		42 million	5 million	1.2%	50%	

*The proportion of adults (15 to 49 years of age) living with HIV/AIDS in 2002, using 2002 population numbers.
**Hetero: heterosexual transmission; IDU: transmission through injecting drug use; MSM: sexual transmission among men who have sex with men.

Source: UNAIDS AIDS Epidemic Update, December 2002.

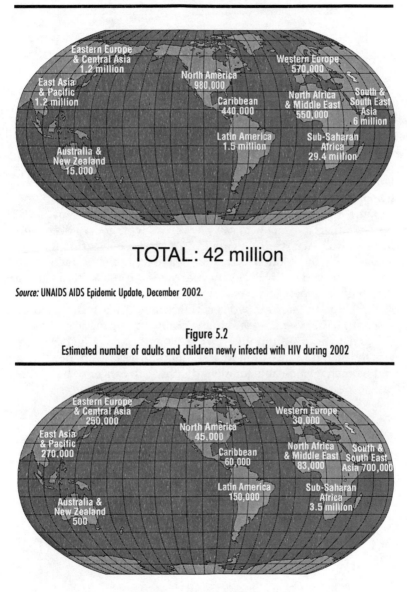

Figure 5.1
Adults and children estimated to be living with HIV/AIDS as of end 2002

TOTAL: 42 million

Source: UNAIDS AIDS Epidemic Update, December 2002.

Figure 5.2
Estimated number of adults and children newly infected with HIV during 2002

TOTAL: 5 million

Source: UNAIDS AIDS Epidemic Update, December 2002.

Although the majority of people currently living with HIV and AIDS are in sub-Saharan Africa, these figures also illustrate the growing epidemics in Southeast Asia and Eastern Europe.

HIV among Women and Minorities in the United States

In regions where HIV has been present since the earliest years of the global epidemic, the most affected populations change over time as the virus spreads beyond the individuals who are initially infected to the general population. The first cases of HIV in the United States were identified primarily among gay men and hemophiliacs in the early 1980s. The first HIV prevention and support initiatives in North America focused on men who have sex with men and medical safety, even as women, children, and heterosexual men were increasingly affected. Long-term HIV surveillance in the United States shows that more women have become infected with HIV every year since the 1980s. Today more than half of all people infected with HIV via heterosexual contact in the United States are women (UNAIDS, 2002b). In addition, rates of HIV have increased dramatically among African American and Latino communities in the United States. By 1998 HIV was the leading cause of mortality among African American men and women, responsible for more deaths than cancer or heart disease (Smith, 2000) (Table 5.3, Figures 5.3, 5.4).

Table 5.3
Death Rates from HIV by Sex and Race in the United States in Individuals Aged 25–44 Years

	White Men	African American Men	Latino Men	White Women	African American Women	Latina Women
1987	19.2	60.2	36.8	1.2	11.6	4.9
1990	35	102	59.3	2.3	23.6	8.9
1995	46.1	179.4	73.9	5.9	53.6	17.2
1998	9.6	58.1	16.6	1.8	25.5	4.6
1999	9.7	59.3	16.5	2.2	26.6	5.3
2000	8.8	55.4	14.3	2.1	26.7	4.6
2001	8.3	53.5	12.4	1.9	26	4.3

Source: Centers for Disease Control and Prevention, National Center for Health Statistics, National Vital Statistics System. National Center for Statistics Data Warehouse: Mortality Tables Available at: http://www.cdc.gov/nchs/datawh/statab/unpubd/mortabs.htm Accessed: January 20, 2004.

Figure 5.3
Female AIDS Cases as a Percentage of Total U.S. AIDS Cases

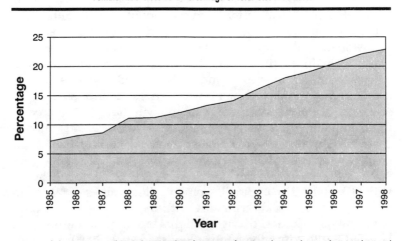

Source: Marlink, R., H. Kao, and E. Hsieh. 2001. Clinical care issues for women living with HIV and AIDS in the United States. *AIDS Research and Human Retroviruses.* Boston: Harvard AIDS Institute.

Figure 5.4
Death Rates from HIV by Sex and Race in the United States in Individuals Aged 25–44 Years

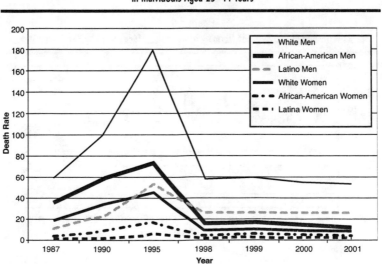

Source: Marlink, R., H. Kao, and E. Hsieh. 2001. Clinical care issues for women living with HIV and AIDS in the United States. *AIDS Research and Human Retroviruses.* Boston: Harvard AIDS Institute.

Figure 5.5 illustrates how women's mortality from AIDS-related complications has outstripped men's almost every year since 1988. In the years after the discovery of protease inhibitors and the advent of triple-combination antiretroviral therapies, HIV and AIDS-related mortality decreased dramatically in the United States. Even during these years, however, women did not benefit equally from new therapies and treatment advances. A lack of access to care and testing along with a need for increased counseling and support services for women might have contributed to this continuing disparity (Marlink, Kao, and Hsieh, 2001). As discussed in Chapter 2, a similar pattern emerged in Brazil when the country's national AIDS care plan began to provide state-sponsored antiretroviral therapy and medical care to all people living with HIV and AIDS. In Brazil, women's illness and mortality did not decrease as quickly as men's with the introduction of anti-retroviral medications, owing to stigma, poverty, and a need for targeted health education efforts (Segurado et al., 2003).

HIV Virology and Medicine

More than twenty years of research has yielded important information about HIV infection and replication, the genome of the

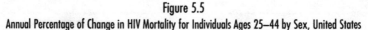

Figure 5.5
Annual Percentage of Change in HIV Mortality for Individuals Ages 25–44 by Sex, United States

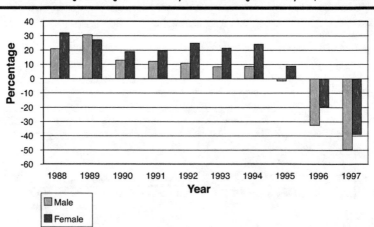

Source: Marlink, R., H. Kao, and E. Hsieh. 2001. Clinical care issues for women living with HIV and AIDS in the United States. *AIDS Research and Human Retroviruses.* Boston: Harvard AIDS Institute.

virus, and how knowledge of HIV's "weak spots" can be exploited to create new therapies. Advances in genetic research and improved patient-monitoring techniques have generated a clearer picture of how HIV evolves and how it affects its host. A better understanding of HIV's genetic structure and the functions of individual genes allows researchers developing new treatments to target specific moments in the viral life cycle, disrupting transmission, replication, and fusion to host cells (Figure 5.6). Despite these discoveries, the complexity of the human immunodefi-

Figure 5.6
Generation of Protective Immune Responses against HIV

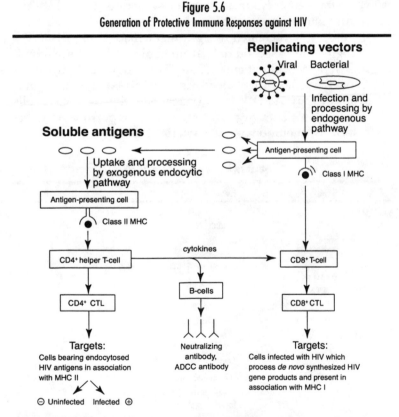

Separate pathways are depicted for (right) self-replicating or (left) inert immunogens. The respective processing (endogenous versus endocytic) and presentation (class I MHC vs class II MHC) pathways are distinguishable. Presentation of a given antigen by an innocuous replicating vector (viral, bacterial or other) would appear to be a favorable option since it could encompass both pathways.

ciency virus continues to pose a serious challenge to researchers designing new antiretroviral drugs and candidate vaccines.

The HIV virion is composed of the nine genes listed in Table 5.4 , each responsible for a different aspect of infection, replication, and transmission. The genes primarily targeted for drug development are *pol* and *env*. Current antiretroviral therapies include protease inhibitors, nucleoside and nonnucleoside reverse transcriptase inhibitors, and fusion inhibitors. The *env* gene is responsible for regulating the formation of a virion's outer envelope, creating the gp120, gp41, and gp160 proteins that candidate HIV vaccines target to stimulate the human immune system to attack the virus upon entry into the body (Klein and Ho, 2000).

Figure 5.7 was created using a mathematical model of disease progression based on data from clinical trials. Each graph tracks a hypothetical patient's CD4+ T cell count and HIV RNA levels over five and one-half years of triple-combination antiretroviral therapy. As HIV RNA increases in the body, CD4 cells decrease and patients begin to experience opportunistic infections such as pneumonia and bacterial infections. When "first

Table 5.4
Key Structural and Regulatory Genes of HIV

Gene	Protein	Function
Structural		
gag	Matrix Capsid Nucleocapsid	Structural core proteins
pol	Protease Reverse transcriptase Integrase	Virus enzymes involved in replication
env	Surface glycoprotein Transmembrane	Viral envelope glycoproteins
Regulatory		
tat	Tat	Activator of viral transcription
rev	Rev	Transports mRNA* to cytoplasm
vif	Vif	Promotes infectivity
nef	Nef	Downregulates CD4 expression Enhances viral activity
vpu	Vpu	Promotes release for viral particles from infected cell
vpr	Vpr	Arrests cell cycle in G2 Increases viral nuclear entry into nondividing cells

*mRNA = messenger ribonucleic acid

Source: Klein, E., and R.J.Y. Ho. 2000. Challenges in the development of an effective HIV vaccine: Current approaches and future directions. *Clinical Therapeutics.*

Figure 5.7
Two Hypothetical Patients Treated with a Three-Drug Antiretroviral Regimen

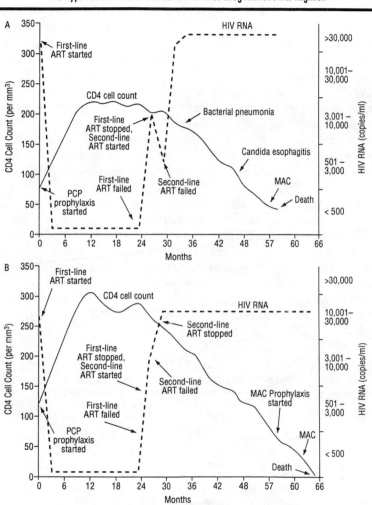

These patients were randomly selected from 1 million simulations with the use of data from the AIDS Clinical Trials Group 320 Study. The patient in Panel A was a 42-year-old man with an initial CD4 cell count of 76 per cubic millimeter and an initialHIV RNA level of more than 30,000 copies per milliliter. After a complicated course, his discounted life expectancy was 56.30 months, his quality-adjusted life expectancy was 48.30 months, and the total discounted medical cost was $89,400. The patient in Panel B was a 24-year-old man with an initial CD4 cell count of 119 per cubic millimeter and an initial HIV RNA level of 10,001 to 30,000 copies per milliliter. His discounted life expectancy was 64.80 months, his quality-adjusted life expectancy was 57.40 months, and the total medical cost was $78,000. PCP denotes *Pneumocystis carinii* pneumonia, MAC *Mycobacterium avium* complex infection, and ART combination antiretroviral therapy.

Source: Freedberg, K.A., E. Losina, M.C. Weinstein, et al. The cost effectiveness of combination antiretroviral therapy for HIV disease. *New England Journal of Medicine.* Copyright © 2001 Massachusetts Medical Society. All rights reserved.

line" antiretroviral therapy begins, HIV RNA decreases dramatically for months or even years. When resistance to first line therapy develops, HIV RNA begins to increase until a "second line" regimen is introduced that will have varying levels of success in restoring immune function depending on individual patient characteristics. This controlled mathematical simulation based on data collected from large cohorts of people living with HIV and AIDS allows policymakers and health care providers to estimate the long-term impact of antiretroviral therapy in populations of people living with HIV who require treatment. This model can be adjusted to account for regional differences such as the effect of HIV subtype on disease progression, common opportunistic infections, and other health concerns, such as malnutrition or drug use (Freedberg et al., 2001).

Scientists have searched for an HIV vaccine since the virus was first characterized, but more than twenty years later no successful candidate has emerged. The seven common vaccines listed in Table 5.5 were each developed between six and eighty years after the cause of the target illness was identified, with an average development period of thirty years. For some diseases, such polio and influenza, further research has led to the creation of new vaccines even after a successful candidate was discovered (Klein, 2000).

Table 5.5
Viral Vaccines Currently Licensed for Use in Humans (2000)

Virus	Family	Type of vaccine	Disease (if different from virus)	Year identified	Year vaccine developed
Polio	Picornavirus		Poliomyelitis	1909	
Oral Sabin vaccine		Live attenuated			1957
Salk vaccine		Inactivated			1953
Measle	Paramyxovirus	Live attenuated		1954	1963
Mumps	Paramyxovirus	Live attenuated		1934	1967
Rubella	Togavirus	Live, partly attenuated	German measles	1962	1971
Rabies	Rhabdovirus	Inactivated		Discovered 1903; isolated 1960	1970
Influenza	Orthomyxovirus	Inactivated, subunit, and live attenuated		1933	1941
Hepatitis B	Hepadnavirus	Subunit	Serum hepatitis	1965	1986

Source: Klein, E., and R.J.Y. Ho. 2000. Challenges in the development of an effective HIV vaccine: Current approaches and future directions. *Clinical Therapeutics.*

Clinical Trials

Clinical trials conducted in developing countries not only further scientific research on HIV treatment and prevention, but can also provide underserved populations with access to care and treatment. Trial design must reflect both the study's research goals and respect for study participants' needs, concerns, and potential vulnerability. International guidelines such as the Declaration of Helsinki and the Belmont Report help research directors to ensure that trial procedures will protect participants' human rights and health to the greatest extent possible. Throughout the course of a study, participants might leave the trial or develop unforeseen medical complications. Researchers must plan for these changes when drafting a project proposal in order to obtain statistically significant data. Figure 5.8 illustrates the stages of a mother-to-child HIV prevention study from initial participant recruitment to final treatment efficacy assessment.

Figure 5.8
Trial Profiles: Study of nevirapine compared with zidovudine to prevent mother-to-child HIV transmission in Kampala, Uganda

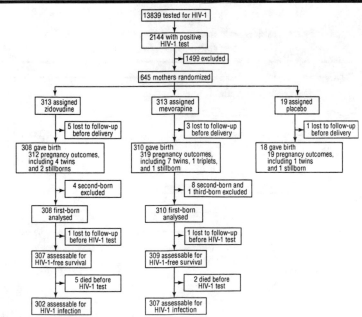

Reprinted with permission from Elsevier (**The Lancet**, 1999, vol. 354, 795–802)

HIV in Developing Countries and Access to Care

Financial constraints often prevent individuals living with HIV and AIDS from receiving antiretroviral treatment, but in many regions access to even basic palliative care (to treat symptoms such as pain without curing a condition) and prevention or prophylaxis is restricted. In countries with large rural populations, individuals might be unable to travel to the nearest health facility. In regions with insufficient health care infrastructure, there might be too few doctors and nurses to treat all individuals requiring care. As the last figure in this section illustrates, however, even the most basic level of health care infrastructure can potentially administer HIV prevention programs, deliver palliative care, and offer HIV counseling and testing services. See Figures 5.9, 5.10, and 5.11.

Figure 5.12 is a hypothetical example of the kinds of HIV care and support that are feasible at three levels of infrastructure, ranging from educational materials and nutrition information, to counseling and testing services, to antiretroviral therapy and complex

Figure 5.9
Per capita public expenditure on health in international dollars (1997) for sub-Saharan African and high-income countries

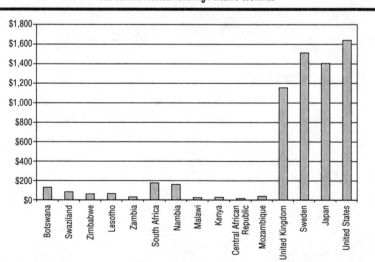

Source: Ramanathan, K., D. Tarantola, and R. Marlink. 2002. Access to HIV and AIDS Care. In M. Essex, P. Kanki, and S. Mboup, eds. *AIDS in Africa,* 2nd ed. New York: Kluwer Academic/Plenum.

Figure 5.10
Percent of population with access to health services in urban and rural areas in
selected sub-Saharan African countries (1990–1995)

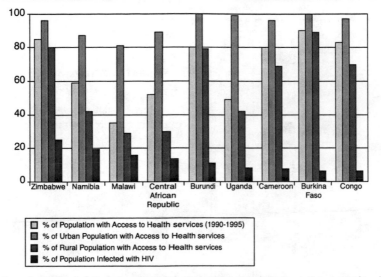

Source: Ramanathan, K., D. Tarantola, and R. Marlink. 2002. Access to HIV and AIDS Care. In M. Essex, P. Kanki, and S. Mboup, eds. *AIDS in Africa,* 2nd ed. New York: Kluwer Academic/Plenum.

patient monitoring. Even in regions with little or no health care infrastructure and limited resources, a range of care and support options can be put into place with community support.

HIV Transmission and the Movement of the Epidemic

As discussed in Chapter 1, international and in-country migrations play a significant role in the spread of HIV worldwide. Global HIV subtype surveys show how different strains of HIV-1 and HIV-2 have "migrated" across and between continents, sometimes forming new recombinants along the way. Civil war, unsafe medical practices, injection drug use and drug trafficking, sex work, labor migration, and international tourism have all played a role in the spread of HIV. Knowledge of these trends can help epidemiologists determine where new HIV epidemics might evolve, potentially allowing national governments to respond quickly to the threat of increasing HIV prevalence.

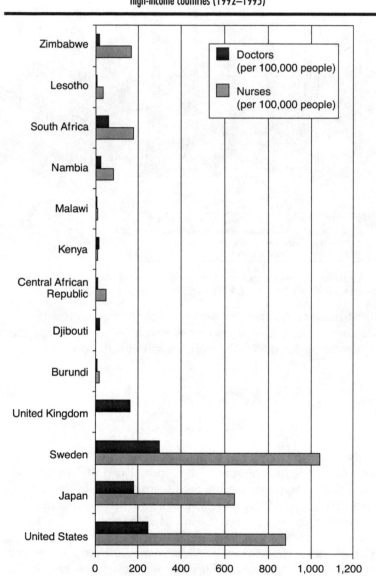

Figure 5.11
Availability of Health Personnel in sub-Saharan African and
high-income countries (1992–1995)

Source: Ramanathan, K., D. Tarantola, and R. Marlink. 2002. Access to HIV and AIDS Care. In M. Essex, P. Kanki, and S. Mboup, eds. *AIDS in Africa,* 2nd ed. New York: Kluwer Academic/Plenum.

Figure 5.12
An Example of a Comprehensive Approach in HIV/AIDS Care

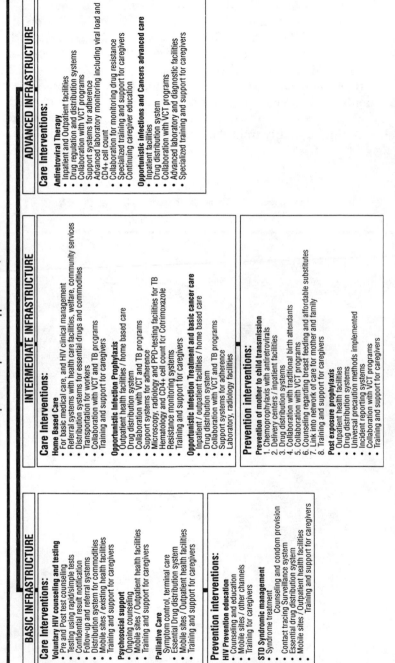

BASIC INFRASTRUCTURE

Care Interventions:

Voluntary HIV counselling and testing
- Pre and Post test counseling
- Testing using rapid/simple tests
- Confidential result notification
- Follow-up and referral systems
- Distribution system for commodities
- Mobile sites / existing health facilities
- Training and support for caregivers

Psychosocial support
- Ongoing counseling
- Mobile sites / Outpatient health facilities
- Training and support for caregivers

Palliative Care
- Symptom control, terminal care
- Essential Drug distribution system
- Mobile sites / Outpatient health facilities
- Training and support for caregivers

Prevention interventions:

HIV Prevention education
- Counseling and education
- Mobile sites / other channels
- Training for caregivers

STD Syndromic management
- Syndrome treatment
  Counseling and condom provision
- Contact tracing Surveillance system
- Essential drug distribution system
- Mobile sites / Outpatient health facilities
  Training and support for caregivers

INTERMEDIATE INFRASTRUCTURE

Care Interventions:

Home Based Care
- For basic medical care, and HIV clinical management
- Referral systems with health care facilities, welfare, community services
- Distribution systems for essential drugs and commodities
- Transportation for workers
- Collaboration with VCT and TB programs
- Training and support for caregivers

Opportunistic Infection Prophylaxis
- Outpatient health facilities / home based care
- Drug distribution system
- Collaboration with VCT and TB programs
- Support systems for adherence
- Microscopy, radiology and PPD-testing facilities for TB
- Hematology and CD4+ cell count for Cotrimoxazole
- Resistance monitoring systems
- Training and support for caregivers

Opportunistic Infection Treatment and basic cancer care
- Inpatient / outpatient facilities / home based care
- Drug distribution system
- Collaboration with VCT and TB programs
- Support systems for adherence
- Laboratory, radiology facilities

Prevention interventions:

Prevention of mother to child transmission
1. Chemoprophylaxis with antiretrovirals
2. Delivery centers / inpatient facilities
3. Drug distribution systems
4. Collaboration with traditional birth attendants
5. Collaboration with VCT programs
6. Counseling regarding breast feeding and affordable substitutes
7. Link into network of care for mother and family
8. Training and support for caregivers

Post exposure prophylaxis
- Outpatient health facilities
- Drug distribution systems
- Universal precaution methods implemented
- Incident reporting systems
- Collaboration with VCT programs
- Training and support for caregivers

ADVANCED INFRASTRUCTURE

Care Interventions:

Antiretroviral Therapy
- Inpatient and Outpatient facilities
- Drug regulation and distribution systems
- Collaboration with VCT programs
- Support systems for adherence
- Advanced laboratory monitoring including viral load and CD4+ cell count
- Collaboration for monitoring drug resistance
- Specialized training and support for caregivers
- Continuing caregiver education

Opportunistic infections and Cancers advanced care
- Inpatient facilities
- Drug distribution system
- Collaboration with VCT programs
- Advanced laboratory and diagnostic facilities
- Specialized training and support for caregivers

Source: Ramanathan, K., D. Tarantola, and R. Marlink. 2002. Access to HIV and AIDS Care. In M. Essex, P. Kanki, and S. Mboup, eds. *AIDS in Africa,* 2nd ed. New York: Kluwer Academic/Plenum.

Figures 5.13 through 5.16 document the connections between in-country migration and the movement and growth of
Uganda's HIV epidemic. HIV prevalence is highest in Uganda's
northern and southern districts, including Gulu, Rakai, and
Masaka. Masaka and Rakai are populous regions near the capital
city of Kampala, whereas Gulu is situated on Sudan's northern
border. All three regions contain major shipping routes from
Kampala to Kenya, Tanzania, and Sudan, and migrant workers
commute regularly from these provinces into the capital. As dis-

Figure 5.13
Reported cumulative AIDS incidence rates per 100,000 population to
February 1990 for 34 districts of Uganda

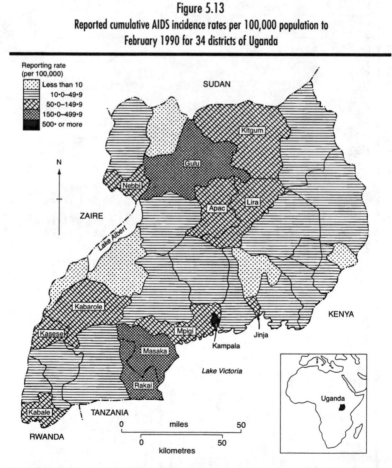

Reprinted with the permission of Cambridge University Press. Smallman-Raynor, M.R., and A.D. Cliff. 1991. Civil war
and the spread of AIDS in Central Africa. *Epidemiology and Infection.*

Figure 5.14
Location of principal roads in Uganda against a backcloth of district
population densities per square mile

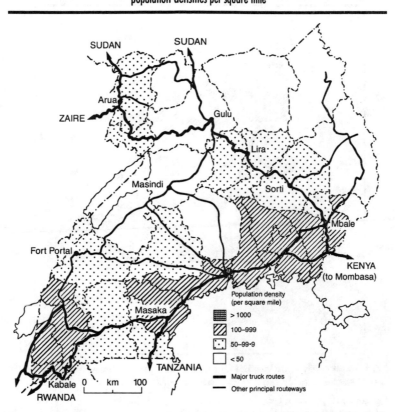

Reprinted with the permission of Cambridge University Press. Smallman-Raynor, M.R., and A.D. Cliff. 1991. Civil war
and the spread of AIDS in Central Africa. *Epidemiology and Infection.*

cussed in Chapter 1, HIV prevalence is often high near shipping routes and paths of labor migration, which partially explains Uganda's north-south concentration of HIV infections. Uganda's civil war, beginning in 1979 with the overthrow of Idi Amin, led to widespread recruitment of troops by the Uganda National Liberation Army (UNLA) between the 1970s and 1980s. UNLA soldiers were predominantly recruited in the north of the country and deployed in the southern districts, returning home to the northern borders at the end of the country's conflict. This pattern of "bipolar" troop movement mirrors the development of HIV prevalence in Uganda: highest in the south where troops were

Figure 5.15
Principal labour supply and labour demand regions in Uganda

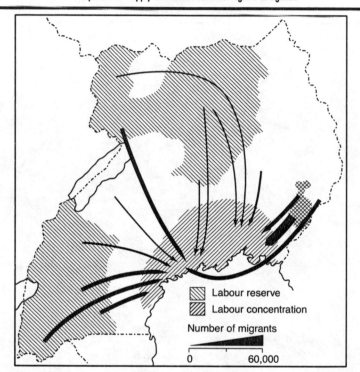

Vectors show inter-censal migration flows, 1959–69, upon which the original formulation of the hypothesis for migrant labour and the spread of AIDS in Uganda is based. *Source:* ref. [12].

Reprinted with the permission of Cambridge University Press. Smallman-Raynor, M.R., and A.D. Cliff. 1991. Civil war and the spread of AIDS in Central Africa. *Epidemiology and Infection.*

stationed during conflict and in the north where many returned at the end of the war (Smallman-Raynor and Cliff, 1991).

HIV infections detected in Romanian children were first documented in 1989. This data is presented in Table 5.6. The majority of these children, most under four years of age, were born to mothers who were not infected with HIV, suggesting that the majority of infections in young children resulted from exposure to contaminated blood and blood products in health care settings. Abandoned children living in Romanian orphanages were routinely treated for anemia and malnutrition with small blood transfusions during the early 1990s, with few precautions taken

Figure 5.16
UNLA recruitment rates in Uganda by district. Levels are proportional
to the volumes of the spheres

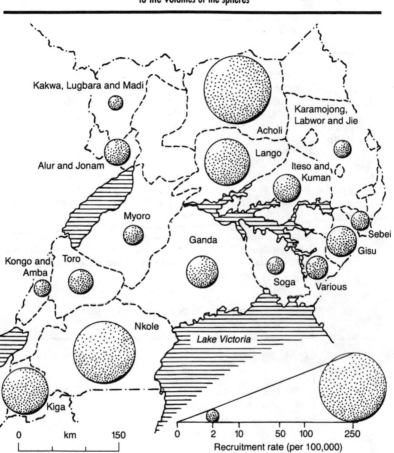

Reprinted with the permission of Cambridge University Press. Smallman-Raynor, M.R., and A.D. Cliff. 1991. Civil war and the spread of AIDS in Central Africa. *Epidemiology and Infection.*

to completely sterilize injection equipment. At the time, average national HIV prevalence was low and Romanian blood banks did not screen donations for HIV (Patrascu and Dumitrescu, 1993).

As illustrated in Figure 5.17, Eastern Europe is one of the fastest-growing centers of HIV prevalence in the world. The earliest "outbreaks" of HIV infection were recorded in the area in 1995 among intravenous drug users in southern Ukraine. Between

Table 5.6
Seroprevalence of HIV Infection in Children and Adults in the Romanian Country Towns (1990)

Group	Constanta No. pos/ tested	%	Focsani No. pos/ tested	%	Craiova No. pos/ tested	%
Adults						
Blood donors	0/32		0/312		0/108	
Orphanage personnel	0/27		0/71		0/62	
Hospital personnel	0/47		0/82		0/41	
Pregnant women	1/102	0.98	0/38		2/100	2.0
Healthy adults	2/3,150	0.063	0/37		0/542	
Teenagers (16–18 yr)	0/36		0/36		0/21	
Total adults	3/3394	0.088	0/576		2/874	
Children						
3–6 yr	0/81		0/80		ND	
Hospital (0–3 yr)	288/382	75.39	4/23	17.39	28/409	6.84
Orphanages	48/175	27.42	35/114	30.7	57/343	16.62
Malnourished	9/128	7.03	ND		14/82	17.07
Total children	345/766	45.03	39/217	17.97	99/766	12.92

Source: Patrascu, I.V., and O. Dumitrescu. 1993. The epidemic of human immunodeficiency virus infection in Romanian children. *AIDS Research and Human Retroviruses.* Bucharest: Romania AIDS Association and Virology Laboratory.

Figure 5.17
Number of newly diagnosed HIV infections by transmission group and
year of report in Eastern Europe, 1994–2001

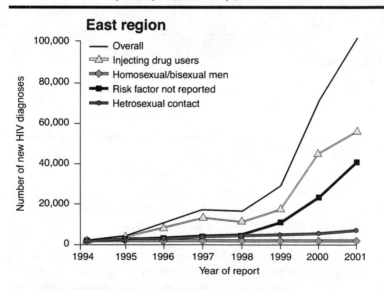

Reprinted with permission from Elsevier (**The Lancet**, 2003, vol. 361, 1035–1044)

Figure 5.18
Four principal heroin trafficking routes and known HIV-1 subtypes (B, C, E, B/C
recombinant) in south and south-east Asia, 1999

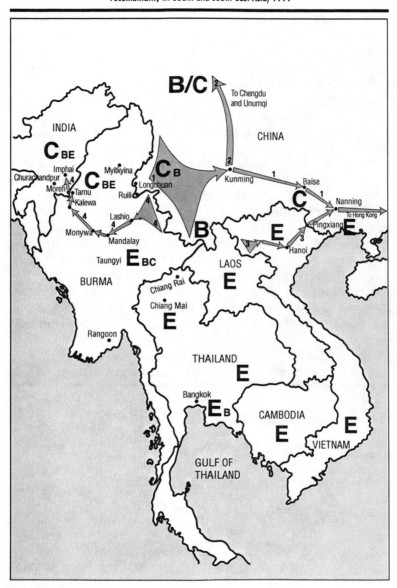

Source: Beyrer, C., M.H. Razak, K. Lisam, et al. 2000. Overland heroin trafficking routes and HIV-1 spread in south
and Southeast Asia. *AIDS.*

1995 and 1999 major increases in HIV prevalence were noted throughout the Russian territories, concentrated in Kaliningrad, Moscow, and Irkutsk. Researchers conducting surveillance in the area attribute rising HIV prevalence to a dramatic increase in intravenous drug use and the illegal drug trade after the fall of the Soviet Union in 1990 destabilized the region. UNAIDS estimates that the number of people living with HIV and AIDS in the east region increased from about 30,000 to 1 million individuals between 1995 and 2001 (Hamers and Downs, 2003).

The region of Southeast Asia traditionally known as the "golden triangle" (northern Thailand, northeastern Myanmar [formerly Burma]), southwestern China, and western Laos) accounts for the production and transport of more than 60 percent of the world's heroin. The majority of opium poppies are grown and processed into heroin in Burma, then shipped east and north into China and Vietnam, or northwest into India. HIV transmission follows these established routes as shown in Figure 5.18, allowing epidemiologists to track both heroin shipping and intravenous drug use by examining relationships among viral strains and subtypes across national borders (Beyrer et al., 2000).

A 1998 survey of tourists (Figure 5.19) in the Dominican Republic shows that most visitors' choice of vacation spot is not influenced by concerns over local HIV risk and prevalence. At the same time, a majority of the survey group felt that receiving HIV

Figure 5.19
Tourists' perceptions of personal risk of HIV infection on vacation and at home

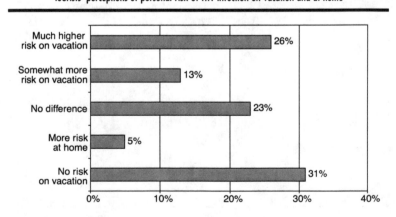

Source: Forsythe, S., J. Hasbún, and M.B. de Lister. 1998. Protecting paradise: Tourism and AIDS in the Dominican Republic. *Health Policy and Planning.*

prevention materials upon entering the country would give them greater confidence that the government was responding appropriately to the epidemic (Forsythe, Hasbún, and de Lister, 1998).

Cost-Effectiveness of HIV Prevention, Care, and Treatment

When creating a national treatment program, policymakers must consider not only the cost of antiretroviral drugs, but also the costs associated with counseling and testing services, treatment of opportunistic infections, and patient monitoring. The costs of HIV prevention initiatives also vary depending on factors such as the program's target community, scope, and desired level of impact.

Figure 5.20 outlines a model of the costs associated with a comprehensive national HIV surveillance and treatment program. Without listing specific costs, which vary from one region to the next, the model accounts for research, productivity losses and gains, educational efforts, and family support as well as treatment and testing costs.

Before committing to a specific HIV prevention or treatment initiative, policymakers and researchers must explore a variety of scenarios to determine which intervention will use available resources most efficiently to the benefit of the greatest number of people. Table 5.7 is based on data developed for a hypothetical cohort of 20,000 pregnant women in sub-Saharan Africa who will receive nevirapine to prevent HIV transmission to their infants. Based on estimated costs for counseling and testing services, patient monitoring, and antiretroviral medication, this model projects how many HIV infections can be prevented and how many "disability adjusted life years" (DALYs) will be saved in regions with either 15-percent or 30-percent HIV prevalence among pregnant women. DALYs measure years of life saved, accounting for quality of life and potential economic productivity lost or gained. As discussed in Chapter 2, the "targeted" prevention model delivers nevirapine only to pregnant women who agree to counseling and test positive for HIV. The "universal" model delivers nevirapine to all pregnant women regardless of HIV status, rendering counseling and testing services unnecessary.

Figure 5.20
Cost Components of AIDS/HIV Infection

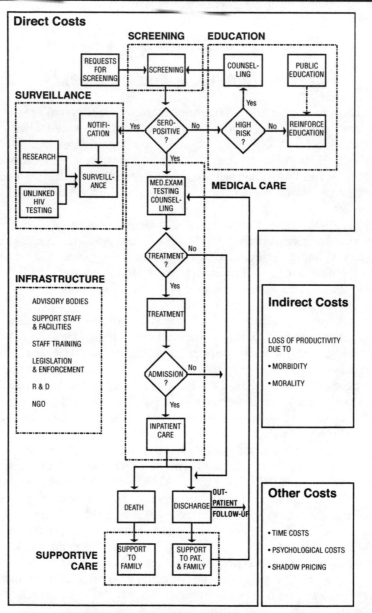

Source: Lim, J.Y., B.W. Chew, and K.H. Phua. 1994. An economic analysis of AIDS—towards a proposed model of costing: a Singapore experience. *Asia Pacific Journal of Public Health.*

Table 5.7
Cost-effectiveness of HIVNET 012 Regimen (one dose nevirapine to mothers and infants)

	Universal Treatment		Targeted Treatment	
	15% HIV-1 Seroprevalence	30% HIV-1 Seroprevalence	15% HIV-1 Seroprevalence	30% HIV-1 Seroprevalence
Program cost per 20,000 women (US$)	83,333	83,333	124,488	141,922
HIV-1 cases averted	302	603	246	476
DALYs saved	7,931	15,862	6,491	12,572
Cost per HIV-1 case averted (US$)	276	138	506	298
Cost per DALY (US$)	10.51	5.25	19.18	11.29

Reprinted with permission from Elsevier (**The Lancet**, 1999, vol. 354, 795–802)

HIV Surveillance and Public Health Responses to HIV and AIDS

Routine HIV surveillance allows local and national governments to monitor the movements of the epidemic countrywide and at the provincial level. Surveillance conducted among intravenous drug users or sex workers might give a good picture of the early stages of an epidemic. Studies of HIV prevalence among young people, pregnant women (as in Figure 5.21), and men attending

Figure 5.21
HIV prevalence by age, South African antenatal clinic attendees: 1991–2001

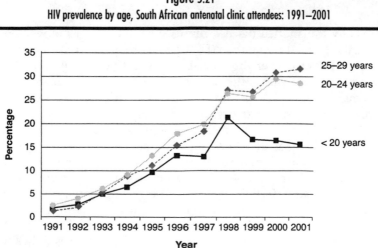

Source: UNAIDS AIDS Epidemic Update, December 2002.

Figure 5.22
HIV Prevalence Among Selected Thai Populations, 1987–2000

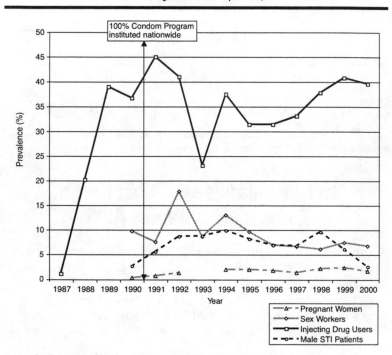

Reprinted with permission from Elsevier (**The Lancet**, 1995, vol. 346, 530–536)

sexually transmitted disease clinics mark the virus's movement into the general population. HIV prevalence and incidence surveys conducted over the course of several years can show the effectiveness of prevention and treatment programs. Some programs (Figure 5.22), such as Thailand's national AIDS control efforts among sex workers, focus on only one sector of society, whereas others, such as the STD prevention trail in Mwanza, Tanzania, focus on the entire population.

One Tanzanian trial examined the effect of treatment for sexually transmitted diseases (STDs) on HIV transmission. Many STDs increase an individual's risk of HIV infection by irritating the genital tract or weakening the immune system. Treatment and prevention of STDs might be possible in regions where HIV treatment is not available because of a lack of resources or health care infrastructure, presenting a new avenue for HIV prevention in resource-scarce settings. In Mwanza, the "intervention" group

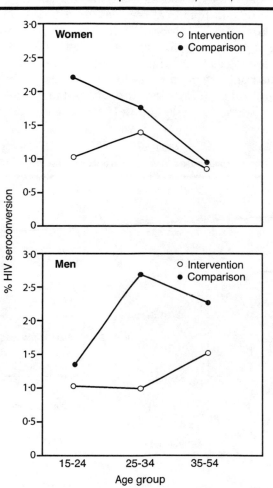

Figure 5.23
Incidence of HIV infection over 2 years by age and sex in STD
intervention and comparison communities, Mwanza, Tanzania

Source: UNAIDS AIDS Epidemic Update, December 2002.

received access to a new STD treatment clinic, including free
drugs and patient monitoring and information on STD prevention and diagnosis. The control group received information on
HIV prevention and safer sex techniques. After two years, incidence of new HIV infections decreased by more than 40 percent
in the group receiving STD treatment, as shown in Figure 5.23.

Stigma and Discrimination

Stigma is one of the most important barriers to accessing diagnosis, support, care, and treatment services for people living with HIV and AIDS (Figure 5.24, Table 5.8). In designing care and prevention programs, it is therefore vital for policymakers to examine public knowledge and attitudes toward HIV and AIDS. AIDS-related stigma might stem from traditional beliefs about sexual relationships, gender roles, race, and class, and these factors should be considered when designing HIV education initiatives.

Figure 5.24
The link between HIV/AIDS and pre-existing sources of stigma and discrimination

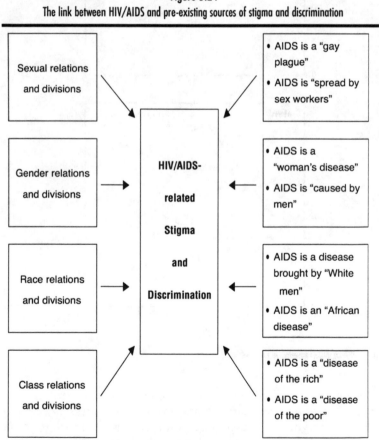

Source: HIV/AIDS related stigma and discrimination: A conceptual framework and an agenda for action. Horizon Program, New York. 2002.

Table 5.8
Levels of Stigma and Discrimination and Intervention Responses

Causal Level	Definition	Examples	Change Mechanism
Super-Structural	Macrosocial and political arrangements, resource and power differences	Gender inequalities, homophobia, poverty, economic underdevelopment	Social movements, empowerment of disenfranchised groups and populations
Structural	Laws and policies	Lack of or poor implementation of human rights laws; laws that promote discrimination, e.g., restrictions on travel and migration	Legislative lobbying, civil and human rights activism, legal reform
Environmental	Living conditions, resources, and opportunities	Lack of rights in workplace, lack of access to information and services	Provision of social and health services, community organization, unionization
Individual	How the environment is experienced and acted upon by individuals	Fear of negative reactions by others, lack of knowledge, low risk perception, moral values	Education, counseling, improved self-efficacy

Source: HIV/AIDS related stigma and discrimination: A conceptual framework and an agenda for action. Horizon Program, New York. 2002.

References

Beyrer, C., M. H. Razak, K. Lisam, et al. 2000. Overland heroin trafficking routes and HIV-1 spread in south and Southeast Asia. *AIDS* 14: 75–83.

Bolognesi, D. P. 1990. Approaches to HIV vaccine design. *Trends in Biotechnology* 8(2): 40–45.

Centers for Disease Control and Prevention, National Center for Health Statistics, National Vital Statistics System. 2001. Death rates for human immunodeficiency virus (HIV) disease, according to sex, race, Hispanic origin, and age; United States, selected years 1987–2001. Available at: http://www.cdc.gov/nchs/datawh/statab/unpubd/mortabs.htm. Accessed: April 20, 2004.

Fauci, A. S. 2003. HIV and AIDS: 20 years of science. *Nature Medicine* 9(7): 839–843.

Forsythe, S., J. Hasbún, and M. B. de Lister. 1998. Protecting paradise: Tourism and AIDS in the Dominican Republic. *Health Policy and Planning* 13(3): 277–286.

Freedberg, K. A., E. Losina, M. C. Weinstein, et al. 2001. The cost effectiveness of combination antiretroviral therapy for HIV disease. *New England Journal of Medicine* 344(11): 824–831.

Grosskurth, H., F. Mosha, and J. Todd, et al. 1995. Impact of improved treatment of sexually transmitted diseases on HIV infection in rural Tanzania: Randomized controlled trial. *Lancet* 346: 530–536.

Guay, L. A., P. Musoke, and T. Fleming et al. 1999. Intrapartum and neonatal single-dose nevirapine compared with zidovudine for prevention of mother to child transmission of HIV-1 in Kampala Uganda: HIVNET 012 randomized trial. *Lancet* 354(9181):795–802.

Hamers, F. F., and A. M. Downs. 2003. HIV in central and Eastern Europe. *Lancet* 361: 1035–1044.

Horizons Program. 2002. HIV/AIDS related stigma and discrimination: A conceptual framework and an agenda for action. New York: Horizons Program.

Klein, E., and R. J. Y. Ho. 2000. Challenges in the development of an effective HIV vaccine: Current approaches and future directions. *Clinical Therapeutics* 22(3): 295–314.

Lim, J. Y., B. W. Chew, and K. H. Phua. 1994. An economic analysis of AIDS—towards a proposed model of costing: a Singapore experience. *Asia Pacific Journal of Public Health* 7(3): 143–150.

Marlink, R., H. Kao, and E. Hsieh. 2001. Clinical care issues for women living with HIV and AIDS in the United States. *AIDS Research and Human Retroviruses* 17(1): 1–33.

Marseille, E., J. G. Kahn, and F. Mmiro, et al. 1999. Cost effectiveness of single-dose nevirapine regimen for mothers and babies to decrease vertical HIV-1 transmission in sub-Saharan Africa. *Lancet* 354: 803–809.

Patrascu, I. V., and O. Dumitrescu. 1993. The epidemic of human immunodeficiency virus infection in Romanian children. *AIDS Research and Human Retroviruses* 9(1): 99–104.

Pomerantz, R. J., and D. L. Horn. 2003. Twenty years of therapy for HIV-1 infection. *Nature Medicine* 9(7): 867–873.

Ramanathan, K., D. Tarantola, and R. Marlink. 2002. Access to HIV and AIDS Care. In M. Essex, P. Kanki, and S. Mboup, eds., *AIDS in Africa*, 2nd ed. New York: Kluwer Academic/Plenum.

Segurado, A.C., S. D. Miranda, M. D. R. D. O. LaTorre, et al. 2003. Evaluation of the care of women living with HIV/AIDS in São Paulo, Brazil. *AIDS Patient Care and STDs* 17(2): 85–93.

Smallman-Raynor, M. R., and A. D. Cliff. 1991. Civil war and the spread of AIDS in Central Africa. *Epidemiology and Infection* 107: 69–80.

Smith, D. K. 2000. HIV/AIDS among African Americans: Progress or progression? *AIDS* 14: 1237–1248.

UNAIDS. 2000. Epidemiological Fact Sheets on HIV/AIDS and Sexually Transmitted Infections: United States of America. Available at: http://www.who.int/emc-hiv/fact_sheets/pdfs/usa_en.pdf. Accessed: April 29, 2004.

———. 2002. AIDS Epidemic Update. Geneva: UNAIDS.

Vidal, N., M. Peeters, C. Mulanga-Kabeya, et al. 2000. Unprecedented degree of human immunodeficiency virus type 1 (HIV-1) group M genetic diversity in the Democratic Republic of the Congo suggests that the HIV-1 pandemic originated in central Africa. *Journal of Virology* 74(22): 10498–10507.

6

Organizations

The following list of international organizations provides examples of the partnerships, funders, research institutions, and community-based organizations at the forefront of the fight against HIV and AIDS today. It would be impossible to list every organization focused on HIV and AIDS worldwide, particularly as growing international awareness of the epidemic leads to the creation of numerous new support, activist, and research partnerships. Institutions listed in this chapter, therefore, are those that maintain a truly international focus, seeking to create partnerships between individuals and governments either across continents or within a specific geographic region. Many of these organizations focus their efforts both on AIDS prevention and care and on clinical and social research, combining direct assistance to communities and individuals with international education and scientific discovery.

African AIDS Vaccine Program (AAVP)
Fax: 41 22 791 4865
E-mail: hvi@who.int
Region: Africa

AAVP is an international network of African researchers and clinicians formed in 2000 to speed the creation and distribution of an effective HIV vaccine in Africa. In partnership with UNAIDS and the WHO, AAVP works to support research, capacity building, and community involvement in new vaccine trials.

AIDS Treatment Data Network
611 Broadway, Suite 613

New York, NY 10012
Phone: (212) 260-8868
Fax: (212) 260-8869
Web site: http://www.atdn.org
Region: United States

The AIDS Treatment Data Network is an advocacy and information source for people living with HIV and AIDS in the United States. The network provides educational materials on HIV and AIDS care and treatment, including information on adherence to antiretroviral regimens.

American Foundation for AIDS Research (AmFAR)
1828 L Street, NW, Suite 802
Washington, DC 20036-5104
Phone: (202) 331-8600
Fax: (202) 331-8606
Web site: http://www.amfar.org
Region: International

This foundation was founded during the early years of the HIV epidemic in the United States to support scientific and medical research on HIV and AIDS prevention, care, and treatment. AmFAR's present mission includes support for research and advocacy efforts in developing countries, as well as in the United States, including support for clinical trials, assistance to community-based nongovernmental organizations, and professional development for health care providers.

Black AIDS Institute
1833 West 8th Street, Suite 21
Los Angeles, CA 90057
Fax: (213) 989-0181
Web site: http://www.blackaids.org
Region: United States

The Black AIDS Institute is dedicated to "fighting AIDS among people of African descent" in the United States through advocacy and information dissemination. The Institute publishes *Kunjisource*, a monthly newsletter reporting on medical advances, political developments, and celebrity activities related to African Americans living with and affected by HIV and AIDS. The institute also supports peer counseling programs, advocacy and outreach, and art exhibits.

Elizabeth Glaser Pediatric AIDS Foundation
1140 Connecticut Avenue NW, Suite 200
Washington, DC 20036
Phone: (202) 296-9165
Fax: (202) 296-9185
Web site: http://www.pedaids.org
Region: International

The foundation supports medical, social, and scientific research focused on children living with or affected by HIV and AIDS. Originally limited to the United States, the foundation currently supports advocacy, research, prevention, and treatment initiatives for children and adults living with HIV and AIDS in developing regions worldwide.

European AIDS Treatment Group (EATG)
Mindener Strasse, 33
40227 Duesseldorf
Germany
Phone: 49 0 211 78 83 481
Fax: 49 0 211 78 85 414
Web site: http://www.eatg.org
Region: Europe

Made up of representatives from twenty-eight countries in Europe, EATG's mission is to increase access to antiretroviral medications, technological advances, and treatment for opportunistic infections for people living with HIV and AIDS. EATG works to facilitate new research on HIV and AIDS treatment and care and seeks to empower Europeans living with HIV to become actively involved in research, testing, and dissemination of new treatments and medical techniques.

Family Health International
2101 Wilson Boulevard, Suite 700
Arlington, VA 22201
Phone: (703) 516-9779
Fax: (703) 516-9781

Web site: http://www.fhi.org
Region: International

Family Heath International (FHI) works in more than seventy countries worldwide to improve public health through access to reproductive services, HIV prevention strategies, counseling, and health-related information services. FHI assists governments and nongovernmental organizations in conducting HIV and AIDS prevalence studies and behavioral surveys. In addition, FHI partners with resource-scarce nations to facilitate introduction of mother-to-child HIV transmission prevention programs, rollout of antiretroviral treatment programs, and development of voluntary counseling and testing services.

Gay Men's Health Crisis
The Tisch Building
119 West 24th Street
New York, NY 10011
Phone: (212) 367-1000
Web site: http://www.gmhc.org
Region: United States

Founded in 1982 in response to rising rates of HIV and AIDS among gay men in New York, the Gay Men's Health Crisis is now a nationwide organization focusing on education, support, and improved access to care and treatment for people living with HIV and AIDS. Although providing services and support to all people living with HIV and AIDS in the United States, Gay Men's Health Crisis emphasizes the fight against homophobia and support for the health and human rights of gay men and lesbians.

Global AIDS Alliance
1225 Connecticut Ave., NW, Suite 401
Washington, DC 20036
Phone: (202) 296-0260
Web site: http://www.globalaidsalliance.org
Region: International

The Global AIDS Alliance works with government and non-governmental partners worldwide to educate policymakers about HIV and AIDS in order to "catalyze" improvements to human rights, access to care and treatment, and funding.

Global AIDS Interfaith Alliance (GAIA)
P.O. Box 29110
San Francisco, CA 94129-0110
Phone: (415) 461-7196
Fax: (415) 461-9681
Web site: http://www.thegaia.org
Region: International

GAIA partners with religious groups in developing countries to create and support community-based, grassroots HIV and AIDS counseling, care, and education initiatives. GAIA's local focus helps individual communities organize a response to HIV and AIDS based on their specific needs, concerns, and traditions. GAIA is not affiliated with any single religious faith, but rather seeks to involve religious leaders and organizations of all faiths in HIV and AIDS education and support.

Global Fund to Fight AIDS, Tuberculosis, and Malaria
53 Avenue Louis-Casaï
1216 Geneva-Cointrin
Switzerland
Phone: 41 22 791 17 00
Fax: 41 22 791 17 01
Web site: http://www.theglobalfund.org
Region: International

The Global Fund supports HIV and AIDS care, treatment, and prevention programs proposed by governments and nongovernmental organizations in developing countries worldwide. The Global Fund is financed by donations from national governments, individuals, and private foundations, and is administered independently from any national government or international organization. The Global Fund supports programs that require partnership between government offices, nongovernmental organizations, local communities, and people living with HIV and AIDS in designing and implementing treatment and education interventions.

Global Network of People Living with HIV/AIDS (GNP+)
P.O. Box 11726
1001 GS, Amsterdam
The Netherlands

Phone: 31 20 689 8218
Fax: 31 20 689 8059
Web site: http://www.gnpplus.net
Region: International

GNP+ seeks to improve the quality of life of people living with
HIV and AIDS through political action, education initiatives targeting governments and communities, and international support
networks for communities of people living with or affected by
HIV and AIDS. GNP+ supports five branches in Africa, Asia and
the Pacific, Europe, Latin America and the Caribbean, and North
America.

Harvard AIDS Institute
651 Huntington Ave., Suite 631
Boston, MA 02115
Phone: (617) 432-4400
Fax: (617) 432-4545
Web site: http://www.aids.harvard.edu
Region: International

The Harvard AIDS Institute is a research organization administered through Harvard University's School of Public Health. The
institute's research and clinical trials focus on HIV vaccine development, a better understanding of the genetics of HIV-1 subtype
C (the most common HIV subtype in southern Africa), and
strategies for treatment delivery in resource-scarce settings.

HIV Vaccine Trials Network (HVTN)
1100 Fairview Ave. N, PO Box 19024
Seattle, WA 98109
Phone: (800) 448-0440
Web site: http://www.hvtn.org
Region: International

The HVTN conducts clinical trials of HIV vaccines in the United
States and internationally under the auspices of the United States
Division of AIDS and National Institutes of Health. As well as
sponsoring clinical trials, the HVTN facilitates international
exchanges of technical information and scientific discovery
related to HIV vaccine development.

Hope for African Children Initiative
House 1/237
Wood Garden, Off Wood Ave.
Kilmani, Nairobi
Kenya
Phone: 254 2 577 487
Web site: http://www.hopeforafricanchildren.org
Region: Africa

The initiative is active throughout Africa, focusing its efforts on regions where the HIV epidemic is particularly severe. Initiative staff, teachers, health care providers, and volunteers work with families affected by HIV and AIDS to find medical care for parents who are ill, assist parents in planning for their children's future, and offering counseling, school programs, and career training to orphans. The Initiative is cosponsored by six international and African organizations, including CARE, PLAN, the Society for Women and AIDS in Africa, and Save the Children.

Horizons Program
1 Dag Hammarskjold Plaza
New York, NY 10017
Phone: (212) 339-0500
Fax: (212) 755-6052
Web site: http://www.popcouncil.org/horizons
Region: International

The Horizons Program is administered by the Population Council and is based in five offices in sub-Saharan Africa, North Africa, South America and the Caribbean, Southeast Asia, and the United States. Horizons works to create research partnerships in developing countries to fight HIV and AIDS, focusing on strategies for service delivery, improving prevention interventions, and studying best practices for treatment and support. In addition, Horizons works to build research and care capacity in resource-scarce regions through training and partnerships.

International AIDS Economics Network
Web site: http://www.iaen.org
Region: International

The International AIDS Economics Network (IAEN) is a research organization dedicated to collecting information on the costs and cost-effectiveness of HIV and AIDS prevention, care, and treatment options. IAEN advises national and local governments on how to use scarce resources to serve people living with HIV and AIDS through locally appropriate initiatives. In addition, IAEN helps developing country governments conduct cost-effectiveness research to evaluate HIV and AIDS care and prevention strategies using state-of-the art statistical software and methods of analysis.

International AIDS Society
Karolinska Institute
Berzeliusväg 8
SE-171 77 Stockholm
Sweden
Phone: 46 8 508 846 40
Fax: 46 8 508 846 64
Web site: http://www.ias.se
Region: International

As a resource for HIV and AIDS researchers, clinicians, counselors, and other health care workers the International AIDS Society sponsors international training and education initiatives, including the International AIDS Conference, which takes place every two years. As a scientific and research partnership, the society works to include the "scientific perspective" in local and international efforts to fight HIV and AIDS, disseminating information on best medical practices, offering consultation on new scientific developments, and encouraging debate on research related to HIV and AIDS care, treatment, and prevention.

International AIDS Vaccine Initiative (IAVI)
110 William Street
New York, NY 10038-3901
Phone: (212) 847-1111
Fax: (212) 847-1112
Web site: http://www.iavi.org
Region: International

Recognizing that "the best long-term solution to the growing AIDS epidemic is a vaccine," IAVI supports international HIV vaccine research and works to ensure that a future vaccine will be accessible in resource-scarce regions worldwide.

International Association of Physicians in AIDS Care
33 North LaSalle Street, Suite 1700
Chicago, IL 60602-2601
Phone: (312) 795-4930
Fax: (312) 795-4938
Web site: http://www.iapac.org
Region: International

Made up of more than 12,000 members from eighty-nine countries, the International Association of Physicians in AIDS Care (IAPAC) seeks to "marshal the coordinated strength of health care professionals worldwide to the benefit of people living with and affected by HIV/AIDS."

**International Community of Women
Living with HIV/AIDS (ICW)**
Unit 6, Building 1, Canonbury Business Centre
Canonbury Yard 190a, New North Road
London N1 7BJ
United Kingdom
Phone: 44 20 7704 0606
Fax: 44 20 7704 8070
Web site: http://www.icw.org
Region: International

The ICW was formed in 1992 by a group of women attending the Eighth International AIDS Conference in Amsterdam. The group aims to create a network of support and communication among women living with HIV and AIDS worldwide to increase visibility of and advocacy for women affected by the HIV epidemic.

International Council of AIDS Service Organizations
65 Wellesley St. E., Suite 403
Toronto, Ontario
Canada M4Y 1G7
Phone: (416) 921-0018
Fax: (416) 921-9979
Web site: http://www.icaso.org
Region: International

Based in Canada with regional secretariats in Latin America, Asia, Europe, and Africa the International Council of AIDS Service Organizations (ICASO) provides a network of support and communication for nongovernmental and community-based AIDS organizations. IACSO seeks to strengthen community organizations in resource-scarce regions in order to support access to HIV and AIDS care and support, human rights protection of people living with HIV and AIDS, and local HIV and AIDS education efforts.

International HIV Treatment Access Coalition (ITAC)
ITAC Secretariat, Department of HIV/AIDS
World Health Organization
20 Avenue Appia
CH-1211 Geneva 27
Switzerland
Phone: 41 22 791 1641
Fax: 41 22 791 4834
E-mail: itac@who.int
Web site: http://www.itacoalition.org
Region: International

The coalition seeks to improve international drug procurement and delivery systems, train health care workers, and increase donations to AIDS care efforts in developing countries. ITAC partners with governments, nongovernmental organizations, people living with HIV and AIDS, and research organizations to increase access to HIV and AIDS care and treatment.

International Red Cross and Red Crescent
P.O. Box 372
CH-1211 Geneva 19
Switzerland
Phone: 41 22 730 42 22
Fax: 41 22 733 03 95
Web site: http://www.ifrc.org
Region: International

The Red Cross has addressed HIV and AIDS in developing countries since the 1980s. Since 1998 the organization has embarked on an initiative to better educate members, volunteers, and partners on issues related to HIV and AIDS in order to strengthen advocacy and disaster relief efforts.

Joint United Nations Programme on AIDS (UNAIDS)
World Health Organization
20 Avenue Appia

CH-1211 Geneva 27
Switzerland
Phone: 41 22 791 3666
Fax: 41 22 791 4187
Web site: http://www.unaids.org
Region: International

UNAIDS is one of the world's most influential AIDS advocacy and support organizations. Jointly supported by the United Nations, the World Health Organization, the World Food Program, the International Labor Organization, and the World Bank, UNAIDS monitors the worldwide HIV epidemic and works to mobilize resources and advocacy efforts to fight HIV and AIDS. UNAIDS also provides technical support and publishes a wide variety of scientific, scholarly, and educational materials.

Network of African People Living with HIV/AIDS
P.O. Box 30218
Nairobi
Kenya
Phone: 254 2 228766
Fax: 254 2 312888
Web site: http://www.naprap.org
Region: Africa

Based in Kenya, Zambia, and Côte d'Ivoire, the Network of African People Living with HIV/AIDS (NAP+) seeks to "strengthen a regional voice of people living with HIV/AIDS" in Africa to improve quality of life and access to care and to influence local and national policy decisions. NAP+ has created a network of support and visibility to combat stigma and to better educate people living with HIV and AIDS in Africa through conferences, training, and information dissemination.

Society for Women and AIDS in Africa
Rue 1 X G, Villa Rose, Point E BP
16425 Dakar-Fann Dakar
Senegal
Phone: 221 824 59 20
Fax: 221 824 49 88
Web site: http://www.swaainternational.org
Region: Africa

The Society for Women and AIDS in Africa is the first pan-African HIV and AIDS support and advocacy program devoted specifically to women and children living with and affected by HIV and AIDS. The society was founded in 1988 by women from Angola, Democratic Republic of Congo, Zambia, Sudan, Nigeria, and Ethiopia in response to sharply increasing HIV prevalence among African women. In 2003 the society supported thirty-nine local chapters in partnership with UNAIDS, the World Bank, the World Health Organization, and others. The society focuses on care and advocacy for orphans and children affected by HIV, combating gender discrimination, increasing women's access to contraception, and improving women's access to antiretroviral therapy.

Student Global AIDS Campaign (SGAC)
1225 Connecticut Avenue NW, Suite 401
Washington, DC 20036
Phone: (202) 296-6727
Web site: http://www.fightglobalaids.org
Region: International

Based in the United States, the SGAC is a lobbying group run by students based in more than fifty colleges and universities. SGAC focuses its efforts on fund-raising to support international AIDS organizations, lobbying and education in support of access to antiretroviral treatment in developing countries, and a campaign to reduce or cancel developing countries' debt burden.

United Nations Children's Fund (UNICEF)
UNICEF House 3
United Nations Plaza
New York, NY 10017
Phone: (212) 326-7000
Fax: (212) 887-7465
Web site: http://www.unicef.org/aids/index.html
Region: International

UNICEF's response to quickly increasing HIV prevalence among people under the age of twenty-five includes support for orphans, programs to prevent mother-to-child HIV transmission, and efforts to educate young people in HIV prevention techniques and "life skills."

United Nations Development Programme (UNDP)
One United Nations Plaza
New York, NY 10017
Fax: (212) 906-5364
Web site: http://www.undp.org
Region: International

UNDP works with national governments to support crisis resolution, technological and communications challenges, poverty reduction, the promotion of democratic governance, and human rights protection. In addition, UNDP specifically focuses on including support for the fight against HIV and AIDS in government development and budgeting plans through greater empowerment of women and through supporting access to clean water, nutrition, and health care.

World Bank HIV/AIDS
Global HIV/AIDS Program
1818 H Street, NW
Washington, DC 20433
Phone: (202) 473-9414
Fax: (202) 522-3235
Web site: http://www1.worldbank.org/hiv_aids
Region: International

The World Bank recognizes the long-term effects that HIV and AIDS will have on resource-scarce countries' economies and economic development, and seeks to support HIV and AIDS care and treatment programs through grants, loans, and credits. The World Bank works with a variety of local and international partners, including the United Nations, UNAIDS, and the Global AIDS Program.

World Health Organization
Avenue Appia 20
1211 Geneva 27
Switzerland
Phone: 41 22 791 2111
Fax: 41 22 791 3111
Web site: http://www.who.int/en
Region: International

The World Health Organization seeks to achieve the "attainment by all peoples of the highest possible level of health." Governed by the World Health Assembly's 192 member states, the World Health Organization works with international partners, including UNAIDS, to support access to HIV and AIDS counseling, testing, care, and treatment. The World Health Organization and UNAIDS cosponsor the "3 by 5 Initiative," a program that aims to treat 3 million people living with HIV and AIDS with antiretroviral therapy by 2005.

7

Selected Print and Nonprint Resources

The resources described in this chapter will assist in further research on specific issues related to HIV and AIDS in the world. On-line resources such as UNAIDS' fact sheets on HIV prevalence and Family Health International's guidelines and training materials are updated frequently to reflect new research discoveries, changes in local and national policies, and recent surveillance and epidemiological findings. Databases of news articles and primary source documents such as AEGIS and AllAfrica contain historical information on social and political responses to the HIV epidemic, adding regional detail to global trends. The primary source materials listed are almost all public domain documents, available in Web-based archives maintained by nongovernmental organizations, international bodies, embassies, and national governments. Access to these documents provides a firsthand view of the decisions, policies, discoveries, and protests that have shaped the world's response to AIDS. All Internet-based resources listed in this chapter are available free of charge to all readers with access to the Internet. Textbooks and other print resources provide an in-depth look at specific aspects of the epidemic, such as human rights, the search for a vaccine, AIDS and women's health, and the socioeconomic impact of the epidemic.

Primary Sources

Abuja Declaration on HIV/AIDS, Tuberculosis and Other Related Infectious Diseases, April 24–27, 2001. Available at: http://www.un.org/ga/aids/pdf/abuja_declaration.pdf

The declaration, drafted at the end of the Organization for African Unity's 2001 summit in Abuja, Nigeria, calls for the creation of a global fund to fight HIV and AIDS in developing countries. This document forms the basis of the Global Fund to Fight AIDS, Tuberculosis, and Malaria proposed by United Nations Secretary-General Kofi Annan in April 2001.

Accelerating access to HIV/AIDS care and treatment in developing countries: A Joint Statement of Intent. Available at: http://www.unaids.org

In 2000, five pharmaceutical companies entered into a partnership with UNAIDS, UNICEF, the WHO, and other international organizations to form the Accelerating Access Initiative. The initiative is the first international partnership with pharmaceutical companies focused on negotiating antiretroviral drug price reductions to make HIV and AIDS treatments available in resource-scarce regions.

Agreement on Trade-Related Aspects of Intellectual Property Rights (TRIPS). Available at: http://www.wto.org/english/tratop_e/trips_e/t_agm3c_e.htm#5

TRIPS was ratified in 1994 by the World Trade Organization to provide international guidelines on patent protection. Although TRIPS specifies that product patents must be respected worldwide, the agreement includes a section that authorizes governments to break patents "In the case of a national emergency or other circumstances of extreme urgency."

The Belmont Report: Ethical Principles and Guidelines for the Protection of Human Subjects of Research. April 18, 1979. Available at: http://www.fda.gov/oc/ohrt/irbs/belmont.html

The Belmont Report, authored by the U.S. National Commission for the Protection of Human Subjects of Biomedical and Behavioral Research, lays out ethical guidelines to govern the design and conduct of clinical research involving human subjects. The report's three key tenets of respect for persons, beneficence, and justice provide the basis for human subjects' protection in research studies.

Declaration of Helsinki Ethical Principles for Medical Research Involving Human Subjects. Available at: http://www.wma.net/e/policy/b3.htm

The World Medical Association's 2001 declaration requires that clinical trials of new drugs and medical procedures avoid the use of placebos if possible, instead comparing new therapies to proven, preexisting techniques.

The Delhi Declaration: Parliamentarians' Commitment towards a World Without AIDS. Available at: http://www.india-seminar.com/2002/520/520%20the%20delhi%20declaration.htm

The Delhi Declaration documents a commitment by the governments of South Africa, Kenya, Uganda, Nigeria, Thailand, Nepal, China, and India to formulate a comprehensive, local and international response to HIV and AIDS.

The Durban Declaration. *Nature*, 2000; 406: 15–16.

The Durban Declaration was drafted in 2000 in response to South African President Thabo Mbeki's public questioning of the causal link between HIV and AIDS. The declaration's 5,000 signatories affirm that "The evidence that AIDS is caused by HIV-1 or HIV-2 is clear cut, exhaustive, and unambiguous."

Energy and Commerce Members Question Sesame Character Introduction. Available at: http://energycommerce.house.gov/107/letters/07122002_667print.htm

Six members of the U.S. government's Committee on Energy and Commerce wrote on July 12, 2002, to the president and CEO of the Public Broadcasting Service to protest any future introduction of an HIV-positive character onto the children's television show *Sesame Street*. The letter requests that the Public Broadcasting Service describe the reasoning behind the introduction of a character living with HIV and to promptly account for how much "public money" was spent on *Sesame Street*.

The Global Fund to Fight AIDS, Tuberculosis, and Malaria Funded Programs Database. Available at: http://www.theglobalfund.org/search/default.aspx?lang=en

Founded in 2001, the Global Fund supports programs to prevent, treat, and study AIDS, tuberculosis, and malaria in resource-scarce regions. The fund's database includes full text of proposals from more than fifty countries worldwide.

International Ethical Guidelines for Biomedical Research Involving Human Subjects. Available at: http://www.cioms.ch/frame_guidelines_nov_2002.htm

Guidelines developed by the Council for International Organizations of Medical Sciences and the World Health Organization to regulate international clinical trials. The guidelines stipulate that study participants must receive clinical care equivalent to the standard of care in the study's sponsoring country.

The London Declaration on AIDS Prevention. *International Nursing Review,* 1988; 35(4): 119.

The London Declaration was composed and ratified by the 1988 World Summit of Ministers of Health on Programmes for HIV Prevention. The Declaration is one of the first international documents to explicitly state that discrimination against people living with HIV and AIDS hampers public health interventions aimed at preventing and treating HIV infection.

The Nairobi Declaration: An African Appeal for an AIDS Vaccine. Available at: http://www.who.int/vaccine_research/diseases/hiv/aavp/en

The Nairobi Declaration, signed by forty African clinicians and researchers, calls for increased support for HIV vaccine development in African countries, including support for local infrastructure, national and local government participation, and international funding and technical support.

Revealing the "Blood Wound" of the Spread of HIV AIDS in Henan Province—Written on the Eve of the First AIDS Day of the New Millennium by He Aifang. Available at: http://www.usembassy-china.org.cn/sandt/henan-hiv.htm

This 2000 article exposes the effects of allegedly unsafe blood and plasma collection practices on HIV transmission in rural China. Composed under a pseudonym, the accuracy of the article's claims cannot be fully established. Nevertheless, "Revealing the 'Blood Wound'" led to the first frank discussion of commercial blood collection and new HIV infections in the Chinese press. Background on the article is available from the U.S. Embassy in China at: http://www.usembassy-china.org.cn/sandt/henan-hiv.htm.

South African Constitutional Court Judgment Compelling Government to Provide Mother-to-Child Transmission Prevention— Delivered 5 July 2002. Available at: http://www.tac.org.za/ Documents/MTCTCourtCase/ConCourtJudgmentOrdering MTCTP-5July2002.pdf

The South African Treatment Action Campaign has published the text of Pretoria High Court Judge Chris Botha's landmark decision compelling the South African government to provide antiretroviral therapy to prevent mother-to-child HIV transmission in public health facilities.

State of the Union Address by George W. Bush, January 28, 2003. Available at: http://www.whitehouse.gov/news/releases/ 2003/01/20030128-19.html

In his January 2003 State of the Union Address, U.S. President Bush calls on Congress to approve US$15 billion over five years to fight HIV and AIDS worldwide. The "Emergency Plan for AIDS Relief" aims to treat 2 million people with AIDS, prevent 7 million new HIV infections, and deliver care to 10 million people living with HIV and AIDS in 15 countries worldwide.

United Nations General Assembly Special Session on HIV/AIDS Declaration of Commitment. Available at: http://www.un.org/ ga/aids/coverage/FinalDeclarationHIVAIDS.html

This United Nations Declaration identifies HIV and AIDS as "a global emergency," stating that without sufficient action, HIV will adversely affect economic development, human rights, and community health worldwide.

United Nations Resolution 1308. Available at: http://www.un. org/Docs/scres/2000/sc2000.htm

Resolution 1308, passed in 2000 by the United Nations Security Council, recognizes the "need to incorporate HIV/AIDS prevention awareness skills and advice in aspects of the United Nations Department of Peacekeeping Operations' training for peacekeeping personnel." This acknowledgment of the effect that armed conflict has on the spread of HIV lays the groundwork for future efforts at HIV education and prevention among military service personnel.

World Health Organization. New offers of low-cost antiretroviral medicines: A statement from the World Health Organization [statement WHO/04]. February 9, 2001. Available at: http://www.who.int/inf-pr–2001/en/state2001–04.html

This statement from the director general of the World Health Organization "welcomes" announcements from Cipla and other drug manufacturing companies that generic antiretroviral therapy could be sold in developing countries for US$600 per person per year. The statement affirms the WHO's interest in "working closely" with generic drug manufacturers to make HIV and AIDS treatment available in resource-scarce regions.

WTO Declaration on the TRIPS Agreement and Public Health. Doha, Qatar, 2001. Available at: http://www.ictsd.org/ministerial/doha/docs/mindeclfinal.pdf

The "Doha Declaration," ratified in 2001 by the World Trade Organization, states that governments may override patents in times of national public health emergency. This amendment to TRIPS authorizes national governments to issue "compulsory licenses" for the production of generic drugs to treat HIV, tuberculosis, malaria, and other diseases.

Print Resources

Alcamo, E. 2003. *AIDS: The biological basis,* 3rd edition. Boston: Jones and Bartlett Publishers.

This medical reference book provides in-depth discussions of the biological aspects of HIV, including the mechanics of virus transmission, virus-host interactions, and the effects of antiretroviral drugs on host and virus. The third edition includes information on prevention strategies, mother-to-child HIV transmission, and HIV epidemics in resource-scarce regions.

Barnett, T., and A. Whiteside. 2002. *AIDS in the 21st century: Disease and globalization.* Hampshire, England: Palgrave Macmillan.

Barnett and Whiteside examine the social and economic impact of HIV and AIDS in developing regions from the perspective of governments, local communities, businesses, and families. *AIDS in the 21st Century* discusses government responses and care and prevention interventions at the national and local level in sub-Saharan Africa.

Bartlett, J. G., and A. K. Finkbeiner. 2001. *The guide to living with HIV infection: Developed at the Johns Hopkins AIDS Clinic,* 5th edition. Baltimore, MD: Johns Hopkins University Press.

This handbook for people living with HIV and AIDS provides basic and comprehensive information on HIV treatment and care, new medications, challenges of living with HIV and AIDS, and information for caregivers. The fifth edition contains new sections on women and AIDS and coinfection with HIV and tuberculosis.

Baylies, C., J. Bujra, and C. Baglies, eds. 2001. *AIDS, sexuality, and gender in Africa: The struggle continues.* London: UCL Press.

Based on personal accounts from women in nine Zambian and Tanzanian communities, this work examines the effects of HIV and AIDS on African women and explores ways that women can affect the course of the epidemic. The editors address the roles that gender norms play in the focus communities' responses to HIV and AIDS and suggest strategies to empower women and men to respond effectively to the epidemic.

Brandt, D. 2001. *The approaching storm: HIV/AIDS in Asia.* Washington, DC: World Vision Publications.

Brandt examines the development of the HIV epidemic in Asian countries, a region long considered to have been spared the worst effects of the virus. By 2001 Asia's nascent HIV epidemic threatened to surpass that of sub-Saharan Africa. This monograph discusses emerging HIV epidemics among Asian sex workers, intravenous drug users, and other vulnerable groups.

Cleland, J., and B. Ferry, eds. 1995. *Sexual behavior and AIDS in the developing world.* London: Taylor and Francis.

Published in collaboration with the World Health Organization, this book investigates HIV prevention strategies and barriers to their success in developing regions. Cleland and Ferry include specific information on condom distribution and family planning, sexual risk taking and behavior change, and the impact of other sexually transmitted diseases on HIV transmission.

Dejong, J. 2003. *Making an impact in HIV and AIDS: NGO experiences of scaling up.* London: Intermediate Technology Publications.

In regions where health care infrastructure is weak or government commitment to health care is insufficient, nongovernmental organizations (NGOs) might be on the front lines of HIV and AIDS prevention, advocacy, and care efforts. Working from case studies and personal accounts from representatives of NGO, Dejong provides strategies for increasing the impact national and community-based NGOs can have on HIV and AIDS.

Dolin, R., H. Masur, and M. S. Saag. 2002. *AIDS therapy,* 2nd edition. Oxford, England: Churchill Livingstone.

AIDS Therapy is a comprehensive guide to HIV and AIDS treatments. The book includes in-depth information on all currently available antiretroviral drugs, including fusion inhibitors such as T-20. In addition, Dolin et al. address the treatment of opportunistic infections associated with AIDS, alternative therapies, and strategies for adherence to antiretroviral regimens.

Essex, M., S. M'boup, P. J. Kanki, R. Marlink, and S. D. Tlou, eds. 2002. *AIDS in Africa,* 2nd edition. Norwell, MA: Kluwer Academic/Plenum Publishers.

This reference book examines the African HIV epidemic from a local and continental perspective, addressing government responses and the challenges of providing adequate care and treatment for people living with HIV and AIDS in resource-scarce regions. The book includes updated epidemiological statistics as well as sections on training programs for health care personnel, the costs and cost-effectiveness of providing antiretroviral therapy, and case studies of national responses.

Fan, H., R. F. Connor, and L. P. Villarreal. 2004. *AIDS: Science and society*, 4th edition. Boston: Jones and Bartlett Publishers.

This reference book includes comprehensive information on the basic biology and social impact of HIV and AIDS, focused on new discoveries in the fields of epidemiology and virology.

Guest, E. 2003. *Children of AIDS: Africa's orphan crisis*. London: Pluto Press.

Using case studies conducted in Zambia, Uganda, and South Africa, Guest examines the effects of HIV and AIDS on African children. The book collects the stories of "AIDS orphans," caregivers and relatives, health care providers, and community service leaders.

Holmes, W. 2003. *Protecting the future: HIV prevention, care, and support among displaced and war-affected populations*. Bloomfield, CT: Kumarian Press.

This practical guide for field-workers working with displaced populations provides information on how to design and implement HIV prevention interventions among refugees. Holmes includes specific strategies and exercises aimed at involving refugees in culturally appropriate, community-based education and prevention programs.

Irwin, A.C., J. Millen, and D. Fallows. 2003. *Global AIDS: Myths and facts: Tools for fighting the AIDS pandemic*. Cambridge, MA: South End Press.

Irwin et al. address twelve common "myths" about the worldwide HIV epidemic, including the belief that "AIDS is an African problem" and that "treatment in developing countries is not technically feasible." Discussion focuses on the effect of partnerships between activists and scientists on global and regional responses to HIV. The book includes an introduction by South African Treatment Action Campaign Chair Zackie Achmat.

Kalipeni, E., S. Craddock, J. Oppong, and J. Ghosh, eds. 2003. *HIV and AIDS in Africa: Beyond epidemiology*. Blackwell Publishers.

This collection of work from African activists, health care workers, scientists, and others examines the causes and impact of the HIV epidemic in Africa from social, scientific, and political perspectives. Book sections address the impact of poverty, war, migration, gender roles, and global economic relationships on the spread of and response to HIV across Africa.

Mann, J., S. Gruskin, M. A. Grodin, and G. Annas, eds. 1999. *Health and human rights.* London: Routledge.

Health and Human Rights collects perspectives from health care providers, lawyers, and policymakers on the connections among public health, access to health care, and individual human rights. The collection includes a section on HIV and AIDS along with more general information on international human rights legislation and guidelines.

Mann, J., and D. J. M. Tarantola, eds. 1996. *AIDS in the World II.* Oxford: Oxford University Press.

After nearly twenty years of HIV and AIDS, international scientific, social, policy, and health care experts reflect on the current state of HIV globally and discuss lessons learned from the first decades of the epidemic.

Matthews, D. D. 2003. *AIDS sourcebook: Basic consumer health information about acquired immune deficiency syndrome,* 3rd edition. Detroit, MI: Omnigraphics.

The *AIDS Sourcebook* provides a detailed overview of HIV diagnosis, progression, and treatment for people living with HIV and AIDS and their caregivers. The book includes sections on antiretroviral therapy, issues for mothers and children living with HIV, HIV prevention science and programs, and statistical information on HIV and AIDS in the United States.

Micollier, E., ed. 2003. *Sexual cultures in East Asia.* London: Routledge.

Using ethnographic, historical, and sociological research perspectives, this book examines HIV risk and prevention in South and Southeast Asia. Contributors discuss the social aspects of gender, power relationships between men and women, commercial sex work, family structures, and religion in relationship to HIV transmission and vulnerability.

Oldstone, M. B. A. 2000. *Viruses, plagues, and history.* Oxford: Oxford University Press.

Oldstone charts the history of viral epidemics in human history from smallpox and influenza to tuberculosis, ebola, and HIV. This popular history examines the impact of "plagues" on science, society, and government and compares past and present responses to health crises precipitated by deadly viruses.

Panda, S., A. Chatterjee, and A. S. Abdul-Quader, eds. 2003. *Living with the AIDS virus: The epidemic and the response in India.* Thousand Oaks, CA: Sage Publications.

Panda et al. have collected a series of perspectives on the history of HIV in India since the virus was first detected more than fifteen years ago, examining the Indian government's response to the nation's increasing epidemic.

Richman, D. D., ed. 2003. *Human immunodeficiency virus.* London: International Medical Press.

This compendium of articles by clinicians and researchers provides a basic introduction to the molecular epidemiology, pathogenesis, transmission, and treatment of HIV.

Singhal, A., and E. M. Rogers. 2003. *Combating AIDS: Communication strategies in action.* Thousand Oaks, CA: Sage Publications.

Focusing on HIV prevention and education efforts worldwide, *Combating AIDS* examines the vital role that communication plays in ensuring the success of prevention interventions. Singhal and Rogers use case studies to illustrate methods of crafting culturally appropriate HIV prevention messages in developing countries.

Stine, G. J. 2003. *AIDS update 2003.* San Francisco, CA: Benjamin Cummings.

This reference book is based on the chronology of the HIV epidemic in the world, tracking twenty-two years of scientific discovery, sociopolitical responses, advances in prevention and treatment, and legal responses.

Stockdill, B. C. 2003. *Activism against AIDS: At the intersections of sexuality, race, gender, and class.* Boulder, CO: Lynne Rienner Publishers.

This handbook details the experience of "minority" groups affected by HIV and AIDS in the United States. Stockdill explores how intersecting identities such as race and gender can affect an individual's experiences with HIV, access to support and care, and ability to become involved in local and national responses.

Thomas, P. 2001. *Big shot: Passion, politics, and the struggle for an AIDS vaccine.* New York: PublicAffairs.

Thomas presents a social history of HIV vaccine design and testing from 1994 to 2001. *Big Shot* examines the political alliances, funding strategies, and personalities behind the slow and often controversial search for an effective vaccine to prevent HIV.

Wong-Staal, F. 2002. *AIDS vaccine research.* New York: Marcel Dekker.

This textbook provides a detailed examination of the current state of HIV vaccine design. Including chapters on vaccine engineering, HIV's viral diversity, and the use of animal models in vaccine testing, *AIDS Vaccine Research* focuses on the technical and scientific challenges of vaccine development.

Nonprint Resources

AEGIS
http://www.aegis.org

Founded in the 1980s, AEGIS is an on-line database of information on HIV and AIDS, including current events, scientific discovery, and policy formulation and change. AEGIS collects scientific articles, conference proceedings, and literature from news media sources, allowing free access to information on the current state of the international HIV epidemic.

AllAfrica
http://allafrica.com/aids

AllAfrica Global Media is one of the world's largest on-line distributors of African news sources. AllAfrica AIDS collects and archives articles published by African news media, giving a continent-wide and local view of responses to HIV and AIDS.

European AIDS Project and Mobility
http://www.aidsmobility.org/

The European AIDS Project Web site includes a list of links to European HIV and AIDS support, research, education, and advocacy organizations. The list includes special sections on migrants, immigrants, and displaced populations in Europe.

Fourteenth International AIDS Conference
http://www.aids2002.com

The Fourteenth International AIDS Conference Web site provides news, full text of speeches and presentations, and a database of abstracts from the 2002 International AIDS Society Conference. The conference abstracts database allows users to search for recent study results from around the world, focusing on a broad range of topics related to HIV and AIDS, including clinical trials of new treatments, prevention studies, community and grassroots organizing, and cost-effectiveness studies. The Fifteenth Conference on AIDS will be held in Bangkok, Thailand, in 2004. The conference Web site is available at: http://www.aids2004.org.

Growthouse.org (Asian AIDS Resources)
http://www.growthhouse.org/asianhiv.html

This set of "regional guides" contains information on HIV and AIDS organizations in Asian countries, including Thailand, Malaysia, Singapore, Indonesia, Hong Kong, Japan, the Philippines, and India. In addition, Growthouse includes a list of resources for Asian immigrants living in the United States.

HIV/AIDS Positive Stories (Southeast Asia Directory of Services)
http://www.hivaids.webcentral.com.au/text/dir5.html

This directory includes contact information for South and Southeast Asian HIV support and education organizations in Cambodia, China, India, Indonesia, Japan, Malaysia, Mongolia, the Philippines, Papua New Guinea, and Thailand.

HIV/AIDS Treatment Information Service
http://www.aidsinfo.nih.gov/

Sponsored by the U.S. Department of Health and Human Services, "AIDS Info" provides information on clinical trials related to HIV and AIDS in the United States and new and existing HIV treatments. AIDS Info collects information for people living with HIV and AIDS and their health care providers on new treatments and medical advances and provides treatment guidelines and educational materials on HIV and AIDS vaccine development, care, and treatment.

Kaiser Family Foundation
http://www.kff.org

The Henry J. Kaiser Family Foundation focuses its research and publications on policymaking related to public health issues in the United States and internationally. The foundation tracks domestic and international spending on HIV and AIDS, the development of new prevention and care programs, public reaction to the epidemic, and trends in the epidemic's movement and development worldwide. The foundation publishes the *Kaiser Daily HIV/AIDS Report* that collects and archives news stories on HIV and AIDS from media sources worldwide.

Latin American Council of AIDS Service Organizations
http://www.laccaso.org/

The South and Central American branch of the International Council of AIDS Service Organizations offers country-specific listings of HIV and AIDS resources. The site is in Spanish.

Program for the Collaboration against AIDS and Related
Epidemics (ProCAARE)
http://www.procaare.org

ProCAARE is an international discussion forum for health care providers, scientists, policymakers, and others. The ProCAARE forum focuses on debate and education related to scientific advances in HIV and AIDS care, treatment, prevention, and vaccine development. In addition, ProCAARE provides synopses of the proceedings of international medical and scientific conferences related to HIV and AIDS.

Pub Med
http://www.ncbi.nlm.nih.gov/PubMed/

PubMed is sponsored by the National Library of Medicine. The PubMed database contains more than 14 million article citations from medical and scientific journals, including a large group of full-text articles available for free download. Database searches provide citation information including article abstracts that are sorted using a standard set of nearly 22,000 keywords.

UNAIDS/WHO Epidemiological Fact Sheets
http://www.who.int/emc-hiv/fact_sheets/

UNAIDS, in partnership with the WHO and UNICEF, collects epidemiological and surveillance data on HIV and other sexually transmitted infections from nearly every country in the world. The "fact sheets" derived from this data include information on literacy rates, access to health care, prevalence of specific sexually transmitted infections, and HIV prevalence statistics for rural and urban areas by sex and age. The fact sheets are updated regularly with new data collected by local and international researchers working with UNAIDS.

UNAIDS/WHO Global HIV and AIDS and STD
Surveillance
http://www.who.int/emc-hiv

This archive of HIV surveillance literature includes the UNAIDS "Reports on the Global AIDS Epidemic" for 1998 through the present. Along with other epidemiological and surveillance materials, the global reports examine the current state of the HIV epidemic worldwide, discussing regional trends and new epidemics as well as changes in established prevalence patterns.

USAID Directory of Associations of People Living with
HIV/AIDS
http://www.usaid.gov/pop_health/aids/Publications/docs/hivaidsdirectory.pdf

This U.S. Agency for International Development guide lists contact information for local and national groups of people living with HIV and AIDS worldwide. The directory includes a synopsis of groups' "key activities," funding sources, and membership.

USAID Network of African People Living with HIV/AIDS
http://www.dec.org/pdf_docs/PNACN456.pdf

This guide focuses specifically on groups of people living with HIV and AIDS in Africa, including contact information, description of organizational goals, and funding sources.

World Economic Forum Global Health Initiative Network Directory
http://www.weforum.org/site/homepublic.nsf/Content/
Global+Health+Initiative%5CGHI+Business+Tools%5CGHI+
Networking+Directory

The directory includes listings of organizations focusing on AIDS, tuberculosis, and malaria worldwide. Users can search for organizations by disease, location, and type of intervention. The database also includes contact information for UNAIDS Country Program Advisors in more than thirty countries worldwide.

Index

About the Authors

Richard G. Marlink, Ph.D., is senior researcher and executive director of the Harvard AIDS Institute at the Harvard School of Public Health in Boston, Massachusetts. His published works include two editions of *AIDS in Africa,* and he has published more than sixty articles in peer-reviewed medical and scientific journals. Dr. Marlink has developed HIV/AIDS research and education initiatives in Botswana, Brazil, Puerto Rico, Senegal, South Africa, Tanzania, and Thailand.

Alison G. Kotin is research publications coordinator at the Harvard AIDS Institute at the Harvard School of Public Health in Boston, Massachusetts.